Playgrounds for Young Children:

National Survey and Perspectives

Editors

Sue C. Wortham
University of Texas at San Antonio

Joe L. Frost
University of Texas at Austin

D0863060

A Project of the
Committee on Play
American Association for Leisure and Recreation
An association of the
American Alliance for Health, Physical Education,
Recreation and Dance

GV

. 6.5

Copyright © 1990
American Alliance for Health, Physical Education,
Recreation and Dance
1900 Association Drive
Reston, VA 22091

ISBN 0-88314-488-3

OLSON LIBRARY
NORTHERN MICHIGAN UNIVERSITY
MARQUETTE. MICHIGAN 49855

Table of Contents

About the Authors

Louis Bowers is professor of physical education at the University of South Florida. He has been the principal person responsible for tabulating and describing the results of the AALR Committee on Play's surveys for elementary school playgrounds, park play structures, and preschool playgrounds.

Lawrence D. Bruya is professor and head of the Department of Physical Education at Washington State University, Pullman. He has edited two volumes about elementary school playgrounds, served as chairperson for the AALR Committee on Play, and consults regarding play structures.

Michael E. Crawford is associate professor of recreation at the University of Missouri, Columbia. He is active in the American Association for Leisure and Recreation, National Recreation and Park Association, and International Play Association and has completed multiple research projects about play structures, children's play, and risk taking. He is currently a research and development consultant to the State of Missouri child care licensing program.

Steen B. Esbensen is professor at the Université du Quebec à Hull, Quebec, Canada. He is author of *Planning Play Spaces for Preschoolers* and *The Early Childhood Playground: An Outdoor Classroom* published by High/Scope Press. In addition to teaching in early childhood teacher education, he has published on various aspects of play and play environments and collaborates with landscape architects and recreation planners to design for play.

Joe L. Frost is Parker Centennial Professor in the Department of Curriculum and Instruction at the University of Texas at Austin. He is past-president of the American Association for the Child's Right to Play and past-president of the Association for Childhood Education International. His work related to play and play environments includes consulting with the U.S. Department of Justice, the U.S. Consumer Product Safety Commission, the U.S. Air Force, and various schools, cities, and equipment manufacturers. His publications include *Children's Play and Playgrounds* (with B. Klein) and *When Children Play* (with S. Sunderlin). He is currently serving on the American Society for Testing and Materials' Public Playground Equipment Task Group.

Tom Jambor is associate professor of early childhood education at the University of Alabama at Birmingham. He currently serves as the American representative to the International Association for the Child's Right to Play (IPA) and president of International Play Association/USA. He has designed numerous community-built developmental playground environments.

Mary S. Rivkin is assistant professor of education at the University of Maryland, Baltimore County. She is a co-editor of *The Young Child at Play: Reviews of Research*, Vol. 4 and has helped design playgrounds.

James Talbot is owner and designer/builder, Neverland Play Designs in Austin, Texas. He has a degree in architecture and has devoted 20 years to creating fantasy environments and places for children, as well as lecturing, giving workshops, and writing on the subject. He is author of "Plants in Children's Environments" in Frost and Sunderlin's *When Children Play*.

Donna Thompson is associate professor of physical education at the University of Northern Iowa, Cedar Falls. She is chairperson of the AALR Committee on Play, contributed to the volumes that reported information about school playgrounds, co-edited the volume on park playgrounds, is secretary of the American Society for Testing and Material's Task Force to develop standards for public use playgrounds, and consults regarding play structures.

Marshal R. Wortham is professor of art at Southwest Texas State University, San Marcos and maintains a private design practice. He has designed custom structures and play environments for elementary schools and child care centers. He is a member of the AALR Committee on Play and the International Play Association.

Sue C. Wortham is associate professor of early childhood and elementary education at the University of Texas at San Antonio. She is a member of the AALR Committee on Play, served as treasurer of the American Association for the Child's Right to Play (IPA/USA), and has researched and published on various aspects of play and play environments, particularly as regards infants and toddlers. She has served as a play environment consultant for public schools, churches, and child care centers.

Thomas D. Yawkey is professor of early childhood education at the Pennsylvania State University. He is co-author of *Play and Early Childhood Development* (with J. Johnson and C. Christie, Scott, Foresman) and *Integrated Learning Activities for Young Children* (with S. Trostle, Allyn and Bacon), and co-editor of *Single Parents and Nontraditional Families* (with G. Cornelius, Technomic Publishing). He serves as co-director, Title VII Academic Excellence Project PIAGET, and specializes in young bilingual and monolingual children's play, cognition, and communications.

1

Introduction

Sue C. Wortham
Joe L. Frost

What is the ideal play environment for young children in the early childhood years? What is the current status of playgrounds for preschool children? This book represents the last of three national efforts undertaken by the Committee on Play, a committee of the American Association for Leisure and Recreation, whose parent group is the American Alliance for Health, Physical Education, Recreation and Dance. The two previous surveys studied elementary school and community park playground equipment.

This volume reports the results of the Preschool Playground Equipment Survey. As a result of 349 surveys conducted by 62 trained volunteers in 31 states, we are able to construct information on the kinds of play equipment and materials available on early childhood playgrounds, whether the setting is a child care facility or other type of preschool setting.

The best early childhood play environment is not just a play area equipped with play structures. An environment for young children includes the natural features of the landscape and opportunities for children to engage in social, fantasy, and creative play, as well as physical play. The editors and authors offer the reader comprehensive information on all aspects of the play environment for young children, with the hope that those who design new facilities or are considering refurbishing existing preschool playgrounds will be challenged to develop play environments that are exciting and rewarding places for young children to play.

In Chapter 2, "The National Survey of Preschool Centers Playground Equipment," and Chapter 3, "Results of the Survey," Lou Bowers discusses the procedures followed to conduct and report the results of the study. Bowers played a major role in all three studies, both in instrument design and processing the data collected.

The issues involved with playground safety are discussed by Joe Frost in Chapter 4, "Young Children and Playground Safety." He presents recent unpublished statistics on the scope and causes of injuries on playgrounds and discusses key safety elements to prevent playground injuries. Attention is given to modifications that can be made to specific types of equipment to improve their safety. The advantages and disadvantages of various types of playground surfacing material are presented, as well as information on hazardous equipment that is still being manufactured and sold.

The design of play environments for young children is described in Chapters 5 and 6. In Chapter 5, "Play Environments For Young Children: Design Perspectives," Steen Esbensen traces the influence on playground design to include adventure playgrounds, the environmental yard concept developed by Robin Moore, work yards using salvaged materials, and creative playgrounds adapted from adventure playgrounds. Esbensen reports that by the 1970s and 1980s safety concerns had a strong influence on safe playground design. He regards early childhood play environments as outdoor classrooms. They should be learning environments that encourage child-initiated, teacher-supported activities and promote the child's influence on space and materials. Esbensen further describes desirable design features of play environments in terms of the types of developmental play they should provide in various zones.

In Chapter 6, "Infant-Toddler Playgrounds," Sue Wortham is concerned with the inclusion of play environments especially designed for the developmental needs of infants and toddlers. She discusses how play interfaces with development in infants and toddlers and how play environments can be designed and arranged to meet babies' needs and abilities for play. Wortham also describes why infants need to be outdoors, especially what they learn from experiences in the natural environment. She concludes that effective infant-toddler playgrounds combine developmentally appropriate features with natural environments that promote motor play, social play, and object play.

The evolution of commercial play equipment is explained by Marshal Wortham in Chapter 7, "Advances in Playground Equipment for Young Children." Like Esbensen, he explains the changes and evolution of play equipment in recent decades that have been influenced by availability of new materials and manufacturing and design possibilities. He notes that many manufacturers are responding to safety research in equipment design. They are also influenced by the growing market in playgrounds for younger children stimulated by the large growth in child care facilities. He reports that in the 1980s more progressive companies availed themselves of current research in child development and began expanding the play value of equipment designed for children in the early childhood years.

Play equipment maintenance is also related to safety. In Chapter 8, "Maintaining Play Environments: Training, Checklists, and Documentation," Donna Thompson, Larry Bruya, and Mike Crawford present guidelines and checklists for assessing playground features for safety and maintenance. The authors discuss how to conduct a safety inspection, including procedures to use in checking for safe equipment, safe installation of equipment, maintenance of equipment and play zones, and how to evaluate the design of equipment. The authors also present a system to document risk on preschool play structures.

Tom Jambor focuses on perceptual-motor development and how it affects the total development of the child. In Chapter 9, "Promoting Perceptual-Motor Development in Young Children's Play," he discusses the relationship of perceptual-motor development to the child's play and how the outdoor environment can be enhanced for children's play. Jambor describes how body awareness, spatial awareness, directional awareness, and temporal awareness develop in the young child. He discusses theories of development and how motor play facilitates perceptual-motor development. Activities to promote perceptual-motor skills are also suggested.

In Chapter 10, "The Role of Adults in Children's Play," Tom Yawkey expands upon information about the adult's influence on children's play discussed in earlier chapters. He proposes that adult involvement in child play has benefits for child development, in pretend play with physical objects, social play, and persistence in play. Adult support and involvement in the child's play also benefits language and intellectual competencies and signals to children that adults approve of their play. He suggests that adults need to consider time, space, materials, and preparatory experiences when planning for involvement in children's play. He also discusses various strategies adults can use to become involved in play activities.

The authors of the final two chapters express a need to expand and enhance "built" play environments with natural features. In Chapter 11, "Outdoor Play—What Happens Here?" Mary Rivkin expresses concern that urban children, particularly, have fewer opportunities to play outdoors. She contrasts the first efforts in developing urban playgrounds in the last century with how city children today are increasingly playing indoors. Rivkin expresses concern about the quality of research on the play of young children, particularly because most research was conducted indoors. She reviews the literature on developmentalist studies on play, outdoor play environments in various cultures, and thoughtfully designed playgrounds. She believes that outdoor play is more than a playground and advocates that we seek to expand its range and opportunities.

In the final chapter, "Magical Playscapes," James Talbot and Joe Frost express their dissatisfaction with the growing trends to replace natural play environments with high-tech, slick mechanical environments and to restrict free play opportunities for children. They encourage those involved in playground design to think back to the impressionable events of their childhoods and to construct play environments that reflect and enhance their most intriguing and magical memories. Finally, they suggest 19 design principles for those who would build magical places for children, with children.

The editors would like to thank Marian Ruomo at the University of Texas at San Antonio and Selina Jasso and Nancy Treffler-Hammonds at the University of Texas at Austin for typing the manuscripts. Their patience and expertise are greatly appreciated.

2

National Survey of Preschool Centers Playground Equipment

Louis Bowers

The Committee on Play of the American Association for Leisure and Recreation of the American Alliance for Health, Physical Education, Recreation and Dance initiated a survey of playground equipment available for use by children in preschool centers in the United States. The study was an extension of the 1985 National Survey of Elementary School Playground Equipment and the AALR 1986 National Survey of Playground Equipment in Community Parks conducted by the Committee on Play. Both the 1985 and 1986 studies were conducted in order to secure accurate information that might be used by educators and designers to improve existing and future playground equipment in schools and community parks. The National Survey of Preschool Centers Playground Equipment was undertaken to secure information specific to the play environments provided for preschool age children.

Survey Instrument Development

The Committee on Play completed in 1985 the development of a survey instrument designed to describe the type and condition of playground equipment in elementary schools. This instrument was constructed by Louis Bowers with review input by members of the Committee on Play. The total process of constructing the survey instrument, experts' review, conducting field trials, and making final revisions, took place between May 1984 and April 1985.

The reliability of the survey instrument was established at the 1985 AAHPERD Convention by means of training volunteers and computing percentage of agreement of rating of items of surveys completed by 44 volunteers of the same playground. After establishing reliability, the survey instrument was named the AAHPERD-AALR-COP National Elementary School Playground Equipment Survey and was utilized in the National Survey of Elementary School Playground Equipment Study. With slight modification, the survey was also used in the 1986 National Survey of Community Park Playground Equipment.

The Committee on Play made the decision to extend the length of the 1985 survey from seven to eight pages so that the new survey would be more appropriate to the equipment and activities of preschool centers.

The eight-page survey instrument was designed to secure information regarding: (a) the type and quantity of play structures and play materials, (b) location of each play structure on the playground, (c) the maintenance status of each play structure, (d) the height and configuration of each play structure, and (e) the type of surface material under each play structure. The survey provides information regarding broken or missing parts, sharp edges and projections, small openings within the structures, and other safety conditions. Conditions related to signs, trees, pathways, shade structures, wheel toys, manipulative materials, and garden areas are also covered.

Survey Instrument Reliability

In October 1988 at the national convention of the National Association for the Education of Young Children, 42 volunteers were trained in the administration of the Preschool Playground Equipment Survey. Joe Frost of the University of Texas instructed the volunteers in the administration of the survey by means of a 35mm slide presentation of examples of assessment items of the survey.

Also explained to the volunteers was the procedure they should use to randomly select preschool centers in their area. This procedure called for them to obtain a list of all state licensed preschool centers within their area and to randomly select on the average of one of ten preschool centers using a table of random numbers provided for them. The volunteers were directed to send all completed surveys to Louis Bowers, Department of Physical Education, University of South Florida, Tampa, Florida 33620.

The volunteers, composed of early childhood and physical education professionals, visited Page Preschool in Garden Grove, California, where each surveyor independently used the instrument to survey the playground at the preschool. Each volunteer returned the completed survey of the Page Preschool playground to Joe Frost before leaving the playground.

Inter-Rater Objectivity

The surveys of Page Preschool completed by the 42 volunteers were given to Louis Bowers for computation of the percentage of exact agreement between each of the raters on each item. This procedure involved tabulating the most frequent response for each item, dividing by 42 and converting the result to a percentage.

For example, if 40 of the 42 surveyors checked yes for an item, the inter-rater agreement was 95 percent. For survey items requiring a quantitative response of "how many" or "how high" the number of responses that were alike was divided by 42 and converted to a percentage.

The average percentage of agreement for items within each section and the average percentage of agreement for all items on the survey was computed. The overall average percentage of agreement for all items on the survey was 86 percent.

The following tables provide the percentage of agreement for each item and the average percentage of agreement for each section of the survey. Considering the large number of volunteer surveyors trained, the limited time for training, and the exacting procedure used to establish the percentage of agreement for each item, the overall objectivity of 86 percent is quite high.

(Text continues on page 15)

TABLE 2.1— Inter-Rater Exact Agreement
Survey Section 1: Types and Numbers of Equipment

Permanent Fixed Equipment	Percentage of Agreement
swings	97.6
slides	94.0
balance beams	98.8
overhead ladders	61.9
rocking apparatus	82.0
tire/net climbers	100.0
firemen's poles	75.0
trapeze bars	91.6
suspended bridges	100.0
seesaws	88.0
merry-go-rounds	100.0
geodesic domes	95.0
monkey bars	51.0
interconnected structures	80.9
	Average 86.8

Portable Materials	Percentage of Agreement
tricycles	57.8
loose tires	76.1
sand	82.1
wagons	79.0
barrels	83.3
loose boards or other	96.4
water	77.3
wheelbarrows	97.6
building materials	100.0
gardening tools	100.0
art materials	98.8
carpentry tools	100.0
	Average 87.4

Other Provisions	Percentage of Agreement
grassy areas for organized games	91.6
accessible water-supply hose or faucets	63.0
separate sand play areas	82.1
hard surface area for games	65.4
shade structures (man-made)	84.5
storage for portable play materials	70.2
play houses	100.0
storage for maintenance equipment	66.2
cars (for dramatic play)	100.0
areas for digging soil	76.1
tables	91.6
trucks (for dramatic play)	100.0
natural areas for plants	59.5
water play areas	63.0
toilet facilities	71.4
provisions for animal care	96.4
boats (for dramatic play)	100.0
amphitheatres	98.8
	Average 82.2

TABLE 2.2
Inter-Rater Exact Agreement
Survey Section 2: Location and Accessibility of Playground Equipment

	Item	% Agreement
2.1	equipment easily viewed	69.0
2.2	four-foot wall surrounding playground	100.0
2.3	wheelchair access to equipment	85.7
2.4	wheelchair access on equipment	95.2
		Average 87.5

TABLE 2.3
Inter-Rater Exact Agreement
Survey Section 3: Placement and Size of Equipment

Item	% Agreement
3.1 ten-foot space between equipment	73.8
3.2 average number of exposed concrete footings per center	85.7
3.3 designated traffic patterns on pathways	71.4
3.4 smaller equipment for younger children	88.0
3.5 large and small equipment separated	98.6
	Average 83.5

TABLE 2.4
Inter-Rater Exact Agreement
Survey Section 4: Swing Equipment, Descriptive Information on Swing Structures

	Item	% Agreement
4.1	separate swing structures	93.8
4.2	swing seats	95.2
4.3	metal/wood seats	100.0
4.4	swivel suspensions for seats	100.0
4.5	swing structures for younger children	64.2
4.6	swing seats for infants and toddlers	76.1
4.7	barriers around swing structures	92.6
4.8	support structures firmly anchored	85.7
4.9	sharp corners, edges, and projections	76.1
4.10	moving parts in good repair	62.0
4.11	plastic-covered chains	100.0
4.12	commercial matting	100.0
		Average 86.0

TABLE 2.5
Inter-Rater Exact Agreement
Survey Section 5: Percentages for Sliding Structures

	Item	% Agreement
5.1	slides present	100.0
5.2	slides with missing or broken parts	78.0
5.3	sharp corners, edges, or projections	68.2
5.4	supporting structures firmly anchored	68.2
5.5	wide slides	92.6
5.6	smooth, stable sliding surface	60.0
5.7	deceleration chute	62.5
5.8	inches from ground at end of slide	78.0
5.9	vertical height of slide	60.0
Surface Materials Reported Under Sliding Equipment		
5.10	commercial matting	100.0
		Average 74.0

TABLE 2.6
Inter-Rater Exact Agreement
Survey Section 6: Percentages for Climbing Equipment with the Following Conditions

	Item	% Agreement
6.1	climbing structures	64.0
6.2	firmly anchored structures	61.9
6.3	securely fastened parts	61.9
6.4	open holes at end of pipes	66.2
6.5	small spaces	64.0
6.6	sharp edges, protrusions	69.0
6.7	spaces between 7 and 11 inches	71.0
6.8	maximum height from ground	57.0
6.9	guard rail around highest platform	78.0
6.10	openings between 4½ and 9 inches	64.0
Materials Found Under Climbing Equipment		
6.11	commercial matting	100.0
		Average 65.7

TABLE 2.7
Inter-Rater Exact Agreement
Survey Section 7: Percentages for Rotating Equipment

	Item	% Agreement
7.1 through 7.8	Answered correctly. No rotating equipment present.	100.0

TABLE 2.8
Inter-Rater Exact Agreement
Survey Section 8: Percentages for Rocking Equipment

	Item	% Agreement
8.1	rocking equipment present	95.2
8.2	firmly anchored structures	69.0
8.3	all parts are present	78.5
8.4	sharp edges, projections	71.4
8.5	3-inch-long hand hold	98.6
8.6	11-inch foot rest	61.9
8.7	spring action pinching possible	60.0
Surface Materials Found Under Rocking Equipment Structures		
8.8	commercial matting	100.0
		Average 76.4

TABLE 2.9
Inter-Rater Exact Agreement
Survey Section 9: Percentages for Seesaw Structures

	Item	% Agreement
9.1 through 9.10	Answered Correctly. No seesaws present.	100.0

TABLE 2.10
Inter-Rater Exact Agreement
Survey Section 10: Percentages for Designated Sand Play Areas

	Item	% Agreement
10.1	separated sand play areas	88.0
10.2	clean and debris free	64.2
10.3	good drainage apparent	69.0
10.4	sand play areas elevated	73.8
10.5	covered or located to exclude animals	97.6
10.6	benches for adult seating	61.9
		Average 75.8

TABLE 2.11
Inter-Rater Exact Agreement
Survey Section 11: Percentages for Wading Pools

	Item	% Agreement
11.1	separate water play areas	97.6
11.2	pool	100.0
11.3	elevated, fenced, and gated pool areas	97.3
11.4	clear and free of debris	69.0
11.5	average depth of pool	61.0
11.6	benches for adults adjacent to wading pool	67.0
		Average 82.0

TABLE 2.12
Inter-Rater Exact Agreement
Survey Section 12: Percentages for Centers with Signs, Trees, and
Pathways

	Item	% Agreement
12.1	overview map of play area	95.2
12.2	accessible facilities designated	73.5
12.3	signs for seeking help in case of accident	78.5
12.4	signs directing wheel toy traffic	64.2
12.5	sign indicators to direct play traffic	97.6
12.6	signs indicating difficulty of play structure	95.2
12.7	signs prohibiting animals from playground	100.0
12.8	signs warning against dangerous play activities	100.0
12.9	sign to expand exploratory play	97.6
12.10	signs written in other languages common to region	100.0
		Average 90.2

TABLE 2.13
Inter-Rater Exact Agreement
Survey Section 13: Percentages for Trees and Shade Structures

Item		% Agreement
13.1	trees located within 50 feet	62.0
13.2	trees planned as part of play structure	93.8
13.3	dead trees used as part of play structure	100.0
13.4	tree houses built	100.0
13.5	trees on perimeter to break wind	71.4
13.6	man-made structures to shade seating	100.0
13.7	drinking fountains near playground equipment	59.6
		Average 83.8

TABLE 2.14
Inter-Rater Exact Agreement
Survey Section 14: Pathways

Item		% Agreement
14.1	lines likely to occur	73.8
14.2	hard surface pathways	97.6
14.3	width of pathway/length of pathway	73.8
14.4	hard surface pathway materials	97.6
14.5	at least one intersection	97.6
Surface Materials		
14.6	commercial matting	100.0
		Average 88.1

TABLE 2.15
Inter-Rater Exact Agreement
Survey Section 15: Wheel Toys

Item		% Agreement
15.1	wheel toys available	90.4
15.2	riding wheel toys available	97.6
15.3	push wheel toys available	76.1
15.4	pull wheel toys available	60.0
		Average 81.0

TABLE 2.16
Inter-Rater Exact Agreement
Survey Section 16: Manipulatives

Item		% Agreement
16.1	wooden building blocks	90.5
16.2	tools and buckets available	83.3
16.3	balls and other sporting equipment available	83.3
16.4	trucks, cars, and other small toys available	83.3
		Average 85.1

TABLE 2.17
Inter-Rater Exact Agreement
Survey Section 17: Garden Area

Item		% Agreement
17.1	garden area planted by children	97.6

Training of a second group of 15 volunteers was conducted by Larry Bruya, a member of the Committee on Play, during a week-long workshop on the study of play environments at the University of Nebraska at Omaha. Bruya surveyed a preschool center playground and compared the independent surveys of the same preschool center playground by the volunteers to his ratings. This procedure resulted in an overall agreement of 83.5 percent. Based on this high objectivity, the data of the surveys of these workshop participants were included in the study.

Data Representation

The 349 surveys received and tabulated were completed by 62 volunteers and represent preschool centers in 31 states. The surveys provided information about 2,447 play structures, 2,783 portable play materials, and 2,919 other provisions on the playgrounds.

While the 349 surveys represent a random selection process within geographical areas, there is not a high representation of surveys from either the northeastern or northwestern states. The distribution and the number of preschool playgrounds surveyed within each state are shown in Figure 2.1.

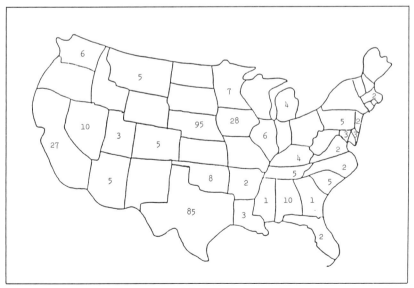

Figure 2.1. A map of the United States showing the number of preschool playgrounds surveyed within each state.

The National Preschool Playground Study provides intensive, important, current information about the type and condition of play structures and portable play objects in preschool centers in the United States. The study also provides a reliable survey instrument, which is appropriate for use in assessing the status of preschool playgrounds. It should assist preschool administrators, teachers, and parents in the process of improving the quality of play environments for preschool age children.

3

Results of the Survey

Louis Bowers

The results of the National Survey of Playground Equipment in Preschool Centers are presented in the following series of 17 tables. These results are based on assessments of 349 preschool centers located in 31 states. The surveys were administered by 62 trained volunteer preschool and physical education professionals. The playgrounds surveyed were located in preschool centers randomly selected from a list of all preschool centers located in each of the communities included in the study. A total of 2,447 play structures were surveyed in 349 preschool centers. In addition, 2,783 portable materials and 2,919 other provisions were recorded. The average amount of time used to administer the survey in each preschool center was 27 minutes.

The results of the 349 surveys reported in this chapter were recorded at the University of South Florida by graduate research assistants Michael Collins and Mark Hirsch under the direction of Louis Bowers. Mark Hirsch, however, tabulated the results with Bowers.

The following tables provide the tabulated results of the survey of playground equipment and portable materials found on preschool centers in the United States.

Section 1 focuses on the type and number of pieces of equipment and other provisions for play. Section 2 focuses on the location and accessibility of the equipment. Section 3 records the placement and size of equipment.

Sections 4 through 11 report on the size, physical structure, condition, and ground covering beneath individual types of equipment.[1] The play equipment was categorized as swinging, sliding, climbing, rotating, rocking, seesaws, sand play, or wading pool type equipment.

Section 12 focuses on centers with signs, trees, and pathways; Section 13 on trees and shade structures; Section 14 on pathways; Section 15 on wheel toys; Section 16 on manipulative materials; and Section 17 on garden area.

TABLE 3.1
Survey Section 1: Types and Numbers of Equipment

Permanent Fixed Equipment	Total No. Present	Average Per Center	Percentage Total Equipment
swings	554	1.58	22.63
slides	531	1.52	21.70
balance beams	219	.62	8.94
overhead ladders	186	.53	7.60
rocking apparatus	175	.50	7.15
tire/net climbers	152	.43	6.21
firemen's poles	142	.40	5.80
trapeze bars	127	.36	5.19
suspended bridges	87	.24	3.55
seesaws	76	.21	3.10
merry-go-rounds	72	.20	2.94
geodesic domes	66	.18	2.69
monkey bars	60	.17	2.45
Total Number of Structures	2,447		

[1]The survey instrument called for the surveyers to indicate the depth of resilient materials underneath play equipment. Because the data were incomplete they were not reported in the results. The editors of this volume participated in surveys in 16 states and found none that met the requirements for resilient surfaces.

TABLE 3.1, continued

Portable Materials	Total No. Present	Average Per Center	Percentage Total Equipment
tricycles	1,039	2.97	37.33
loose tires	536	1.53	19.25
sand	276	.79	9.91
wagons	231	.66	8.30
barrels	167	.47	6.00
loose boards or other	151	.43	5.43
water	100	.28	3.59
wheelbarrows	97	.27	3.48
building materials	59	.16	2.12
gardening tools	54	.15	1.94
art materials	51	.14	1.83
carpentry tools	22	.06	.79
Total Portable Materials	2,783		

Other Provisions	Total No. Present	Average Per Center	Percentage Total Equipment
tables	372	1.06	12.74
grassy areas for organized games	318	.91	10.89
accessible water-supply hose or faucets	296	.84	10.14
separate sand play areas	276	.79	9.45
hard surface area for games	255	.73	8.73
shade structures (man-made)	253	.72	8.66
storage for portable play materials	175	.50	5.99
play houses	156	.44	5.34
storage for maintenance equipment	137	.39	4.69
cars (for dramatic play)	128	.36	4.38
areas for digging soil	125	.35	4.28
trucks (for dramatic play)	110	.31	3.76
natural areas for plants	104	.29	3.56
water play areas	100	.28	3.42
toilet facilities	68	.19	2.32
provisions for animal care	17	.04	.58
boats (for dramatic play)	16	.04	.54
amphitheatres	13	.03	.44
Total Other Provisions	2,919		

TABLE 3.2
Survey Section 2: Location and Accessibility of Playground Equipment

Item	Percentage Yes	Percentage No
2.1 equipment easily viewed	72	28
2.2 four-foot wall surrounding playground	85	15
2.3 wheelchair access to equipment	18	82
2.4 wheelchair access on equipment	5	95

TABLE 3.3
Survey Section 3: Placement and Size of Equipment

Item	Percentage Yes	Percentage No
3.1 ten foot space between equipment	55	45
3.2 average number of exposed concrete footings per center = 1.00		
3.3 designated traffic patterns on pathways	75	25
3.4 smaller equipment for younger children	47	53
3.5 large and small equipment separated	36	64

TABLE 3.4
Survey Section 4: Swing Equipment, Descriptive Information on 554 Swing Structures

Item	Number	Average/Center
4.1 separate swing structures	554	1.58
4.2 swing seats	1,455	Average/Swing Structure 2.62
4.3 metal/wood seats	73	Percentage of Total Swing Seats 5.0
4.4 swivel suspensions for seats	194	Percentage of Total Swing Seats 13.4
4.5 swing structures for younger children	191	Percentage of Total Swing Structures 34.0
4.6 swing seats for infants and toddlers	245	17
4.7 barriers around swing structures	60	11
4.8 support structures firmly anchored	509	83

TABLE 3.4, continued

Item	Number	Average/Center
4.9 sharp corners, edges, and projections	119	21
4.10 moving parts in good repair	419	76
4.11 plastic covered chains	58	10
4.12 Surfacing Materials Under Swings		
sand		29.00
grass		20.00
hand-packed dirt		15.00
pea gravel		12.00
clay		6.00
mulch		5.00
commercial matting		4.29
tan bark		3.00
rocks, pebbles, stones		1.87
carpeted turf		1.74
asphalt		.58
concrete		.29
other		.87

TABLE 3.5
Survey Section 5: Percentages for 531 Sliding Structures

Item	Average	Number	Percentage
5.1 slides present		531	21.7
5.2 slides with missing or broken parts		34	6.0
5.3 sharp corners, edges, or projections		94	18.0
5.4 supporting structures firmly anchored		446	84.0
5.5 wide slides		110	21.0
5.6 smooth, stable sliding surface		479	90.0
5.7 deceleration chute		264	50.0
5.8 inches from ground at end of slide	7⅓"		
5.9 vertical height of slide	5'5"		
5.10 Surface Materials Under Sliding Equipment			
sand			34.0
grass			19.0
packed dirt			11.0
pea gravel			10.0
clay			6.0
mulch			5.0
commercial matting			4.0
bark wood			3.0
concrete			2.0
carpet turf			1.7
asphalt			.8
other			3.1

TABLE 3.6
Survey Section 6: Percentages for 1,046 Pieces of Climbing
Equipment with the Following Conditions

	Item	Average	Percentage
6.1	climbing structures	3.00	33
6.2	firmly anchored structures		84
6.3	securely fastened parts		91
6.4	open holes at end of pipes		10
6.5	small spaces		16
6.6	sharp edges, protrusions		15
6.7	spaces between 7 and 11 inches		29
6.8	maximum height from ground	5 feet	
	Percentages for Climbing Equipment Height		
	0 feet to 2 feet 11 inches		11.44
	3 feet to 3 feet 11 inches		10.99
	4 feet to 4 feet 11 inches		21.53
	5 feet to 5 feet 11 inches		16.60
	6 feet to 6 feet 11 inches		14.43
	7 feet to 7 feet 11 inches		10.65
	8 feet to 8 feet 11 inches		8.59
	9 feet to 9 feet 11 inches		2.40
	10 feet to 10 feet 11 inches		2.40
	11 feet to 11 feet 11 inches		.34
6.9	guard rail around highest platform		61
6.10	openings between 4½ and 9 inches		44
6:11	Surface Materials Found Under Climbing Equipment with an Average Maximum Height of 5 Feet 4 Inches		
	sand		33.0
	grass		22.0
	dirt		14.5
	pea gravel		8.7
	clay		5.0
	mulch		5.0
	commercial matting		3.0
	wood/bark		2.5
	gravel		1.5
	asphalt		1.2
	concrete		1.2
	carpet turf		.7
	weeds		.7
	other		

TABLE 3.7
Survey Section 7: Percentages for Rotating Equipment

	Item	Number	Percentage
7.1	rotating apparatus present	72	2.9
7.2	firmly anchored structures		65.0
7.3	securely fastened parts		40.0
7.4	sharp edges, protrusions		14.0
7.5	rotation-post area open		16.0
7.6	shearing action under structure		9.0
7.7	gear boxes which could crush fingers		4.0
7.8	perimeter clearing of 20 feet		9.0

7:9	Surface Materials Found Under 72 Pieces of Rotating Equipment	
	grass	25.0
	dirt	22.3
	sand	15.7
	pea gravel	14.4
	clay	11.8
	concrete	5.2
	commercial matting	1.3
	stone	1.3
	asphalt	1.3
	brick	1.3

TABLE 3.8
Survey Section 8: Percentages for 175 Rocking Equipment

	Item	Number	Percentage
8.1	rocking equipment present	175	7
8.2	firmly anchored structures		33
8.3	all parts are present		83
8.4	sharp edges, projections		17
8.5	3-inch-long hand hold		76
8.6	11 inch foot rest		59
8.7	spring action pinching possible		47
8:8	Surface Materials Found Under 175 Rocking Equipment Structures		
	grass		24.7
	sand		24.7
	dirt		12.3
	mulch		11.2
	pea gravel		10.1
	concrete		6.7
	clay		6.7
	bark		2.2
	commercial matting		1.1

TABLE 3.9
Survey Section 9: Percentages for 76 Seesaw Structures

	Item	Average	Number	Percentage
9.1	seesaw structures present		76	3
9.2	seesaws present		103	1.6 per structure
9.3	highest height of seats	37 inches		
9.4	firmly anchored structures			44
9.5	internal moving parts accessible to fingers			40
9.6	secure joints and fasteners			72
9.7	sharp corners or projections			26
9.8	cushions impact of seat landing			19
9.9	3-inch-long hand holds			68
9.10:	Surface Materials Found Under 76 Seesaw Structures			
	grass			38.0
	sand			20.8
	dirt			6.9
	clay			6.9
	pea gravel			5.5
	asphalt			5.5
	concrete			5.5
	stone			5.5
	wood/bark			2.7
	carpet			1.3

TABLE 3.10
Survey Section 10: Percentages for 276 Designated Sand Play Areas

	Item	Number	Percentage
10.1	separated sand play areas	276	9.9
10.2	clean and debris free		81.0
10.3	good drainage apparent		62.0
10.4	sand play areas elevated		30.0
10.5	covered or located to exclude animals		18.0
10.6	benches for adult seating		38.0

OLSON LIBRARY
NORTHERN MICHIGAN UNIVERSITY
MARQUETTE, MICHIGAN 49855

TABLE 3.11
Survey Section 11: Percentages for 100 Wading Pools

Item	Number	Percentage
11.1 separate water play areas	100	3.59
11.2 pool 65%; waterfall 0%; water cascade 0%; spray 0%; sprinkle 15%; water canal 2%; water wheel 2%; water table 10%; other 6%		
11.3 elevated, fenced, and gated pool areas		45.6
11.4 clear and free of debris		52.0
11.5 average depth of pool	5½"	
11.6 benches for adults adjacent to wading pool	25	

TABLE 3.12
Survey Section 12: Percentages for 198 Centers with Signs, Trees, and Pathways

Item	Percentage Yes	Percentage No
12.1 overview map of play area	1	99.0
12.2 accessible facilities designated	3	97.0
12.3 signs for seeking help in case of accident	1	99.0
12.4 signs directing wheel toy traffic	3	97.0
12.5 sign indicators to direct play traffic	3	97.0
12.6 signs indicating difficulty of play structure	.6	99.4
12.7 signs prohibiting animals from playground	.6	99.4
12.8 signs warning against dangerous play activities	.3	99.7
12.9 sign to expand exploratory play		100.0
12.10 signs written in other languages common to region		100.0

TABLE 3.13
Survey Section 13: Percentages for Trees and Shade Structures

Item	Average Per Center	Yes	No
13.1 trees located within 50 feet	6.23		
13.2 trees planned as part of play structure		17	83
13.3 dead trees used as part of play structure		4	96
13.4 tree houses built		3	97
13.5 trees on perimeter to break wind		23	77
13.6 man made structures to shade seating Measurements: width 14' height 9' length 23' depth 7' Material Type: wood 60%; metal 22%; plastic 11.1%; concrete 16.6%; cloth 0%; other 0%	.82		
13.7 drinking fountains near playground equipment	.23		

TABLE 3.14
Survey Section 14: Pathways

Item	Average	Yes	No
14.1 lines likely to occur		47	53
14.2 hard surface pathways		53	47
14.3 width of pathway	12'		
length of pathway	76'		
14.5 at least one intersection		25	75

14.4	hard surface pathway materials	Percentage
	concrete	66.1
	asphalt	27.4
	fine gravel	2.1
	brick	1.6
	dirt	1.0
	crushed limestone	.5
	sand	.5
	wood	.5

TABLE 3.15
Survey Section 15: Wheel Toys

	Item	Percentage Yes	Percentage No
15.1	wheel toys available	54	46
15.2	riding wheel toys available	55	45
15.3	push wheel toys available	44	56
15.4	pull wheel toys available	37	63

TABLE 3.16
Survey Section 16: Manipulatives

Item	Percentage Yes	Percentage No
16.1 wooden building blocks	19	81
16.2 tools and buckets available	51	49
16.3 balls and other sporting equipment available	54	46
16.4 trucks, cars, and other small toys available	56	44

TABLE 3.17
Survey Section 17: Garden Area

	Item	Percentage Yes	Percentage No
17.1	garden area planted by children	15	85

4

Young Children and Playground Safety

Joe L. Frost

In 1981, following more than a decade of intensive study, the United States Consumer Product Safety Commission published voluntary guidelines for public playground safety (USCPSC, 1981a, 1981b). Although the guidelines are incomplete and imperfect, they are the most carefully developed and most widely used guidelines yet developed in this country. They are addressed primarily to children ages 5 to 12 and public playground equipment, but the guidelines are relevant, with modifications for children's age, size, and developmental levels, to preschool playgrounds.

With the initiation of the National Electronic Injury Surveillance System (NEISS) in 1972, systematic injury data for playground injuries were collected from a sample of hospital emergency rooms across the United States, and the public became aware of the scope of these injuries.

Playground Injuries

The NEISS data revealed a gradually increasing number of playground injuries during the 1980s, growing from 154,828 in 1980 to

208,488 in 1985 and 202,346 in 1988 (Figure 4.1). The slight decline in injuries reported between 1985 and 1988 may be due to growing awareness of safety problems on playgrounds and increasing numbers of lawsuits.

The NEISS data are clustered by age groups: 0–4-year-olds; 5–14-year-olds; and older (Table 4.1). Young children are at far greater risk on playgrounds than older children. Probable causes are relatively poor coordination and logical reasoning and inappropriate equipment (e.g., sized for older children).

Equipment Involved in Injuries

During 1988, the equipment most frequently implicated in injuries was swings (all children), followed in descending order by climbing equipment, slides, other categories, and seesaws (Table 4.1). The injuries on swings involved children ages 0–4 in 33 percent of the cases and 5–14-year-olds in 60 percent. The injury ratio on slides was equally divided between the two age groups. Older children (5–14) were far more frequently injured on climbing equipment (79 percent) than were 0–4-year-olds (19 percent).

More boys were injured than were girls. Clearly, the high incidence of injuries on swings, climbers, and slides was in large part a function of their frequency on playgrounds. Other equipment, such as seesaws, merry-go-rounds, etc., *may* have been implicated in injuries on an equivalent, proportional basis.

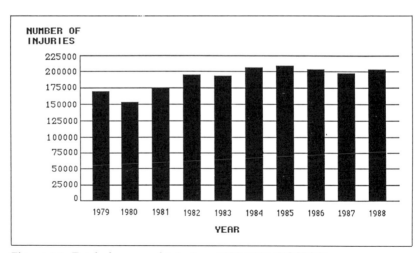

Figure 4.1. Total playground injuries—1979–1988 (USCPSC)

The AALR National Survey of Preschool Playgrounds, reported in this book, revealed that the most common equipment on playgrounds, in descending order, was climbers, swings, slides, seesaws, and rotating equipment. Using these data (Table 4.2) and CPSC injury data for all ages, we determine that seesaws, in proportion to

TABLE 4.1
Equipment Involved In Injuries—1988 (USCPSC)

| | | Percentages by Age | | |
Equipment	Number	0–4 yrs.	5–14 yrs.	Older
Swings	76,089	33.1	59.8	7.1
Climbing equipment	57,217	18.7	78.5	2.8
Slides	42,806	48.1	48.8	3.1
Seesaws	9,686	32.2	63.0	4.8
Other	16,548			
Total	202,346			

TABLE 4.2
Equipment on Preschool Playgrounds and Proportion of Injuries (Survey of 349 Sites—1988)

Type	Number	Injuries All Ages	Percent Implicated
Climbing equipment	1,046	57,217	1.8
Swings	554	76,089	0.7
Slides	531	42,806	1.2
Seesaws	76	9,686	0.8
Rotating equipment	72	N.A.	N.A.

frequency on playgrounds, were implicated in slightly more injuries than were swings, but only about half as frequently as were climbers and slides.

The three AALR National Surveys of Playgrounds (public schools, public parks, preschools) revealed that preschool playgrounds contain a far wider array of equipment and materials than do public schools and public parks (Tables 4.3, 4.4, 4.5).

The relative absence of "portable materials" and "other provisions" (Tables 4.4, 4.5) on public school and public park playgrounds reflects the absence of storage for portable materials and the emphasis on motor development and organized games. Assuming that children's play is spread over a wider range of equipment and materials, attention to preschool safety must be expanded to match equipment selection, playground zoning, installation, maintenance, and supervision of these more complex play environments.

TABLE 4.3
Playground Equipment

Permanent fixed equipment	Preschool equipment	Public schools equipment	Public parks equipment
Swings	554	397	370
Slides	531	300	363
Balance beams	219	249	64
Overhead ladders	186	323	92
Rocking apparatus	175	84	192
Tire/net climbers	152	26	—
Firemen poles	142	281	95
Trapeze bars	127	904	132
Suspended bridges	87	38	55
Seesaws	76	183	70
Merry-go-rounds	72	44	97
Geodesic domes	66	109	41
Monkey bars	60	240	66
Total number	2,447	3,178	1,637

TABLE 4.4
Playground Equipment

Portable materials	Preschool equipment	Public schools equipment	Public parks equipment
Tricycles	1,039		
Loose tires	536		
Sand	276		
Wagons	231		
Barrels	167		
Loose boards or other	151		
Water	100		
Wheelbarrows	97		
Building materials	59		
Gardening tools	54		
Art materials	51		
Carpentry tools	22		
Total number	2,783		

TABLE 4.5
Playground Equipment

Other provisions	Preschool equipment
Grassy areas for organized games	318
Accessible water-supply hose or faucets	296
Separate sand play areas	276
Hard surface area for games	255
Shaded structures (man-made)	253
Storage for portable play materials	175
Play houses	156
Storage for maintenance equipment	137
Cars (for dramatic play)	128
Areas for digging soil	125
Tables	118
Trucks (for dramatic play)	110
Natural areas for plants	104
Water play areas	100
Toilet facilities	68
Provisions for animal care	17
Boats (for dramatic play)	16
Amphitheatres	13
Total number	2,665

Injuries and Fatalities

During 1988 the frequency order of injuries for all age groups treated at emergency rooms was, most to least, fractures, lacerations, concussions, strains/sprains, hematomas, dislocations, punctures, dental injuries, foreign bodies, avulsions, crushing, amputations, ingestion, hemorrhage, and burns. Fractures lead the list of serious injuries, accounting for over one-fourth of all injuries. The large majority of fractures were to the arms, followed by leg fractures.

Overall, head area injuries were the leading types of injury. They were especially prevalent among young children. Head first falls from heights of 3 or more meters is "almost always likely to result in fracture or concussion" (King & Ball, 1989). Some United States studies indicate that concussion and/or skull fracture can result from a fall of 6 inches onto hard surfaces such as concrete. A range of studies from various countries, reported by King and Ball (1989) show that falls from heights account for most playground injuries. Such data support the need for resilient surfacing under and around playground equipment.

The CPSC reported 28 playground fatalities occurring betweei. March 1985 and February 1987. The leading cause of these fatalities was asphyxiation/strangulation, resulting from such accidents as head/neck entrapment, entanglement in suspended elements, and clothing entrapment on S-hooks and protruding elements. The data available for the 1970s show that falling onto hard surfaces was the principal cause of playground fatalities. Growing awareness of the need for resilient surfacing under and around playground equipment may have affected the fatality data over the past decade.

The single most common cause of death in 1985–87 was hangings in swing chains and ropes. Four children were strangled on slides because clothing was caught in protruding elements or because they were entangled by ropes. Two children died of skull fractures inflicted by swings. Most of the fatalities occurred at home playgrounds. Children are less likely to be closely supervised at home than at school. Further, most back-yard equipment is of cheap, poorly designed construction.

Concern over playground injuries and fatalities prompted the CPSC in 1987 to develop a broad-based playground safety program. The program includes: updating injury data, defining hazard patterns, identifying children's developmental patterns and age characteristics, revising safety handbooks, developing information materials, and developing safety guidelines for preschools. In addition, playground specialists are working with the American Society for Testing and Materials to develop safety standards for playground equipment (all ages) and for playground surfacing. Since no American guidelines or standards for preschool playgrounds are yet available, the author draws from existing guidelines/standards of various countries and agencies and from personal experience in developing the next topic, Preventing Playground Injuries.

Preventing Playground Injuries

This section is presented in two parts: General Hazard Analysis and Playground Equipment Analysis. The content is not intended to be exhaustive but key safety elements often implicated in injuries are discussed. The key information sources and guidelines/standards from the United States and other countries deal more specifically with older children than with preschool children, so modifications for young children have been made by the author. These modifications were gleaned from safety literature, personal interactions with play/ safety specialists, and experience in legal litigation involving playground injuries.

General Hazard Analysis

Entrapment

Over the past two decades a number of children have been entrapped in playground equipment. The consequences of head and/or neck entrapment can be brain damage or death. Most of the children implicated are preschool children. The CPSC guidelines warn that accessible components of moving apparatus and climbing or sliding structures should not be of a configuration that can entrap any part of the user's body. No component or group of components should form an angle or opening that can trap a user's head. The CPSC does not give specific dimensions except for exercise rings. The guidelines from various agencies and countries range from warning against 5 inch to 10 inch inside diameter to 3½ inch to 9 inch diameter openings. The critical dimensions are width of child's head and distance from tip of chin to the top back of the head. Taking into account all ages, two- to twelve-year-olds, an opening may be considered to present an entrapment hazard if the distance between interior surfaces of openings is between 3½–4 inches to 8–9 inches. This criterion should be applied to all adjacent surfaces, including space between ladder rungs, space between steps, space between horizontal ladder rungs, and space between deck railings. Flexible nets should also be examined for entrapment areas.

Heights

The NEISS data show that most injuries and some fatalities on playgrounds result from falls onto hard surfaces. Height is a critical factor because the farther the child falls, the more likely the child will be injured. All major playground guidelines, CPSC and those of other countries, require that protective surfacing be placed under and around all equipment to protect children. The height of equipment should not exceed the capacity of the installed surface to protect the child in a fall. European standards restrict climbing heights to 8 to 9 feet. The CPSC guidelines do not specify a maximum height. Given the number of injuries resulting from falls, the poor maintenance of playgrounds, and the improper surfacing existing on playgrounds, the maximum fall height for children should not exceed the European standard. Fall heights should be reduced for younger age groups. A general rule of thumb is that equipment fall heights should not exceed by more than a few inches the reaching height of children when standing on the protective surface underneath the equipment. It is important for play value that decks be of sufficient height for children to play underneath.

Pinch, Crush, and Shearing Points

Life and limb threatening shearing points are sometimes found on the undercarriage of rotating apparatus, such as merry-go-rounds. Pinch or shearing actions are also found on seesaws, glider swings, and pulleys of cable rides. The CPSC guidelines state: "There should be no accessible pinch, crush, or shear points caused by components moving relative to each other, or to a fixed component when the equipment is moved through its anticipated use cycle." The standards of other countries contain similar statements. In normal play, children use play equipment in ways not intended. Consequently, designers, installers, and users must be alert to detect unusual circumstances that can endanger children. Merry-go-rounds should not have openings or holes in the base that allow children to insert any part of the body, including the fingers. The fulcrum of seesaws should be totally enclosed or designed with springs that do not allow pinching or crushing.

Protrusions and Sharp Areas

The CPSC guidelines specify that there should be no protrusions or sharp areas that are likely to cut or puncture the body or catch clothing. Common violations include exposed bolt ends, exposed ends of tubing, and protrusions on upper portions of support posts that may catch clothing and result in strangulation. Metal slide beds should be checked carefully to ensure that sharp edges are not exposed. Large splinters, protruding nails, and open ends of wire ropes are frequent violations. Nails should not be used in playground equipment. Common remedies for protrusions include countersinking or recessing potential hazards on hardware and covering protruding bolts or tubing with permanent caps or plugs that can be removed only with tools. Protrusions on suspended members of swing assemblies are particularly hazardous since small area impacts can cause skull fracture or skull penetration. All S-hooks should be completely closed to avoid clothing entrapment hazards. It is likely that S-hooks will be prohibited by future standards. Satisfactory substitutions for S-hooks are already available.

Suspended Hazards

The CPSC guidelines prohibit suspended cables, wires, ropes, or similar components within 45 degrees of the horizontal and less than 7 feet above the ground surface. The Canadian (Canadian Institute of Child Health, 1984) and Seattle (Seattle Department of Parks and Recreation, 1986) guidelines specify that no suspended elements less than 1 inch in diameter should be installed in such a manner that allows contact by the user in motion. Such guidelines are not intended to eliminate items such as guard-rails, cargo nets, and climbing grids. Visibility of suspended elements can be enhanced by use of bright colors. Plastic coatings may have some positive effect.

Protective Railings

The CPSC guidelines prescribe protective barriers at least 38 inches high around elevated walking surfaces above 30 inches in height. These should surround the surface except for necessary exits and openings. Dimensions are not prescribed for preschool children. Maximum hand-rail heights can be reduced for younger children. Based on elbow heights of 95th percentile twelve-year-old children (38 inches) and 95th percentile five-year-old children (26 inches), the maximum rail height should correspond to these dimensions. Hand-rail height would vary from about 20 to 26 inches for preschool age children. Hand-rail heights are particularly critical for younger children because of their relatively low levels of motor coordination and strength.

Consumer Information

All playground equipment should be clearly marked with the name, address, and telephone number of the manufacturer. Although not presently required, it is expected that in the future, manufacturers will attach vendor certificates specifying that the equipment conforms to national guidelines or standards. Complete installation and maintenance specifications should also be provided by the manufacturer. These should include guidelines for surfacing.

Toxic Materials and Poisonous Plants

Before beginning a playground, the site should be checked for the existence of toxic materials such as previous land-fill materials or drainage from industrial plants. In addition, children may be exposed to pesticides sprayed in play areas or to toxic wood preservatives in playground equipment. The CPSC recommends that manufacturers ensure that play equipment not contain any hazardous substances that children can ingest, inhale, or absorb through the body. No federal agency presently protects against toxic wood preservatives. A report by Consultants in Epidemiology and Occupational Health, Inc. (1984) concluded that the maximum arsenic exposure for children from using playground equipment is "within the normal variation of carcinogenic exposure for children" (p. 21). On the other hand, the federal Environmental Protection Agency (*Parents Magazine*, May 1985) concluded that infants and toddlers crawling or playing on decks or playground equipment treated with wood preservatives "may be especially susceptible to ill effects since their tolerance to toxins is lower than that of adults" (p. 10). The EPA recommends that decks containing these substances be sealed with at least two coats of shellac or other sealant. In addition, many plants commonly used on playgrounds are poisonous. The prospective playground developer should consult with expert plant nursery operators or other qualified people in the local area to ensure that no plants used on playgrounds are poisonous.

Electrical Hazards

The issue of electrical hazards on playgrounds is not addressed by any of the standards or guidelines of industrialized countries. Nevertheless, electrical hazards on playgrounds are very common. These hazards include exposed air conditioners, electrical switch boxes, and guy wires or other support or access members that allow children to climb into contact with electric wires. All electrical equipment on playgrounds should be fenced or made inaccessible to children, and children should be alerted to potential hazards.

Playground Signs

Because of the growing frequency of lawsuits from playground injuries, signs are appearing on playgrounds with increasing frequency. The Seattle guidelines recommend placing signs for parents and teachers at the entry to all playgrounds. These signs would indicate: (a) special features of the area, (b) suggestions for adult interaction, (c) age group or developmental skills served, and (d) degree of difficulty. Others (Pale Incorporated, 1986; Bruya, 1988) recommend expanding the functions of signs to include information, directions, identification, regulations, and promotion of curriculum.

Playground Equipment Analysis

In the following section, safety problems relevant to the most common playground equipment are examined. A growing practice in schools and cities is to destroy or remove playground equipment that is implicated in injuries. In most cases, this represents poor judgment, for hazardous equipment can often be made safe by modification of the structure or by providing the appropriate resilient material underneath the structure. Equipment is frequently blamed for injuries that are caused by improper surfacing. A second important factor to keep in mind is that playground equipment can be made more challenging without sacrificing safety.

Climbing Equipment

Both metal and wood are common materials used in manufacturing playground equipment. Wood is softer and more forgiving in contacts with bodies but it is prone to splintering, rot, and wear. Metal, on the other hand, may be hot and unattractive. The newer powder-coated metals, including both steel and aluminum, however, resist heat build-up and offer a satisfactory alternative to bare or painted metal. Until recently, exposed bolts were common on almost all commercial metal equipment. Now, efforts are being made to install smooth bolt assemblies or to use materials that do not protrude.

A common hazardous feature that is still being perpetuated by numerous manufacturers is the design of equipment that allows children to fall from one point onto another part of the equipment. For example, the support structure at the bottom entry to chain climbers presents a hazard in the fall zone, as do the ladder rungs lending access to horizontal ladders. Access routes to climbers and decks may include ladders, steps, and stairways. Ladders with rungs should be installed at a 75 degree to 90 degree angle, ladder type steps at 50 degrees to 75 degrees, and stairways at 35 degrees or less. Climbers should not have components that obstruct falls to protective surfacing from the top of the structure or from the inside or outside of the structure. They should not have projections that can entrap clothing, or openings that can entrap portions of the body, including fingers and heads. For example, the distance between rungs on horizontal ladders should be greater than 9 inches and less than 12–14 inches to satisfy entrapment requirements for older children. Nine to 12 inch distances between rungs is appropriate for preschool children, based upon age and developmental levels. A general practical guideline for height of horizontal ladders should be slightly above the reaching height of 95th percentile users. Climbing structures should be zoned to avoid interference with adjacent structures or components. Equipment design should not facilitate climbing on the top of support bars of trapeze-type equipment.

Swings

Swings are frequently involved in playground injuries. Common accidents/injuries include the child falling from the swing to a hard surface, the child falling from the swing and being hit by the seat, and the child running into the path of a moving swing. Most serious swing injuries can be prevented by installing and maintaining proper surfacing underneath the equipment and by providing proper swing seats. The acceptable swing seats are made of light-weight, flexible materials such as rubber and plastic. Heavy glider-type projectiles such as animal-form seats with protruding elements are *extremely* hazardous.

Swings are typically installed too close together. The CPSC recommends 18 inches between seats and between seats and support posts. Standards of other countries take a more conservative position, recommending 24 to 36 inches between these elements. The present author recommends 24 inches between swings and 36 inches between swings and support structures. Swings should be selected according to the various age and developmental needs groups. Infant swing seats need safety straps. Special swings for wheelchairs may be needed for special children. The height of swing beams should be sized to age groups (the higher the swing beam the higher the swinging potential). The beam height of swings should follow the general height requirement for all playground equipment. In general terms, the swing beam should not exceed about 8 feet with 6 to 7 feet being more appropriate for preschool children. The height of the swing seat from the ground should vary from about 16 inches to 18 inches for school-age children; 12 inches to 15 inches for preschool children. Seats for toddlers are placed at a height convenient for adults who are supervising the play activity. The swings should be placed away from traffic areas. Attaching swings to a superstructure increases the possibility of conflicts during play. Extra protection from traffic can be provided by low fences or vertically embedded tires around swing areas. Surfacing materials should be extended to the extent needed to protect children from falls from the swing seat at its maximum height, or at least twice the length of the swing chain.

Slides

Some of the most common hazards on slides include excessive heights, lack of transition decks between ladders and slides, lack of safety railings, insufficient height of slide sides, and inappropriate or poorly maintained surface material underneath. Over 300 children received burns severe enough to seek emergency room treatment in 1988 from playing on slides. The modern, high quality plastic slides are recommended as a solution to this problem. Since toddlers may "freeze" to a hot surface and receive very severe burns, the author recommends that no bare metal decks or slides be installed in toddler playgrounds in hot climates. The CPSC specifies a platform deck of at least 10 inches width at the top entrance to the slide. However, such a small deck area is not sufficient for this purpose. Most modern super-structures employ decks 4 feet square to provide entry and exit surfaces to slides and other exercise options. The CPSC recommends that exit surfaces of slides be at least 16 inches long and parallel to the ground and that the exit itself be 9 to 15 inches above the ground. The length of the exit region and the height above the exit should vary according to age and size of potential users. Protective railings should be provided at the top of the slide chute; they should be at least 24 inches long for both younger and older children. The current CPSC height recommendation of 21 inches for protective barriers is appropriate for twelve-year-old users, but for preschoolers a 16-inch height is more appropriate.

The CPSC recommends a slope not exceeding 30 degrees but in actual play applications, speed of descent varies with the type of slide material and the length of the slide. The German standard (Deutsche Institut fur Normung, 1985) specifies a maximum slope of 40 degrees; this may be more realistic under certain conditions. The speed of the slide should be tested by installers during installation to determine the appropriate angle.

In high impact areas such as the exit of slides, surface materials should be given special consideration. Loose surfacing materials are needed, up to 2 feet deep, because of the frequent displacement of materials and the inadequacy of most maintenance programs. The CPSC guidelines recommend that the sides of slides be at least 2½ inches in height for the entire length of the sliding surface. This is an inadequate dimension. Other countries (Kompan, 1984) require the sides of slides to be 4 to 6 inches high and preschool slides are required to be even higher (7½ inches in Australia). Minimally, slides for all ages should have sides at least 4 inches high.

Merry-go-rounds

Merry-go-rounds have a reputation for being hazardous and for having limited play function. However, available data do not support these contentions. They are more limited in certain play functions than some equipment and some merry-go-rounds are extremely hazardous, particularly those with open spaces in the platform where children can place parts of the body inside and receive severe shearing type injuries. Shearing actions in the undercarriage of badly designed devices severely injure children when they climb underneath the structure. On the other hand, numerous manufacturers produce reasonably safe merry-go-rounds that can add fun and challenge to the playground. Merry-go-rounds are useful for vestibular stimulation (sense of balance), motor activity, and dramatic play. The acceptable types have solid circular bases with strong rigid hand-holds and are free of shearing mechanisms underneath the circular base. At the present time, poorly designed, badly worn, and ill-maintained merry-go-rounds are crushing and amputating fingers and crushing legs. Such outmoded devices should be removed from playgrounds. Serious attention needs to be given to design, installation, maintenance, and supervision of merry-go-rounds. Excessive rotational speed should be limited by supervision and/or by design of the equipment. Protective surfacing should be provided under and around the equipment.

Seesaws

Seesaws are functionally narrow as play devices but they do provide for social activity of children, cooperative play, balance activity, and a limited degree of motor activity: they may be retreats for relaxation and quiet activity. Injuries involving seesaws result from falls, being hit by moving devices, being punctured by splinters, being cut by exposed bolts, having hands crushed by fulcrums, and having feet crushed between the ends of seesaws and the ground.

Car tires are commonly used to cushion the effect of seesaws hitting the ground. These may be attached to the bottom of the seesaw or buried in the ground. Fulcrums of seesaws should be completely enclosed unless they are of the spring type, in which case the spring should not allow for crushing of fingers. The distance between seesaws should be twice the arm length of users and the height should be sized to the age group. The Australian standard specifies a maximum of 6 feet from the ground to the end of the seesaw at maximum height. This appears to be excessive, certainly for preschool children. Rocking type seesaws, spring mounted seesaws, or scaled down seesaws are appropriate for preschool children. Protective surfacing should be provided.

Portable Play Materials

The high quality preschool playground contains a wide variety of portable play materials, including barrels, crates, tires, etc. These materials, like the heavy-duty playground equipment, should be subjected to regular inspection, including examination for loose parts, broken parts, and parts that may be dislodged and swallowed. All such material should be kept in good repair. A supply of parts for wheeled vehicles is needed to ensure safe equipment. A storage facility adjacent to the playground may be needed to protect the materials from the elements and from vandalism and theft.

Playground Surfacing

The Consumer Product Safety Commission identified falling from equipment onto hard surfacing as the major cause of playground injuries. Between 60 and 70 percent of all injuries occur as children fall onto surfacing material beneath the equipment or fall from one part of equipment onto another part. Recent CPSC data show that 90 percent of serious injuries in playgrounds result from falls to hard surfaces (Tinsworth & Kramer, 1990). Consequently, the most direct means for reducing playground injuries is by installing resilient surfacing material under and around the playground equipment as recommended by CPSC.

Although no large-scale scientific studies have been conducted regarding the effectiveness of surfacing material in real life playground conditions, data from the Los Angeles school system give indications of its effectiveness. Over a 20-year period, ending in 1951 with the fall of a six-year-old boy from a swing onto an asphalt surface, the Los Angeles school system recorded 11 playground deaths. In 1955 the Los Angeles school system installed rubber surfacing under playground equipment, and no additional deaths were reported during the next decade. Further, the incidence of fractures and concussions was reduced from 1.25 per school in 1951 to 0.47 in 1965 (Butwinick, 1974).

Commercial surfacing material is only one of several types available that meet the requirements of the CPSC. Others can be categorized under "loose organic materials" and "loose inorganic materials."

Loose organic materials include bark nuggets, mulch, coco shell mulch, and shredded wood. Inorganic loose materials include sand and pea gravel. All of the available materials have both advantages and disadvantages.

Loose Organic Materials

Advantages:
- These materials present an esthetically pleasing appearance.
- These materials are usually inexpensive.
- These materials are not carried into buildings as readily as are inorganic loose materials.

Disadvantages:
- These materials decompose over time.
- The trapped air necessary for protective cushioning is affected by rain and humidity.
- These materials will freeze.
- When wet these materials may allow for micro-organism growth.
- Wind may blow these materials.
- These materials may be blown into children's eyes.
- They may harbor insects.
- They may lose their cushioning properties as dirt and other materials are combined with them.
- They require constant maintenance.

Proper installation of these materials requires that they be kept in place 10 to 12 inches deep in all areas, particularly in high impact areas such as ends of slides and underneath swings.

Inorganic Loose Materials

Advantages:
- Sand is an excellent play material. (Pea gravel has relatively little play value.)
- These materials are inexpensive in most areas.

Disadvantages:
- These materials are displaced by children's playing and must be replenished regularly.
- These materials may be blown or thrown into children's eyes.
- These materials may become compacted.
- They may harbor insects or broken glass.
- They may lose their cushioning properties as they are combined with dirt or other materials.

- These materials may freeze (sand is particularly prone to freezing).
- Pea gravel is particularly hard to walk on.
- These materials require continuous maintenance.
- Wheel chairs will not roll on these materials.
- When installed adjacent to wheeled vehicle tracks they create slippery areas on the hard surface.

Proper installation of inorganic loose materials requires that they be kept in place, 10 to 12 inches deep, with particular attention given to high impact and high use areas such as ends of slides and underneath swings.

Loose materials or inorganic materials should never be installed over concrete or asphalt because with use, and the "pitting effect," hard surfaces are not properly protected.

Commercial Materials (e.g., rubber mats, synthetic turf)

Advantages:
- Some of these materials appear to be very durable. Durability tests in real playground situations have not been conducted over sufficient time to allow clear conclusions.
- These materials are easier to keep clean than are the loose materials. In most applications hosing down is all that is required to clean the surface areas.
- These materials require less maintenance than loose materials.

Disadvantages:
- These materials are subject to vandalism.
- They must be used on level, compact surfaces such as asphalt, concrete, or packed aggregate.
- These materials may be flammable.
- Performance of these materials depends upon the base foundation.
- They may be constructed using toxic materials.
- These materials are very expensive, ranging in price from $8.00 to $14.00 per square foot (1990 prices) plus the cost of a solid base foundation.

Depth of surfacing materials must vary with height of equipment. The surface materials must meet approved G Tests of the CPSC and installation must be done by trained installers. A variation of commercial materials, not mentioned above, is the chopped rubber material that is poured into place and remains in a relatively loose state. These materials have additional disadvantages compared to other commercial materials. They are subject to shifting, must be replenished regularly, and may be ingested by small children.

A great deal of controversy is currently revolving around the appropriateness of various surfacing materials. Laboratory test data submitted to the National Recreation and Park Association (1976) by the Franklin Testing Institute resulted in the following conclusions:

Extremely Hazardous
concrete, asphalt, packed earth

Conditionally Acceptable
gym mat 2″, double thick gym mat, rubber mat, double thick rubber mats, pea gravel, wood chips

Acceptable
sand 8–10″

In its February 1979 report (Mahajan & Beine, 1979) *Impact Attenuation Performance of Surfaces Under Playground Equipment*, the National Bureau of Standards concluded that pea gravel failed the 200g drop test for heights under 4 feet. This finding contradicts tests by the Franklin Institute, just described, and other published data by playground and surfacing companies. Recent tests conducted by the Consumer Product Safety Commission (Ramsey & Preston, 1990) found that pea gravel met the 200g drop test to heights of approximately 6 to 7 feet.

Consequently, questions must be raised about the quality and size of the pea gravel tested. Pea gravel ranges in size from about 1/16 to 1/2 inch in diameter and in some cases crushed rock may be designated "pea gravel." Fine (1/4 inch) river-washed pea gravel appears to be the most desirable type.

The American Society for Testing and Materials is currently developing playground surfacing standards. With the publication of these standards, clearer direction will be available. It must be remembered by all playground developers and users that surfacing material, no matter how excellent initially, is useless unless it is properly maintained. For loose materials this means constant attention to inspection and repair. It is very likely that high-use playgrounds at public parks and public schools will increasingly use commercial materials since the maintenance requirements are considerably less than for loose materials.

Safety Responsibilities

The results of the national survey of preschool playgrounds, reported in this book, reveal an overall pattern of poor equipment design, neglect, abuse, and lack of maintenance. Another major contributing factor to playground injuries is the on-going sale of hazardous equipment by manufacturers and their representatives.

Frost (1990) compared the equipment in the 1989 catalogs of 24 national distributors against the Consumer Product Safety Commission guidelines. He found that half of these companies marketed equipment with "extensive violations" or "extreme violations"; nine of the companies marketed equipment with "limited violations" or "some violations"; only three companies marketed equipment with no violations. Despite the fact that such violations were confirmed in independent, blind analyses, many manufacturers continue to deny that their products are unsafe or that they violate CPSC guidelines.

Fortunately, a growing number of manufacturers are improving the safety features of their equipment. A few interact regularly in national and international conferences, workshops, and professional organizations with play specialists from various disciplines. A large representation is involved in the development of national safety standards/ guidelines, sponsored by the Consumer Product Safety Commission and the American Society for Testing and Materials. A few manufacturers are improving their involvement in consumer education by providing information on child development, installation, maintenance, and supervision to prospective purchasers of their equipment.

It is clear that no single group, working alone, can significantly improve the safety of children's playgrounds. National agencies can develop and monitor safety guidelines/standards and manufacturers can improve equipment design and offer educational services. But educated consumers are needed to ensure that high quality programs of maintenance (Chapter 8) and play leadership (Chapter 10) are available. Finally, we must provide safety education for all children and build strong physical fitness programs to help them meet playground challenges with intelligence and skill.

References

Butwinick, E. (1974). Petition requesting the issuance of a consumer product safety standard for public playground slides, swinging apparatus and climbing equipment. Washington, DC: United States Consumer Product Safety Commission.

Canadian Institute of Child Health. (1984). *Draft for children's play spaces and equipment*. Canadian Institute of Child Health.

Consultants in Epidemiology and Occupational Health, Inc. (1984). *Evaluation of risk to children using arsenic-treated playground equipment*. Sacramento, CA: California State Department of Health Services.

Deutsche Institut fur Normung (DIN). (1985). *Playground equipment for children: Concepts, safety requirements, testing*. Berlin, West Germany: Deutsche Institut fur Normung. Translation by British Standards Institution.

Frost, J.L. (1990). How safe is American playground equipment. *Texas Child Care Quarterly*.

King, K., & Ball, D. (1989) *A holistic approach to accident and injury prevention in children's playgrounds*. London: LCS, Great Guildford House.

Kompan, Inc. (1984). *Playgrounds and safety: Comparisons between various playground equipment standards—American, Australian, British, German*. Windsor Locks, CT: Kompan, Inc.

Mahajan, B.M., & Beine, W.B. (1979). *Impact attenuation performance of surfaces installed under playground equipment*. Bethesda, MD: Consumer Product Safety Commission.

National Recreation and Park Association. (1976). Proposed safety standard for public playground equipment. Arlington, VA: National Recreation and Park Association.

Parent's Magazine. (1985). Beware! Wood preservatives can kill. *Parent's Magazine*, May 1985.

Ramsey, L.F., & Preston, J.D. (1990). *Impact attenuation performance of playground surfacing materials*. Washington, DC: U.S. Consumer Product Safety Commission.

Seattle Department of Parks and Recreation. (1986). *Draft design guidelines for play areas*. Seattle, WA: Seattle Department of Parks and Recreation.

Tinsworth, D.K., & Kramer, J.T. (1990). *Playground equipment related injuries and deaths*. Washington, DC: U.S. Consumer Product Safety Commission.

U.S. Consumer Product Safety Commission. (1981a). *A handbook for public playground safety. Volume 1: General guidelines for new and existing playgrounds*. Washington, DC: U.S. Government Printing Office.

U.S. Consumer Product Safety Commission. (1981b). *A handbook for public playground safety. Volume II: Technical guidelines for equipment and surfacing*. Washington, DC: U.S. Government Printing Office.

5

Play Environments for Young Children: Design Perspectives

Steen B. Esbensen

A child said to the Universe, I exist!
That, replied the Universe,
has created a sense of obligation for adults.

Those of us working with and on behalf of young children have a shared professional objective—to use our talents and skills to help improve the quality of their lives. Play environments for young children serve a crucial role in this context, providing us with a means of channeling our efforts to improve the quality of children's life experiences. Outdoor play environments for young children have been the focus of considerable professional attention over the last 20 years and the evolution of what is considered good professional practice is substantial. In this chapter we will provide an overview of the issues and a perspective on the emergence of the design of safe, stimulating, and appropriate play environments.

Over the years, numerous early childhood educators—Dewey, Froebel, Montessori, Prescott, Read, Stone, and many others—have advocated and brought to the attention of teachers of young children the need for outdoor play environments. Despite the efforts of these educators, however, the outdoor play space has historically been perceived as primarily providing an opportunity for young children to become actively involved in physical exercise and to replenish their bodies with fresh air. There is nothing particularly wrong with this, but from the perspective that we wish to offer, such a perception provides a limited view of the purpose of the outdoor play experience. The outdoor play environment, in our view, should provide young children with experiences that enable them to increase their knowledge of and contacts with nature, and to have opportunities to explore play and learning situations designed to enhance their personal well-being.

Historical Perspective

The history of formal playgrounds for young children can be traced back to the end of the nineteenth century. At that time, the corner sandbox playgrounds provided a swing, a slide, a square sandbox, and a wooden climbing frame. The early equipment was generally built to suit the size of young children and was placed on a sand or grass surface. While such playgrounds were few and far between, they nonetheless influenced the design of playgrounds for day nurseries in cities throughout North America.

The demand for child care experienced by western industrial societies in the course of the twentieth century contributed to the increased need for outdoor play environments. Prior to the existence of formal early childhood education programs, outdoor play environments for young children were either the sandbox playgrounds built in some inner-city neighborhoods or the area in front of or behind people's homes. Children of all ages used the streets, sidewalks, and alleys as play areas before the automobile took over these spaces. As parents began to enroll their children in group experiences such as cooperative nursery schools and day care centers, play environments for young children began to evolve and the standard playground equipment of slides, swings, and climbing frames was augmented by blocks, boards, dress-up clothes, and other loose materials.

The advent of Head Start in the United States and a corresponding increase in the number of day care centers in other western societies over the last 20 years has had an influence on playground design worldwide. Playgrounds for young children, as well as the design of playground equipment, have been developed over the course of these decades. A brief overview of theoretical and practical influences will help us to understand current practice.

Adventure Playgrounds

One group of playground designers was influenced by the "back to nature movement," which had such a profound impact on the evolution of play environments that nature is no longer ignored in their design. Although it was not one specific theory or the work of any one individual that brought nature back into vogue, it is appropriate to recognize the contribution of the landscape architect T.H. Sørenson. In 1931, he introduced the concept of the "adventure playground" (*skrammellegeplads*) and saw his idea realized in 1943 in Emdrup Banke, a new suburban community north of Copenhagen. This playground concept was intended to serve the needs of children aged 6 to 13 by providing them with an opportunity to play with old cars, boxes, boards, fire, water, and animals in a supervised setting within the community. Numerous early childhood educators and playground designers adopted the design and play principles advanced by this concept. Indeed, many dedicated professionals advocated the concept of the adventure playground as part of their efforts to balance the relationship between the child, nature, and the urban environment. Unfortunately, the concept was not always well understood and, in many cases, efforts to create adventure playgrounds failed as a result of misunderstandings and insufficient community support. The concept of the adventure playground did, however, influence theoretical debate and practical considerations within the playground design community.

Environmental Yards

The concept of the "environmental yard" was advocated by those who saw the schoolyard as a potential outdoor extension of the school environment. Among the best known is Robin Moore (1973, 1985), who initiated a project to make a schoolyard a communal place for learning, recreation, and creative play, for the school population and everyone in the larger community. The project, located at Washington (a university laboratory school) near the center of Berkeley and called the Washington Environmental Yard (WEY), has continued to inspire designers and teachers interested in environmental education. The WEY is a good example of a school site being redeveloped to meet the educational and play needs of children in the city, and for many years a balance among natural elements, loose parts, built playground equipment, and supervision-animation was achieved there.

Work Yards

The movement toward "playgrounds for free" or recycled playgrounds with lots of "loose parts" emerged in part from the adventure playground concept and from Simon Nicholson's "theory of loose parts" (1971). During this era, playground designers used recycled telephone poles, tires, railroad ties, and the like to build playgrounds for children, including young children. These playground designers were directly influenced by the concept of "work yards" introduced by Rudolph in 1974. The proposed guidelines for such playgrounds were very similar to those of the adventure playground concept proposed by Sørenson in 1931, but the concept was developmentally inappropriate for young children. While children should be provided with opportunities to build their own playgrounds and influence playground design, the work yards concept was age-inappropriate. However, for better or worse, it had an impact on playground design throughout North America.

Creative Playgrounds

Playgrounds for young children were considerably influenced by both the adventure playground concept and the subsequent trend of the "creative playground." Both these concepts were geared to the play and developmental needs of school-aged children. However, as the creative playground evolved from the "build your own" to a ready-made consumer product, multi-level, multi-purpose, high-density-use "creative" playground equipment was increasingly placed in settings for young children. During the 1970s, playground equipment was constructed from massive timber, and the height and platform sizes were built to the scale of the adult builders—far too massive for the smaller users. For nearly a decade, it was virtually impossible to distinguish between playground equipment for school-aged children and playground equipment for preschool children. It was almost as if there had been a collective loss of memory as to the size, developmental needs, and play behaviors of young children. However, many concerned early childhood educators and playground designers were working to promote the development of ecologically balanced playgrounds. Cooperative nursery schools, day care centers, public parks, and school playgrounds all experienced various degrees of influence from these trends within the playground movement.

Safety Concerns

Toward the end of the 1970s, practitioners and professionals began to focus on safety issues. This was in part due to studies undertaken by the medical profession on the causes of accidents that brought children to the emergency units in hospitals. These studies, combined with an increase in the number of playground accidents generating liability suits and subsequent insurance settlements, caused safety to become a most important consideration in the playground industry for several years. In 1981, the United States Consumer Products Safety Commission (USCPSC) published guidelines for playgrounds and play equipment that included safety factors for location, accessibility, placement, and size of equipment. *A Handbook for Public Playground Safety* (USCPSC, 1981) was used extensively to assess safety on public playgrounds.

Publications of the Canada Mortgage and Housing Corporation (CMHC) also provided extensive recommendations for the design of play environments for young children and school-aged children. *Play Spaces for Preschools* (CMHC, 1978) provided design criteria and recommendations for the operation of play spaces for young children in housing developments. Safety considerations were related to the overall design concept; details relating to the type of material used were not elaborated upon in these documents. Responsible professional practice advocated in these publications advised playground designers to provide for four different play zones—creative-cognitive play, social play, physical play, and quiet-retreat play—and to utilize as much soft surface material as possible, using hard surfacing only for specific purposes. Incorrect positioning and poor organization of the play area and equipment can serve to make the environment unsafe as well as unusable. Discussions of general design considerations and of the arrangement of equipment on the site, as well as suggestions for surfacing around and underneath the equipment, dominated much of the literature on playground design.

Specific consideration of playground safety intensified in the early 1980s. In 1983, the Child Accident Prevention Foundation of Australia published the work of Jill Root, *Play Without Pain: A Manual for*

Playground Safety. In 1984, *Hidden Hazards on Playgrounds for Young Children* (Esbensen, 1984) was widely disseminated in Canada, and the Canadian Institute of Child Health submitted its report and guidelines to the Canadian Standards Association in the hope of generating a national standard for safe playground design (final document for circulation still pending). The focus on safe playgrounds was further reinforced by the *Play for All Guidelines* document by Moore, published in 1987. This publication represents the cumulative efforts and results of the most active playground designers, consultants, and manufacturers in the United States. The guidelines provide an excellent tool to assist with the planning, design, and ongoing management of children's play environments. However, the one shortcoming of the publication is that, in its effort to design for all children, it has not sufficiently recognized the unique needs of preschool children. In this respect, *The Early Childhood Playground: An Outdoor Classroom* (Esbensen, 1987) complements the previous publication by Moore by calling attention to the specific developmental characteristics of young children and by dealing with safety issues in the context of organizing an outdoor play environment to reflect the curriculum objectives of the early childhood education center.

Past experiences have indeed influenced contemporary practice. We can identify substantial changes to the design of play spaces for young children over the last decade. We have seen significant changes in the attention given to safe play, and the recent National Survey of Playground Equipment in Preschool Centers attests to the ongoing concern for improvements. It is noteworthy that the manufacturers of playground equipment have also responded to the concern for safe, fun, and quality play experiences by making improvements to the manufactured products. Yet, notwithstanding this sense of optimism, there are still many challenges ahead for planners, designers, early childhood educators, and playground manufacturers.

The Outdoor Classroom

The outdoor space adjacent to an early childhood facility, be it a nursery school, day care center, or a kindergarten in a public school building, has been strongly influenced by the trends in playground design. Read (1966) reminded us that supplying plenty of space and outdoor equipment helps to provide young children with essential living and learning experiences. If there is insufficient play space outside, children may well be reluctant to go outdoors. To develop an appropriate outdoor play environment on the same site as an early childhood center, a minimum of 100 square feet per child should be allocated (Esbensen, 1990). This would suggest that many day care licensing standards for outdoor play space in North America are inadequate.

Esbensen (1987) suggested that a playground attached to an early childhood education facility should be considered an outdoor classroom. It should be a learning environment designed to meet curriculum objectives by encouraging child-initiated, teacher-supported play activities that are both stimulating and safe. It should also be an environment in which the children are able to influence the evolution of the space and the materials provided for their use. Basic principles for the development of new early childhood centers must be considered when a comprehensive facility to accommodate young children is planned. Nash (1976) provided a practical approach to planning the classroom space. Hohmann (1983) elaborated on how to arrange and equip the classroom and encourage indoor-outdoor activities. Esbensen (1990) provides specific design considerations for buildings and indoor classroom organization, as well as for their complementarity with the outdoor classroom.

The indoor space in a preschool center should have a door opening directly onto the outdoor play environment. It is most desirable that the indoor and outdoor play and learning environments be adjacent, as this has the benefit of reducing the time spent in supervision of the children as they flow back and forth between the two areas. It also has the advantage of giving teachers time to concentrate on the task of facilitating learning through play and to spend quality time with the children, as opposed to being their custodians.

The amount of time young children spend outdoors varies according to the teacher's perceptions of the importance of outdoor play experiences. The quality of the outdoor experience depends in part on the amount and quality of the space available. Historically, the cooperative nursery school movement and health practitioners have stated that young children should spend half the duration of a program in outdoor play. Unfortunately, neither this amount of time nor the appropriate amount of outdoor space is available in early childhood education centers in North America. Most children attending day care centers, kindergartens, and nursery schools now spend the major part of the day inside.

The challenge for early childhood educators and play advocates is twofold: to allocate a sufficient quantity of time to outdoor play experiences, and to ensure that a high-quality outdoor play environment is available. The outdoor play space should be designed so as to provide opportunities for children to develop physical dexterity as well as social, emotional, and intellectual skills.

The need for outdoor play experiences for young children is not new. For decades, teachers and advocates of quality early childhood experiences for young children have written about the need to provide plenty of outdoor play space and equipment to offer children essential living and learning experiences. Space is the first and most essential ingredient for developing a quality outdoor environment. Without ample space, young children will have no desire to go out and there will be no possibility of developing the outdoor classroom according to child-centered design principles. Furthermore, if the outdoor space is not designed to attract the children to use it, they will prefer to stay inside and will not benefit from the outdoor experiences so essential to their well-being. Finally, but not least important, the site selected for a center should be located away from congested streets so as to minimize the potential hazard of automobiles and to reduce the dangerous effects of exhaust fumes.

Practical Considerations

Any well-designed preschool center building in North America should have an overhanging roof to provide filtered light and to create a porch or patio-like setting for use on excessively hot or rainy days. Such a feature should be large enough to allow the use of a variety of play materials: wheeled toys, hollow blocks, and woodworking, clay, and painting materials.

Unfortunately, these recommendations, which date from the early years of the nursery school movement, have only recently begun to be incorporated into the design criteria for new early childhood education centers. Currently, young children are being cared for in buildings initially designed to accommodate school-aged children and are thus forced to experience adult supervision and control as they change their clothes, wait in line to go to the bathroom, wait for others to be ready to walk down the corridor together, and wait for everyone to be quiet before going down the stairs and outside, eventually arriving at the outdoor play setting. What will this outdoor play setting be—a quality outdoor environment with interesting and varied materials or a space without character?

Sadly, the National Survey of Playground Equipment in Preschool Centers confirms that the majority of outdoor play environments are less than ideal pedagogically. Only 19 percent of 349 preschool centers located in 31 states provided wooden blocks in the outdoor classroom and only about half of the centers provided other manipulative play materials such as tools, buckets, balls, trucks, cars, and other small toys. Even such equipment as wheeled toys for riding, pushing, or pulling was available in only about half of the centers. Garden areas in which children could plant and nurture their crops were virtually non-existent; 85 percent of the centers did not provide such an area in the outdoor environment. This statistic alone should be cause for alarm among early childhood educators and advocates of quality play experiences for children, as increasing numbers of young children are growing up in apartment buildings, small housing units, and narrow city or suburban lots.

Social Perspectives

The majority of North American children are growing up in an urban environment and more than half of mothers with young children are now active in the work force. More and more young children are being care for in supervised early childhood programs and therefore the need for quality outdoor play environments is becoming more and more vital. While contemporary practice is less than ideal, it is necessary to establish what we consider to be essential in providing inviting, well-equipped, and stimulating play and learning environments for young children. The following suggestions for designing the outdoor play environment are offered to assist early childhood educators faced with the challenge of creating a new play space or redesigning less than adequate space to make the curriculum work.

The Play Space

A fence at least 4 feet high must surround the playground to create an enclosed outdoor play space. The fence should be built so as to discourage children from climbing over it. It should also conform to the specific safety considerations applied to equipment. The fence can also serve as a screen to reduce the force of frigid winter winds. Evergreen hedges and trees, along with see-through fencing, will help to balance the perception of size as well as to create microclimatic conditions amenable to outdoor play.

Surfacing Textures

A variety of surfacing textures should be provided. Play should be possible on grassy areas, in sand, on gravel, at different heights, and on surfaces that allow for the use of wheeled toys. As sand can be used as both an impact-absorbing material and as a play material, it is important to select the appropriate grade of sand for specific use and to contain it according to its function. A hedge or similar windscreen can serve to prevent the sand from being blown or carried over the entire site. Other materials that have been used as impact-absorbing surfacing include granulated pine bark, rubber matting, and shredded rubber. Such materials should be selected on the basis of a thorough analysis of the site, the age of the users, and the test reliability for absorbing falls from equipment. Sand continues to be the most frequently used surfacing material under swing structures, sliding structures, and climbing equipment (32.16 percent in the National Survey).

Nature

Nature is at risk of disappearing from the daily life experiences of young children growing up in urban North American settings. The competing forces for land use and the development of revenue-generating space make it exceedingly difficult to design playgrounds with an abundance of natural materials. The climatic conditions of a play space can be affected by the presence of trees, bushes, and hedgerows, and a variety of nontoxic vegetation, including edible fruit-bearing bushes, can also serve to enhance the curriculum. Unfortunately, the National Survey confirms that the majority of playgrounds do not include trees, either to deflect the wind or to serve as part of the play structure. In fact, the survey revealed that only 9.91 percent of the 276 centers with designated sand play areas indicated that they were separate from the other play areas. An area for digging, a pile of either soil or sand, or a more generous garden area where children could dig and plant to their heart's content were reportedly very scarce, as was the availability of water play. It appears that much work has to be done to convince the responsible adults of the need to provide these essential curriculum materials in the outdoor classroom.

Design Perspectives

The variety of play experiences and materials that have been suggested for the development of the outdoor classroom prompts us to propose a design framework based on zones (Esbensen, 1980, 1987).

One can choose from a variety of zone frameworks to organize the playground. Frost and Klein (1983) proposed that the playground be organized in zones based on four forms of play: physical, social, dramatic, and cognitive. In 1978, the CMHC published *Play Spaces for Preschoolers*, prepared by Hill, Esbensen, and Rock, in which it was proposed that the playground should be organized according to four categories of development: emotional, intellectual, social, and physical. Esbensen (1980) illustrated the application of this zoning, and many landscape architects and playground designers worked with these frameworks. As a result of the many applications of the four-zone framework, a more detailed framework evolved specifically for use in the design of an outdoor environment for an early childhood education center. Seven different zones were proposed to provide a way of conceptualizing the layout of the play space (Esbensen, 1987). Each of the zones accommodates play materials and equipment to facilitate the range of play experiences that most stimulate young children. With the aid of this design framework, the designer can set the stage for play and introduce a range of loose play materials to complement and enhance the play value over the course of the year. The seven zones suggested to help conceptualize the space use are: transition, manipulative/creative, projective/fantasy, focal/social, social/dramatic, physical, and natural elements.

Transition Zone

The area immediately outside the building is referred to as the transition zone. It serves essentially as an area where children have an opportunity to look out onto the space, assess their options, and make choices. The zone is low-key in character, providing relatively quiet activities such as easel or table painting and play opportunities with clay, a water table, and/or some wheeled toys ready for use. The zone serves to enable children to make the move from indoors to outdoors at their own pace. As with all zone elements, the transition zone may partially overlap with others, most probably with the following three.

Manipulative/Creative Zone

The play behaviors observed in this zone are characterized by relatively quiet and concentrated activities, and the materials provided support such play behaviors. The outdoor manipulative/creative materials could include clay, plasticine, play dough, and paints, as well as such equipment as a water table, easels, and a

carpentry bench for woodworking outdoors. These materials, when available outdoors, provide young children with additional opportunities for creative expression and concentration.

Projective/Fantasy Zone

A separate sand area, sandbox, or sand table that allows children to mix sand and water and to use small objects to pretend and project their ideas can enhance their play. Attention to detail in providing small wooden or plastic vehicles and animals, cartons, containers, spoons, small shovels, and buckets will also influence the quality of the play experience in this zone. A range of more elaborate design ideas is possible for this area—for example, a water pump situated on a small mound from which water can cascade down into the sand/water area or a water wheel adjacent to the sand area. There are many options for projective/fantasy play in a relatively quiet concentrated area.

Focal/Social Zone

An area where teachers and children can quietly sit together, talk, and observe the activities going on around them should be provided in a relatively central place on the site. In a formal design, one could imagine a small, raised gazebo with a round table and stools accommodating both children and adults. In a more informal design, one could imagine a round table centrally positioned near a shady tree. A couple of single-seat rockers or loose rocking chairs could be placed adjacent to the table (within a safe distance). This zone offers children an opportunity to observe without any obligation to take part in the more active play. It also enables the more withdrawn, shy, or new child to gradually become interested in participating in the play activities.

Social/Dramatic Zone

This zone can be developed either in a formal architectural way or in a non-structured way. The designer may choose to set up a small village with small-scale play houses and stores furnished with tables and benches; this will enable the children to engage in parallel, associative, or cooperative play activities. Large hollow blocks and boards, along with dress-up clothes, household utensils, and other such props, can serve to enhance the quality of play in either a formal or a non-structured environment. Proximity to a wheeled toy pathway, with a parking area for tricycles and wagons, along with a water

faucet or fountain, will have a striking impact on the quality of the dramatic play activities. The surface in this zone could be either grass or sand, but if the play houses are built up as on a "creative playground" play structure, sand is the recommended surfacing material for the zone.

Physical Zone

This zone should provide opportunities for running, climbing, rolling, sliding, and balancing. A site that has been landscaped to provide a variety of topographical changes—mounds, small hills, trees, bushes, and/or tree stumps—can help to provide a number of motor challenges for children to dodge around, over, and behind. In addition, the zone should provide fixed equipment to enable them to swing, slide, and climb. The materials in this zone take up considerable space and the activities generate active and rambunctious behaviors; therefore the zone should be situated at some distance from the quieter activity zones.

Natural Elements Zone

It has already been noted that nature is at risk of disappearing from the daily life experiences of children. It is desirable to provide natural elements—trees, bushes, flowers, grass, sand, and water—throughout the outdoor play environment. In order to complement these natural elements, a more defined garden area should be provided. This will enable young children to plant, water, and weed their own garden and to reap the benefits of the harvest. The garden plots should be easily accessible and set out in such a way as to minimize the chance of children accidentally walking or running over the vegetation. The garden plot should be close to a water source and a storage shed for garden tools.

A non-structured area to allow children to dig in piles of dirt should also be planned for on the site. Likewise, areas with tall grass and wild flowers will encourage a variety of insects and birds to visit the yard. A wide variety of natural elements can only serve to enhance the overall quality of the play and learning experiences in the outdoor classroom.

Perspectives on Zones

The zone framework has been used by designers of playgrounds for young children, early childhood educators, and researchers to conceptualize the layout of the various play elements on a site. Designers of playgrounds begin their work by undertaking a thorough assessment of the site, measuring the perimeter, and analyzing the surface materials, climatic and sun-shade conditions, and the relationship of surrounding buildings to the potential playground. Once this analysis is complete and the client has been consulted, the designer and the client proceed to lay out the various zones and to evaluate them in accordance with the stated curriculum objectives and the site assessment. In this way, teachers of young children become involved as one of the clients in the design process and their views of play help to determine the initial focus given to the outdoor play environment. Thus, the quality of the outdoor play environment is directly related to the interest and importance given to it by the early childhood educators. Playground design consultants also play an important role. However, if teachers think of the outdoors as merely a space to allow children to let off steam and/or to allow the teachers themselves to get a break from interacting with the children, then the sites will not be developed as proposed in this chapter.

Researchers have used the framework to develop assessment tools and to guide observation of play patterns on the playground, and teachers have used the framework to help plan their activities. Zoning the play area serves to facilitate the organization of the space in such a way as to incorporate the developmental needs of young children, safety considerations such as size and surfacing of areas, and the learning opportunities available. The design perspective that utilizes a zone framework, whether it be a four- or seven-zone model, provides the flexibility for teachers to elaborate on each zone by introducing new components to each area over time. They can group play areas by analyzing the kinds of activities occurring in the zones and thus determine whether such activities are compatible with the stated objectives.

If the outdoor play environment is to provide safe and challenging play and learning opportunities, it is not enough to give attention only to the design and organization of the site. Attention must also be given to the furniture and playground equipment selected for the different zones. With good design and proper furnishings and careful and regular maintenance, the early childhood outdoor classroom will be a good place for children and adults to enjoy interacting with each other and the materials.

The attention given to designing and organizing the space for play will permit teachers to focus their attention on enhancing the quality of the experiences available in the child care setting. Quality time in a quality environment produces quality early childhood experiences and serves to improve the standard of professional practice.

Research Perspectives

The National Survey of Playground Equipment in Preschool Centers is based on the assessment of 349 preschool centers located in 31 states. Some of the results presented by the survey are alarming, and others are reassuring.

First, if we are concerned with the need to provide natural elements in the playground, it is alarming that, as previously indicated, 85 percent of the centers had no garden area and that 88 percent of the centers did not include trees either as part of the play setting or as natural windbreaks. Furthermore, it is discouraging that relatively few centers provided water and that only about 10 percent of the 276 centers with designated sand play areas provided these as separate areas.

Among the items relating specifically to good professional practice, and less to the playground design component, is the section of the survey concerning loose parts, such as wheeled toys and manipulative materials. It is alarming to find that only about half of the centers provided a range of manipulative materials. Only 19 percent provided wooden building blocks, and the only indication of woodworking or carpentry materials is found in the portable materials survey, which reveals that only 22 carpentry tools were recorded in the entire survey (.06 per center). Art materials and gardening tools represent 1.83 percent and 1.94 percent respectively of all portable equipment —hardly a good sign that the outdoor play environment is being used to enhance essential living and learning experiences for young children. Other loose parts, such as wheeled toys, were available in only about 50 percent of the centers.

The sections of the survey focusing on the materials necessary to support the quality of play activities for young children provide results indicating great shortcomings in the field. If we attempt to find more encouraging results by looking at the other provisions for play in Section 1 of the survey, we are disappointed. In the 349 centers only 118 tables were provided. As we do not know how many tables were in each of the centers, it is impossible to determine what percentage of centers provided tables. However, tables did account for 4.42 percent of the other play provisions in the playgrounds. Again, this is hardly encouraging. The variety of equipment and other materials listed in the survey is not impressive in terms of absolute numbers or in terms of the percentage of equipment available. The materials and equipment identified as most supportive of the transition, manipulative/creative, projective/fantasy, focal/ social, social/dramatic, and natural elements zones were unfortunately rarely provided in this sample of preschool playgrounds. When these results are compared with the design recommendations presented earlier in this chapter, it becomes very clear that there is room for much improvement in the field.

An attempt to ascertain whether or not the physical zone was more adequately furnished required cross-analysis of various sections of the survey. In general, it appears that all centers provided swings, slides, and some form of climbing equipment. Almost all centers had grassy areas for running and organized games. Indeed, it appears the equipment that most encourages gross motor activity was numerically well represented in the 349 centers. Although it was ascertained that 55 percent of the centers provided 10 feet between equipment, the quality of their placement on the site, their complementarity to other materials, and their play value cannot be determined from the survey. However, some conclusions can be reached on the relative quality of the equipment. For example, of the 1,046 pieces of climbing equipment identified, 44 had head entrapment openings of between 4½ and 9 inches. Another 29 percent had openings of between 7 and 11 inches on hand holds or foot supports (ladders, steps). Depending upon the specific height, depth, and angle of these openings, they may or may not constitute a hidden hazard. Likewise, the fact that 61 percent of all climbing equipment had guard rails around the highest platforms would not preclude the risk of falls. Indeed, if the guard rails consist of a single horizontal bar, connected above the platform and with a clear opening of between 18 and 28 inches, then children between the ages of two and five years could fall off the equipment from a sitting position. Such information is not available in the survey but would be helpful in subsequent studies. The surfacing material found under 33 percent of climbing equipment with an average maximum height of 5 feet 4 inches was sand. Fortunately, only 6.5 percent of surfacing found under climbing equipment was gravel, asphalt, or concrete.

Swings averaged more than one per center (a total of 554, or 1.58 per center), with an average of 2.62 swing seats per center. Only 60 swings, or 11 percent, had barriers around the swing structures to prevent children from running into and colliding with the swings. Furthermore, 44 percent of the surveyed centers provided unacceptable surfacing materials underneath the swings. These preliminary observations indicate that there is still a great need for education on the issues of safety and on ways to reduce accidents in playgrounds for young children.

Sliding structures were also very common in the playgrounds surveyed. Only 50 percent had deceleration chutes to enable children to get off the end of the slide slowly. Only 34 percent of 531 pieces of sliding equipment had sand as a surfacing material, while 40 percent of the surfacing material was clearly unacceptable. While 21 percent of the slides were wide enough to accommodate more than one child sliding side-by-side at the same time, no information was available as to the protective siding on these or on the single-child slides. Did they have a 3- to 6-inch siding along the sliding surface to prevent children from falling off? How many of the slides were attached to climbing equipment? Did they have an enclosed "take-off" platform, making it virtually impossible for a child to fall? These are some of the additional questions that need to be asked in future studies and that could help to ascertain the extent to which attention has been given to safety and to quality in the design of playground equipment.

There are a number of other questions that should be considered in future surveys: (a) Is the equipment made of wood, steel, aluminum, plastic, or other material? (b) How is the equipment anchored in the ground? (c) How are the component parts fastened? (d) Is color used on the equipment? If so, which colors and how are they applied? (e) Are there movable parts on the equipment? If so, what are they and what is their purpose? (f) How is the surfacing material maintained? For example, if it is pea gravel, is it soft or compressed?

These are specific questions concerning the safety of playground equipment; many others should be raised regarding the scale, density, and play value of playground equipment. However, the National Survey is an excellent example of how the research community is interested in gathering data and evaluating the quality of playground equipment in preschool centers in the United States. More studies are needed, as their results will enable the practitioners and research community to collaborate to make certain that professional practice improves dramatically in the next decade.

Conclusions

The National Survey has served to demonstrate that many flaws can be found in the design of playgrounds for young children. The lack of attention to detail in the design and construction of playground equipment continues to make the play environment dangerously unpredictable for young children. The statistics on play equipment and surfacing materials in the playgrounds surveyed raise additional questions for future research, but it is clear that design flaws and hidden hazards are to be found both on the equipment and on the surface under much of the equipment.

The design of playgrounds is a complex process involving knowledge and input from early childhood educators, psychologists, landscape architects, playground designers, parents, and engineers. It is a process that also benefits from the knowledge and research of scientists interested in the biosciences, preventative medicine, and the analysis of anthropometrical data to establish human factors criteria for the design of equipment for young children. It is fair to state once again that "planning comfortable, safe, and stimulating early childhood playgrounds is more than child's play. It is a dimension of the early childhood program that must not be overlooked or left to a later date. The design of the outdoor learning environment is as important to the establishment of an early childhood program as are the other elements—staff, materials, and philosophical orientation of the curriculum. The hazardous playgrounds which have prevailed in the past—bad surfacing, incorrect scaling, excessively high structures, poor construction methods, and lack of maintenance—must not be repeated in the coming years" (Esbensen, 1987).

The 1989 survey of preschool playground equipment indicates that we have much work to do through preservice education programs for new early childhood educators and through inservice education for practicing teachers of young children. There is a need to increase awareness and knowledge of the outdoor environment as a place not only to provide opportunities for children to become involved in physical exercise but also to increase their knowledge of and contacts with nature and explore play and learning situations that serve to enhance their personal well-being. Playground designers and manufacturers also appear to need more education. Critical analysis and research on the environments we create for young children will, over time, help us to solve some of the problems overlooked in the past. "The attention we pay to the overall site, the furnishings, the relationship of the site and the equipment to the curriculum, and the opportunities for dynamic interaction between children and adults will all contribute to the provision of high-quality early childhood programs" (Esbensen, 1987).

References

Canada Mortgage and Housing Corporation. (1978). *Play spaces for preschoolers* (advisory document prepared by P. Hill, S. Esbensen, & W. Rock). Ottawa: CMHC.

Canadian Institute of Child Health. (1984). *Draft for children's play spaces and equipment.* Canadian Institute of Child Health.

Esbensen, S. (1980). *Planning play spaces for preschoolers.* Ypsilanti, MI: High/Scope Press.

Esbensen, S. (1984). *Hidden hazards on playgrounds for young children.* Hull, Quebec: Université du Québec à Hull.

Esbensen, S. (1987). *The early childhood playground: An outdoor classroom.* Ypsilanti, MI: High/Scope Press.

Esbensen, S. (1990). Designing the setting for the early childhood education program. In I. Doxey (Ed.), *Child care and education: Canadian dimensions.* Toronto: Nelson.

Frost, J.L., & Klein, B. (1983). *Children's play and playgrounds.* Austin, TX: Playscapes International.

Hohmann, M. (1983). *Young children in action.* Ypsilanti, MI: High/Scope Press.

Moore, R. (1973). *Open space learning place.* In *New School of Education Journal, II(4)/III(1).* Berkeley: Dept. of Landscape Architecture, University of California.

Moore, R. (1985). *Childhood domain.* Kent, UK: Croom Helm Publishers.

Moore, R. (1987). *Play for all guidelines: Planning, design and management of outdoor play settings for all children.* Berkeley, CA: MIG Communications.

Nash, C. (1976). *The learning environment.* Toronto: Methuen Publications.

Nicholson, S. (1971). The theory of loose parts. *Landscape Architecture, 62,* (1) (October).

Read, K.R. (1966). *Let's play outdoors.* Chicago, IL: National Association for Nursery Education. (Revised edition available from NAEYC, Washington, DC).

Root, J. (1983). *Play without pain: A manual for playground safety.* Melbourne: Child Accident Prevention Foundation of Australia.

Rudolph, N. (1974). *Workyards.* New York: Teachers College Press, Columbia University.

Stone, J.G. (1970). *Play and playgrounds.* Washington, DC: National Association for the Education of Young Children.

U.S. Consumer Product Safety Commission (1981). *A handbook for public playground safety. Vol. I: General Guidelines for New and Existing Playgrounds.* Washington: U.S. Government Printing Office.

Bibliography

Bengtsson, A. (1974). *The child's right to play.* Sheffield, UK: Tarta Press/International Playground Association.

Bowers, L. (1979). Toward a science of playground design: Principles of design for play centers for all children. *Journal of Physical Education and Recreation, 8,* 51–54.

Bruya, L.D., & Langendorfer, S.J. (1988). *Where our children play: Elementary school playground equipment.* Reston, VA: American Alliance for Health, Physical Education, Recreation and Dance.

Eriksen, A. (1985). *Playground design.* New York: Van Nostrand Reinhold Co.

Kritchevsky, S., Prescott, E., & Walling, L. (1977). *Planning environments for young children: Physical space.* Washington, DC: National Association for the Education of Young Children.

6

Infant-Toddler Playgrounds

Sue C. Wortham

Infants and toddlers have always enjoyed being outside in the natural environment. Before they are able to move about on their own, babies are taken outdoors in a pram or stroller or placed on a pallet to exercise when the weather permits. Infants who are able to creep or crawl soon find much in nature to intrigue their curiosity. Toddlers expand their exploration into a wider area under the constant supervision of an older child or adult. A sandbox and swing are available in many backyards to extend the possibilities for toddler play.

Playgrounds designed for infants and toddlers in a setting outside the home appeared in the United States shortly after the turn of the twentieth century. In 1908 Emil Bonner built a playground for neighborhood children in New York that included wooden cradles for babies (Jones, 1925). In 1926 it was reported that there were toddlers corners at large playgrounds in Washington, D.C. (*Playground*, 1926), and the first of a series of "tot-lots" were opened in Philadelphia by 1929 (*Playground*, 1931).

In recent decades babies have increasingly been placed in out-of-home care as mothers have entered the work force. Those who are involved with settings that provide care for infants have needed to consider how to include provisions for infants and toddlers within the outdoor play environment.

This chapter, devoted to infant and toddler playground design, addresses that concern. The national survey of preschool play environments has included the collection of data on infant and toddler play areas. In addition to reporting the status of infant and toddler play opportunities within preschool playgrounds, the issue of appropriate design of infant-toddler playground facilities will be discussed. The following questions will be addressed. How do changing developmental levels affect how infants and toddlers play? How do infants and toddlers benefit from outdoor play? What do infants and toddlers need from the play environment in an outdoor setting? Finally, how are playgrounds for infants and toddlers different from those designed for older preschool children and how should the playground be designed to meet the unique needs of infants and toddlers? The first topic of discussion will be how infants and toddlers develop with implications for how they engage in play concurrent with their stages of development.

Relationship Between Development and Play

Literature on children's development and play frequently poses the question of why children play and how play facilitates development. These questions are equally relevant for infants and toddlers during the first three years of life. McCall (1980) proposed that two ideas predominate as to why children play. One reason is that through play the child learns about objects and social relations. Play also provides a safe and relaxed context where the child can explore objects and social relationships.

Basic to the understanding of the relationship between play and development is the phenomenon of the reciprocal nature of the relationship. Vedeler (1986) explained how the work of Piaget (1962) and Erikson (1963) contributed to an understanding of how play and development interact. At the same time that play, imitation, and social interaction are central to the child's development during the first two years of life, they are also prerequisites for further development. Vedeler explained that through observation of infant and toddler play one can discover sequences and characteristics of development that give clues to the level of development the child has reached, what the child is interested in, and how the child can be motivated to learn. If the adult understands how play, imitation, and social interaction develop, much can be learned about the child's abilities and competence.

The play of infants and toddlers can also be described from a more developmental approach. Development during the first three years can be studied through physical development, social development, and cognitive development. Because it is difficult to separate development from play, the interaction between the two can be organized into motor play, object play, and social play (Johnson, Christie, & Yawkey, 1987).

Infant Development and Play

The child is wonderfully prepared for active learning from birth. Children approach the world with all senses open, all motors running—the world is an invitation to experience. Their job is to develop and test all their equipment, make sense of the confusing world of people and things and unseen mysterious forces and relationships like gravity, number, and love. (Greenman, 1988, p. 30)

Piaget (1962) perceived that play provides the vehicle for the infant to be able to make sense of the world. Through play the infant could advance to more sophisticated ways of achieving that understanding. The infant explores to learn about the world, and plays because it is pleasurable to make an impact or have an effect on the surrounding environment (Weisler & McCall, 1976). A first effort at play occurs when the newborn baby uses senses and available physical resources for play such as engaging in mouth play by bubbling saliva on the lips.

Physical development during the first year is focused on gaining control over the body. During the first three months infants learn to lift their heads. Within the next three months they can achieve and maintain a sitting position. During the second six months babies begin to crawl, stand, and perhaps take their first steps (Vedeler, 1986). At first, infants play with their body parts. As they achieve mobility they use their emerging physical abilities to explore the environment. Play allows the baby not only to master physical skills but also to enjoy using them after they have been mastered (Johnson, Christie, & Yawkey, 1987).

Infants engage in social play at a very early age. From birth the infant is a social person. By six weeks of age they attempt to establish eye contact with the mother (Vedeler, 1986). Early interactive games with caregivers such as peek-a-boo not only teach the infant about alternating turns but also introduce the infant to communication skills and make believe (Johnson, Christie, & Yawkey, 1987).

Play with objects is related to cognitive development as well as to social development. Object play also has a role in the child's ability to engage in symbolic play. Play with objects begins when the caregiver attracts the newborn's attention with a rattle or toy. When in the crib, infants learn that they can have an effect on a crib toy such as a mobile by kicking and waving their arms. Once they can grasp a toy, object play becomes more deliberate. The infant's play with objects begins with simple exploration. The child explores the object to understand it, then manipulates it to find out what can be done with it (McCune, 1986).

Object play facilitates symbolic play. Piaget's practice play is a first step when the child uses repetitive motor actions and simple manipulation of objects. When the infant demonstrates by gestures that the meaning is familiar, symbolic play is emerging (McCune, 1986). Symbolic play can be engaged in when the infant understands that one object can represent another. In the beginning stages of symbolic play objects are needed for pretend play to occur. The symbolic play is taken from the child's own experiences.

At the end of the first year the infant has achieved physical mobility and can explore a larger environment. Social interactions with others have established a foundation for more complex forms of social play. The ability to use toys for play has facilitated both cognitive development and social play.

There is evidence that individual differences in play can be identified between 6 months and 12 months. The physical environment has an effect on the quality of infant play. Caruso (1988) summarized research on the effect of early environment on infant play and reported that infants in less stimulating environments explored less. Further, the exploration was of a lower quality. Studies found that the social and physical responsiveness of the environment were the most important factors in the quality of the exploratory play of infants.

Toddler Development and Play

Neither infants nor preschoolers, toddlers are furiously becoming; increasingly mobile, autonomous, social, thoughtful creatures with language and insatiable urges to test and experiment. (Greenman, 1988, p. 52).

During the second and third years, refinement and advances in development enable the toddler almost unlimited opportunities to expand the possibilities for play. Once the infant attains mobility by walking, toddlerhood begins. The ability to engage in exploratory play that began in infancy evolves in a continuous progression that follows a sequence. Belsky and Most (1981) conducted a comprehensive study that enabled them to describe the sequence of exploratory play behaviors in infants between the ages of 7 ½ months and 21 months. Developmental progression began with mouthing and simple manipulation of objects followed by play with objects that was functionally correct. After functional play came relational play and then functional and relational play combined. At this point the earliest form of pretend play could begin. The sequence of pretend play included pretend with the self and then pretend with others. These researchers demonstrated how learning and development are integrated in play, and the sequence or progression in skills involves more sophistication in cognitive development.

In all categories of development and play, toddlers are progressing from focus on self to inclusion of others in play activities. They are evolving from an egocentric view of the world to a more prosocial position. As they become more aware of the thoughts and feelings of their peers, they are gradually becoming able to be a part of a play group. In motor play, object play, and social play, they are developing skills in the ability to interact with others.

During the second year motor development is continuous. The toddler is rapidly developing both gross- and fine-motor skills. In addition to improving walking skills, they are learning to step up and down and run (Johnson, Christie, & Yawkey, 1987). Fine motor skills are also advancing as they engage in grasping, putting objects in containers, dumping toys, and carrying more than one object at a time. Motor play occurs with objects, people, and natural and man-made features that promote physical activities.

Toddler object play becomes more complex. Toddlers are able to play with more than one toy at a time. Simple pretending can be used with objects. The toddler increasingly is able to use objects to substitute for other objects (Piaget, 1962). Fein (1975) described how symbolic play moves from simple to complex. In early make-believe play, realistic objects are needed to facilitate pretense and imagination. With more experience in pretend play, less realistic objects allow the child to be more innovative.

Progress in object play partially depends upon the child's development in language and social skills. Language development parallels progress in symbolic play. Simple pretending begins at about 8 months and reaches its most complex form by about 30 months. Language development also progresses rapidly during the second and third years. Studies of the relationship between language development and symbolic play development determined a strong correlation between the two. Children who learned language early engaged in more representational play than other children. As development in the two continued, the correlation was consistent (McCune-Nicolich & Bruskin, 1982).

It is in social play where the interaction of development and play is the most significant. Object play, motor play, and symbolic play are all affected by the progress of the child's social development, and social play is likewise facilitated by progress in object play, motor play, and symbolic play.

Social development has been described in stages as the infant and young child increasingly are able to play with others. Parten (1932) described stages of social play to include solitary, parallel, associative, and cooperative play. Infants and toddlers were thought to engage in solitary and parallel play; they primarily play by themselves or alongside others. Those who have studied toddler play have refined the understanding of the social levels of toddler play. Cherry (1976) explains that toddlers who appear to be engaged in parallel play are really playing with each other. The toddlers are interacting using body language. Because the toddlers are having their first experiences in playing with their peers, they are learning how to socialize with them by indirect communication.

Figure 6.1. Play equipment can encourage social interaction

Research supports this explanation that parallel play in two- and three-year-olds is a bridge to social play rather than a developmental stage. Studies of toddler play demonstrated that they went from solitary to group play. Parallel play was used as a transient adjustment to a social situation (Johnson & Ershler, 1982).

The nonmobile infant is severely limited in the ability to relate to other infants; however, once mobility has been attained it is possible to initiate social interactions. The toddler can both initiate and retreat from social play. The first attempts at social interaction involve the use of toys. Because a toy is predictable and a peer is not, the toddlers will use toys as the medium of contact (McCall, 1980). The mediating role of toys as mechanisms of social interaction has been described as "social butter" because of their use to facilitate social play (Johnson, Christie, & Yawkey, 1987).

Toddlers may first alternate in using a toy. A child observes another child playing with an attractive toy. When the toy is discarded, the child picks it up and plays with it. Two toddlers may both reach for a toy and end up in a struggle for possession. A toddler may offer a toy to another child. A child may watch another child play with a toy and later imitate the play behaviors that were observed. Mutual imitation is engaged in as toddlers learn that they can influence each other. Advanced use of toys occurs when the toddler plans a play activity with a toy and watches the play partner while carrying out the activity to see what the partner's reaction will be (McCall, 1980).

Development plays a major role in the play of infants and toddlers. While infants are born with resources for play, the first three years of development result in a vast array of skills and competencies that can be used for play. In the next section the relationship between infant-toddler play and how the outdoor play environment affects that play will be discussed. There are benefits to infants and toddlers from playing outside. They have play needs that should be provided on their own playground. These needs and benefits are considered along with developmental capabilities when the infant-toddler playscape is designed and constructed.

Infant-Toddler Play and the Play Environment

What is significant or different about outdoor play for infants and toddlers? Why is it important for babies to have opportunities for outdoor play in addition to indoor play? Many caregivers in group

Figure 6.2. Infants and toddlers enjoy equipment with wheels, sound elements, and chutes that can be acted upon.

settings question the need to take babies outdoors, when toys and equipment needed for infant and toddler play are readily available in the indoor play area. The inconvenience of taking babies outside is also a factor that is frequently mentioned by infant caregivers.

There are many things babies can learn from playing outdoors. Experiencing the natural environment is different from living and playing inside a building. Some of the features of the natural environment can include climate changes, landscape characteristics, openness, wildlife, and the outdoor activities of people (Greenman, 1988). Miller (1989) described outdoor sensory experiences that allow babies to learn about the world to include the sun, shadows, wind, birds, butterflies, and textures such as grass.

When considering the outdoors, another distinction needs to be made between the natural environment and man-made environments. Tuan (1978) proposed that young children have an innate kinship with nature. He described the man-made environment as inanimate as compared to the natural environment, which is both animate and inanimate. In an increasingly urban society, children have fewer opportunities to experience nature. Urban children are surrounded by man-made environments with occasional natural environment elements included. Tuan explained that children around the world enjoy basic earth substances such as water, clay, and sand. Children need to climb trees and slide down slopes in an unstructured environment that is not possible in "manicured" spaces in cities.

The outdoor environment also contributes to infants' and toddlers' sense of self. The child's experiences with rooms, clothes, and playthings contribute to their understanding of their identity. Proshansky and Fabian (1987) believe that environmental locations such as indoor spaces and outdoor places that provide environmental experiences contribute to the child's definition of identity. The settings that constitute daily life become part of the individual's self-identity with a place.

The outdoor play environment also has an influence on the child's play. Darvill (1982) discussed children's play as being affected by toys, play equipment, and other people, as well as the spatial density or social density of the play area. Darvill suggested that researchers should not only be aware of the effects of the setting on children's play but also be aware of possible effects of the environment beyond the play setting.

Infants and toddlers are learners through their senses. Experiences in outdoor play spaces contribute to their recognition of their position in space and their relationship to space. Cherry (1976) proposed that babies develop a sense of laterality and kinesthesia, as well as large and small muscle control and eye-hand coordination, through play. These developmental skills are acquired in indoor and outdoor play activities; nevertheless, the outdoor play space with its openness and freedom of movement enhances these areas of development.

Infant and toddler development and play are affected by the environment where they play. The outdoor playground has unique qualities that cannot be duplicated indoors. Infants and toddlers learn about nature and their relationship to nature by experiencing outdoor play in a natural setting. Their sense of their own identity and their relationship to space and place is also learned through outdoor play. Designers of infant-toddler playgrounds should understand how these factors affect the benefits that babies receive from playing outside.

Infant-Toddler Playground Design

The design of an infant-toddler playground must combine an understanding of child development and the relationship between development and play with an awareness of how the outdoor play area must be organized with the unique needs of that age group in mind. A good infant-toddler playground is not a scaled-down commercial climbing structure located at one corner of a preschool playground. It is not a collection of plastic seesaws, slides, and playhouses scattered about on a small outdoor space covered with artificial turf. Kritchevsky and Prescott (1969) reported that playyards they studied that served younger children were generally less interesting than those designed for three- and four-year-olds. They also described problem playground design as resulting from elements that were pleasing to adults but not very useful to children.

An effective infant-toddler playground combines developmentally appropriate features with a natural environment that promotes motor play, social play, and object play. The design must consider what infants and toddlers need from the play environment to be able to benefit from outdoor play. Environmental design results from relating the child's developmental level into provisions for good outdoor play experiences.

The playscape design should combine the child's need for sensory experiences and experiences in the natural environment. A combination of natural and man-made elements can incorporate opportunities for sensory exploration. Pathways with different surfaces and tex-

Figure 6.3. A walk of different textures challenges emerging locomotor skills

tures, play structures with a variety of elements that can be physically acted upon, and items such as wind chimes or colored banners are man-made design components that are sensory in nature. Natural environment features such as animals, plants, sand, water, and other opportunities for experiences with living things and landscape elements add to the possibilities for sensory exploration.

Outdoor motor play or movement experiences provide infants and toddlers with the widest range of possibilities for physical development. Greenman (1988) proposes that children need the physical challenges of reaching new heights and running wild that the outdoor playground provides. He suggests that young children, including toddlers, need outdoor places for swinging, sliding and rolling, climbing, jumping, running, throwing, kicking, traveling, riding, and transporting. Cherry (1976) added rocking, teeter-tottering, and crawling through to the list of possibilities that should be available in outdoor places.

Playground components for physical play can be provided through both natural and man-made elements. A toddler play structure can contain experiences for crawling, standing, walking, stepping up and down, and sliding. In their study of outdoor play, Steele and Nauman (1985) found that mobile infants and toddlers played on structures

Figure 6.4. Toddlers enjoy the combination of sand and dramatic play possibilities

with simple slides and tunnels. Other playground features that encourage physical experiences are porch swings, infant swings, push and pull toys, and wheeled vehicles for riding. Natural terrain changes can also facilitate crawling, standing, running, jumping, and rolling.

The child also needs to feel that he/she is physically powerful and competent. Provisions for motor play should include features that the child can act upon. Movable parts such as wheels, levers, pulleys, and chutes that can be used to drop sand or toys through, all give the child a sense of control over the environment.

Toys or objects are favorite playthings for infants and toddlers. Objects that facilitate exploratory play, presymbolic and symbolic play, social play, and play with language should be part of the outdoor play environment. Toys are the preferred choice of toddlers in outdoor play. Winter (1985) studied toddler play behaviors and equipment choices on an outdoor playground and found that toys, particularly when combined with sand, were preferred over climbing equipment. Indeed, toys combined with sand can become the major resource for play with other facilities such as play structures serving a supporting role. Informal observations of toddler play revealed that the primary activity was to use toys to transport sand to all areas of the play environment and deposit it in some fashion on pathways, swings, slides, and other structures.

Small toys and objects facilitate social interactions; however, larger toys have a different social role in play from smaller toys. As was mentioned earlier, toddlers use toys to initiate social contact. They show toys to each other, and interest in a toy can extend episodes of social play. Large, shareable toys that allow more than one child to be involved encourage social interactions (Mueller & Brenner, 1977).

Toys can also enhance symbolic play. Watering cans, toy lawn-mowers, doll carriages, and vehicles are just some of the props that suggest opportunities for pretend play. Housekeeping equipment, playhouses, and cardboard boxes encourage role playing and other forms of symbolic play.

In summary, the infant-toddler playscape should include developmentally appropriate features that facilitate play and development for children under three. It should include a balance of natural and man-made elements that allow the child to maximize play experiences when outdoors. The playground structures and features should be uniquely geared to the developmental needs and play characteristics of the children served.

Finally, the infant-toddler playground needs to be safe and secure.

The area must be fenced to prevent children from wandering off. In addition, the child will feel secure because a caregiver is nearby, but also from a sense that the play area is within a protective enclosure. Safety measures should include structures and equipment that are all of safe design, appropriate size, and maintained frequently.

Infant-Toddler Playground Arrangement

Spaces provided for infant and toddler outdoor play are generally smaller than preschool playgrounds. There are fewer facilities for play, and space arrangement is less complex. Greenman (1988) describes an area that has soft, level surfaces with good drainage. The small area can be transformed into a site for infant and toddler play by incorporating planks, boulders, branches, tires, and fabric. Kritchevsky and Prescott (1969) discussed play spaces in terms of units that had variety and complexity. For younger children, they advocated that some complexity is needed, but should not be too stimulating for them. They proposed that there should be opportunities for experiences with choice without providing too many units or variety beyond the coping capacity of the children.

While Kritchevsky and Prescott used pathways in a system of playground layout, linking of playground elements for older children has also been described in terms of zones connected by areas of transition. This conceptualization is less appropriate for infants and toddlers because of the nature of their play. Infants and toddlers do not differentiate between types of play that can occur in various playground areas. Because mobile infants are in a continual state of movement and exploration, playground arrangement follows their style of play. The arrangement of play experiences can be pictured as a cellular matrix with each cell containing a major play event (Wortham & Wortham, 1989). The layout provides for spontaneous multidirectional movement that is integrated.

Survey Results Related to Infant-Toddler Areas of Preschool Playgrounds

The results of the National Survey of Playground Equipment in Preschool Centers does not include tables for types and numbers of equipment for infants and toddlers separate from other preschool equipment. Information for this part of the report was sometimes difficult to identify. When the reliability for the survey instrument was established, the reliability for that part of the survey was low in several categories, indicating errors could be made when data were gathered for the survey. Another difficulty making it difficult to evaluate the infant-toddler equipment was that while the total number of children attending a preschool setting was recorded, there was no information on numbers of infants and toddlers relative to the number of preschool children.

In spite of these inherent difficulties or weaknesses in the available data, it is possible to describe information about some equipment that was found in infant-toddler play areas.

Table 6.1 shows the infant-toddler percentage of total equipment surveyed. Rocking apparatus represented the highest percentage when compared with preschool percentages. Swings and slides each represented only 20 percent of the total equipment. However, results of Section 1 revealed that swings and slides were the types of equipment most frequently found on preschool playgrounds; the two categories together totaled about 44 percent of all permanent equipment surveyed. It seems likely that swings and slides were also more frequently found on infant-toddler playgrounds than other types of permanent equipment. The equipment least represented on infant-toddler playgrounds when comparing percentages were balance beams, overhead ladders, fire poles, trapeze bars, and suspended

TABLE 6.1

Types and Percentages of Permanent Equipment Found in Infant-Toddler and Preschool Areas

	Infant-Toddler Percentage of Total Equipment	Preschool Percentage of Total Equipment
Slides	20	80
Swings	20	80
Balance beam	7	93
Overhead ladders	6	94
Tire/net climbers	10	90
Rocking apparatus	43	57
Fire poles	5	95
Trapeze bars	9	91
Seesaws	18	82
Suspended bridges	7	93
Merry-go-rounds	21	79
Geodesic domes	14	86
Monkey bars	22	78

bridges. Since most of these are generally developmentally inappropriate for young children, their absence is not surprising.

Table 6.2 has a more consistent balance of three to one between preschool percentages and infant-toddler percentages of total portable equipment. Although tricycles on infant-toddler play areas represented only 27 percent of the total, they were probably the most frequently noted portable equipment in actual numbers. Tricycles represented 37 percent of all portable materials counted on the survey. Sand, wagons, barrels, boards, water, and wheelbarrows were also included on many infant-toddler areas (Table 6.3).

The balance and distribution of percentages for other provisions tallied on preschool playgrounds was fairly consistent between infant-toddler and preschool areas. For infant-toddler areas water play had the highest comparative percentage and amphitheatres the lowest. However, there were only 13 amphitheatres recorded for all the playgrounds surveyed. The comparison of shade structures is interesting in that shade structures on infant-toddler playgrounds represented only 11 percent of the total. Since 253 man-made shade structures were tallied, you might expect that they would be present more frequently on infant-toddler play areas.

Besides information presented in the tables above, the survey had additional information related to infant-toddler play. Section 3: Placement and Size of Equipment included information comparing equip-

TABLE 6.2
Types and Numbers of Portable Equipment Found in Infant-Toddler and Preschool Areas

	Infant-Toddler Percentage of Total Equipment	Preschool Percentage of Total Equipment
Tricycles	27	73
Loose tires	18	82
Sand	25	75
Wagons	29	71
Barrels	23	77
Loose boards	23	77
Water	34	66
Wheelbarrows	30	70
Building materials	24	76
Gardening tools	13	87
Art materials	30	70
Carpentry tools	27	73

TABLE 6.3
Types and Percentages of Other Provisions Found in Infant-Toddler and Preschool Areas

	Infant-Toddler Percentage of Total Equipment	Preschool Percentage of Total Equipment
Grassy areas	25	75
Accessible water	20	80
Separate sand play	25	75
Hard surface area	20	80
Shade structures	11	89
Storage-portable play	19	81
Play houses	18	72
Storage-maintenance	23	77
Cars	27	73
Digging areas	15	85
Tables	21	79
Trucks	16	84
Natural area-plants	19	81
Water play area	34	66
Toilet facilities	24	76
Provisions for animal care	18	82
Boats	19	81
Amphitheatres	8	92

ment for younger and older children. Surveyors recorded that almost half of the playgrounds (47 percent) had smaller equipment for younger children. Less positively, only slightly more than a third of the playgrounds surveyed (36 percent) had large and small equipment separated. Section 4 noted that of the 554 swing structures, 191, or 34 percent were swing structures for younger children; 17 percent (245) of the swing structures had swing seats for infants and toddlers.

Limitations of Survey Information

Limitations of the reliability of data collected in the National Survey of Playground Equipment in Preschool Centers were explained previously. In addition to the cautions that must be observed when interpreting the reported information related to infant and toddler play areas, there are other restrictions that have implications for understanding and using the data.

The survey instrument used was adapted to identify and record some of the unique characteristics of playgrounds for preschool

Figure 6.5. Transporting sand is a major interest of infants and toddlers.

children. This was necessary because the instrument was previously used to survey public school and public park playgrounds. Even with modifications, there are differences between playgrounds developed for infants and toddlers and for children three- to six-years-old. The survey instrument could not identify these differences.

It was also difficult to identify the unique characteristics of the play areas for the two age groups. As reported earlier, play areas for the two age groups were not always separate. In addition, even when separated, the similarity between the equipment selected for both age groups made it difficult to identify for whom the play area was intended. At some centers different age groups used all play areas at different times of the day whether combined or separated.

Another limitation of the survey instrument was that the need to have general descriptions of equipment precluded the possibility of identifying differences in materials used to construct equipment. A common practice in child care centers is to use plastic portable play equipment for infants and toddlers. Also, the survey instrument was not designed to identify whether equipment and materials met the developmental needs of infants and toddlers. Information on appropriateness of size of equipment or quality of play experiences provided by the play environment was not measured.

Summary and Conclusions

In spite of the difficulty in reporting survey information specific to infant and toddler play areas, much positive information can be interpreted from the data collected. First of all, preschool or early childhood centers are making provisions for infants and toddlers in some form. Some of the basic materials and equipment that are appropriate for babies that were found in the survey were infant swings, smaller equipment of various types, and provisions for sand and water play. Although they were not specifically identified as present for infant and toddler use, the frequency of tricycles, push and pull toys, and small vehicles and balls indicates those toys and materials appropriate for infants and toddlers were available on many early childhood playgrounds.

Photographs taken at some of the centers surveyed revealed the disparity in quality of play environments. Some locations lacked minimum provisions for play, while others reflected extensive effort and expense. Some centers demonstrated little knowledge of developmental play experiences for younger children, and other locations limited playground design to a collection of equipment and materials without any apparent planning for either early childhood age group. It is hoped that this survey of preschool playgrounds will serve as a stimulus to locations serving infants and toddlers to exercise careful and knowledgeable planning when designing outdoor play areas for infants and toddlers.

Figure 6.6. Few of the preschool playgrounds surveyed had shaded areas for infants and toddlers

References

Belsky, J., & Most, R. (1980). From exploration to play: A cross-sectional study of infant free play behavior. *Developmental Psychology, 17*, 630–639.

Caruso, D.A. (1988). Play and learning in infancy: Research and implications. *Young Children, 43*, 63–69.

Cherry, C. (1976). *Creative play for the developing child*. Belmont, CA: Fearon Pitman.

Darvill, D. (1982). Ecological influences on children's play: Issues and approaches. In D.J. Pepler & K.H. Rubin (Eds.), *The play of children: Current theory and research* (pp. 144–153). Basel, Switzerland: S. Karger.

Erikson, E.H. (1963). *Childhood and society*. New York: W.W. Norton.

Fein, G. (1975). A transformational analysis of pretending. *Developmental Psychology, 11*, 291–296.

Greenman, J. (1988). *Caring spaces, learning places: Children's environments that work*. Redmond, WA: Exchange Press.

Johnson, J.E., & Ershler, J. (1982). Curricular effects on the play of preschoolers. In D. J. Pepler & K.H. Rubin (Eds.), *The play of children: Current theory and research* (pp. 130–143). Basel, Switzerland: S. Karger.

Johnson, J.E., Christie, J.F., & Yawkey, T.D. (1987). *Play and early childhood development*. Glenview, IL: Scott, Foresman.

Jones, H.S. (1925). A playground established by Emil Bonner. *Playground, 19*, 388–389.

Kritchevsky, S., & Prescott, E. (1969). *Planning environments for young children: Physical space*. Washington, DC: National Association for the Education of Young Children.

McCall, R. (1980). *Infants*. New York: Vintage.

McCune, L. (1986). Symbolic development in normal and atypical infants. In G. Fein & M. Rivkin (Eds.), *The young child at play* (pp. 45–52). Washington, DC: National Association for the Education of Young Children.

McCune-Nicolich, L., & Bruskin, C. (1982). Combinatory competency in symbolic play and language. In D. J. Pepler & K.H. Rubin (Eds.), *The play of children: Current theory and research* (pp. 30–45). Basel, Switzerland: S. Karger.

Miller, K. (1989). Infants and toddlers outside. *Texas Child Care Quarterly*, summer, 20–29.

Mueller, E., & Brenner, J. (1977). The origins of social skills and interactions among playgroup toddlers. *Child Development, 48*, 854–861.

Parten, M. (1932). Social participation among preschool children. *Journal of Abnormal and Social Psychology, 27,* 243–269.

Piaget, J. (1962). *Play, dreams and imitation.* New York: W.W. Norton.

Play and play material (1931). *Playground, 25,* 18–19, 50.

Playgrounds for toddlers (1926). *Playground, 19,* 568–569.

Proshansky, H.M., & Fabian, A.K. (1987). The development of place identity in the child. In C.S. Weinstein & T.G. David (Eds.), *Spaces for children* (pp. 144–153). New York: Plenum Press.

Steele, C., & Nauman, M. (1985). Infant's play on outdoor equipment. In J. Frost & S. Sunderlin (Eds.), *When children play* (pp. 121–128). Wheaton, MD: Association for Childhood Education International.

Tuan, Y. (1978). Children and the natural environment. In I. Altman & J.F. Wohlwill (Eds.), *Children and the environment* (pp. 5–23). New York: Plenum Press.

Vedeler, L. (1986). The role of play in the education of handicapped children. *Prospects, 16,* 481–493.

Weisler, A., & McCall, R. (1976). Exploration and play: Resume and redirection. *American Psychologist, 31,* 492–508.

Winter, S. (1985). Toddler play behaviors and equipment choices in an outdoor playground. In J. Frost & S. Sunderlin (Eds.), *When children play* (pp. 129–138). Wheaton, MD: Association for Childhood Education International.

Wortham, S., & Wortham, M. (1989). Infant/toddler development and play: Designing creative play environments. *Childhood Education, 65,* 295–299.

Figure 6.7. A low slide constructed from a material that does not burn sensitive skin in warm climates

7

Advances in Playground Equipment for Young Children

Marshal R. Wortham

In researching the advances made in recent years in playground equipment for preschool children, play value is the most important and ultimate consideration, assuming safety needs are met. However, how the equipment meets the established needs of motor development, fantasy play, social development, and creative play is tied in the commercial marketplace to pressures and expectations not always recognized by designers and researchers of play environments. Although manufacturers are becoming increasingly cognizant of research being published about outdoor play environments that include safety concerns, they are also affected by materials and methods of large scale manufacturing. Additionally, they must also successfully analyze and compete in the commercial market.

An analysis of manufactured play equipment must consider advances in new materials, the market for the sale of equipment, research in the developmental parameters of equipment in learning situations, and play value in general, as well as concern for an environment that is challenging and yet relatively safe for play. This

analysis will consider products from the catalogs of major manufacturers, some of which span over a ten-year period. Also included in
the research are responses to a questionnaire sent to representatives
of major companies.

Materials

An interview conducted with representatives of four major playground equipment companies in 1985 (Miracle Recreation Equipment, Inc., Landscape Structures, Inc./Mexico Forge, Quality Industries, Inc., and Game Time) revealed a growing demand for durable
materials as a major trend in meeting customer expectations in the
1980s (*Parks and Recreation*, 1985). Durability in itself is not a problem
given the history of outdoor equipment. Unfortunately, many traditional pieces of equipment of galvanized structural steel pipe and
stainless steel are still to be found on playgrounds after 30 or more
years, even though research in play and safety has long proven them
inadequate or dangerous in their function. The question of durability,
although not new, apparently has gained renewed concern for at least
two reasons: (a) the fastenings and multiple parts have made the
structures more complex with correspondingly more things to break
down and (b) manufacturers of steel equipment have tried to enhance
their product position in the market by pointing out its durability
when compared to wooden structures.

The 1960s saw the creation of play equipment addressing the
child's need for fantasy play, a change from the heretofore exclusive
attention to physical activity. This equipment, unlike the traditional
seesaws, slides, merry-go-rounds, swings, and jungle gyms of past
years, necessitated a more complex material structure. There were
roofs, side panels and rails, decks, animal heads or bodies, and other
miscellaneous formed shapes. The increase in parts meant an increase
in connecting devices and a corresponding increase in the possibility
of vandalism. Accordingly, more sophisticated connectors have
evolved, not only to thwart vandals but also to eliminate protruding
parts that create a safety hazard for children.

Another primary technical problem was the use of color as applied
to metal surfaces, either steel or aluminum. Three early proponents of
color in playground equipment were Miracle, Mexico Forge, and
Game Time. By 1965, these companies were applying specially
prepared paint mixtures to structural steel surfaces and cast aluminum. The use of color was mainly in the context of fantasy or
make-believe structures. As the design of equipment tended to move

away from such structures, color became more an end in itself, applied to all metal surfaces. By the 1980s, a baked-on polyester powder coating of increased durability was being applied to steel structural parts (Landscape Structures, Inc., 1988), and a powder-coated paint to aluminum structures (Game Time, 1988). These new paints are not only long lasting, but are also free of poisonous lead ingredients.

Beyond the important characteristics of aluminum alloys as light-weight and rust resistant, the metal could be cast into three-dimensional heads of animals or clowns to embellish equipment to create a fantasy or make-believe context (Game Time, 1976). From the point of play value, the manufacture of cast metal riding animals mounted on heavy coil or strap springs may have contributed the most to the play of small children because of their fantasy element and the child's self-initiated opportunity for movement. Although spring animals of plastic material, as well as wood, are in use, cast aluminum with a powder-coated, painted surface still remains a durable choice in the current market.

The most recent development of major importance to playground equipment has been the continuing improvement of plastics, a general term used in this chapter to refer to numerous chemical compounds developed for a myriad of uses. Plastics can be molded to form any desired shape, as well as rolled into long sheets. Moreover, color can be integrated into the material itself, along with ultraviolet light stabilizers.

Before the development of stronger plastics, fiberglas reinforced plastics were dominant. The material is still used by Miracle Recreation Equipment Company for slide beds supporting stainless steel sliding surfaces. Although stainless steel is superior as a durable material, slides of plastic, because of their resistance to heat absorption, have become more popular in recent years. The primary concern about slides voiced by researchers in playground safety is that metal slides can cause serious burns in hot summer climates. Although plastic slides may not have the durability of stainless steel, they correct this safety hazard. Today, most companies include tube or half-tube plastic slides in their inventories. The concept, however, dates back to the 1960s when tube slides were made of metal or fiberglas.

Outdoor play equipment can be purchased in materials as diverse as metal and wood or a combination of both. Metal has not affected play factors directly except as noted above in the use of cast aluminum. Among the major manufacturers currently active in the United States, two build exclusively wood products. They are significant because their products do affect the play environment.

Kompan, a Danish manufacturer, represents the tradition of European wood painted play equipment that has long been ahead of American manufacturers, especially in structures for very young children. While it was typical of American manufacturers to stress physical event play structures at the beginning of this decade, European manufacturers were including learning situations such as outdoor chalkboards and large scale abacus counting frames. Play-

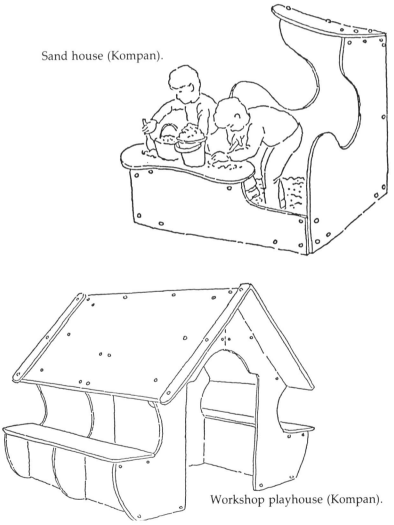

Sand house (Kompan).

Workshop playhouse (Kompan).

Figure 7.1. Alternate contemporary structures.

houses were more complex and along with other structures were
intended for location in sand areas. These structures included shelves
and tables to play on, as well as sand chutes and buckets on pulleys
to carry sand or water. In short, the opportunity for manipulative
play for toddlers was included, as well as traditional play events,
pretend vehicles, and spring riding animals. Plastics were combined
with paint pigments to create very durable surfaces for the wood,
which was often impregnated with salt. Because of the planar
characteristics of multi-ply wood, Kompan has been able to cut out
various shapes with relative ease to create innovative structures for
play. Larger shaped panels also appear to be possible compared to
plastic panels used by other manufacturers.

Another wood manufacturer of note is Children's Playgrounds,
Inc. The guiding concepts in design for this company have European
roots, although the structures are manufactured in Canada. Unlike
Kompan with its brightly painted structures, Children's Playgrounds
uses natural wood, the only color being in plastic slides. The
significance of materials in this context is that wood used in this
manner, although not as durable and long lasting as steel, allows for
more flexibility in updating changes and in custom-built situations.
Some specific structures made possible with this medium of material
include a wooden pyramid, long, gently sloping ramps for handicap
access, open-shade structures, play walls, infant play pens, and a

Figure 7.2. Play pyramid (Children's Playgrounds, Inc.).

shaded infant play yard 40 feet by 20 feet built on a raised ground-level platform covered with rubber matting. Such extensive structures are not practical in a typical manufacturing situation.

An important concept for more traditional manufacturing has been the modular concept, which allows for relative flexibility. Landscape Structures, Inc. is a successful example of this idea. By making decks, railings, and panels conform to a rectangular grid, the total structure can be added on to, enlarged, and arranged relative to space, budget, and specific needs. The materials used in the AdventureScapes system (Landscape Structures, 1988) for preschool children are plastic panels, plastic-coated, expanded metal-type decks, and powder-coated steel roofs and structural frames. In keeping with recent trends, slides are made of molded plastic. Plastic activity panels that conform to the modular grid allow for variation and, perhaps more importantly, change, a factor not present in most manufactured equipment.

The use of materials has affected the parameters for play. Modular designs have provided the designer of play environments with highly durable and vandal-resistant structures to locate within the play environment, although wood has allowed for a maximum of change and alternation in a long-lasting but ultimately less durable context. Plastic, the material of the 1980s, has provided a lightweight, colorful, flexible, and safe material lending itself to multiple manufactured uses. The ability to apply color in a relatively permanent manner has increased the aesthetic appearance of play structures and provided children with an added sensory component to their development. Additionally, in response to pressures for a safer surface under structures, manufactured soft-fall matting continues to be developed to make play a safer activity.

The Playground Equipment Market

It is not within the scope of this analysis to ascertain the complex conditions which have determined the market for play equipment over the years. However, one must recognize in a consideration of changes in equipment that market factors drive manufacturing. Obviously, structures are not likely to be built unless they can be sold. The National Survey of Elementary School Playground Equipment (Bruya & Langendorfer, 1988) supplies at least indirect data in attempting to define market conditions. From that survey, as well as additional surveys of public parks and preschool settings, we have an indication of what is being purchased. One must admit, however, that the question of which came first, the equipment made available (a decision of the manufacturer) or the requirements set forth by school systems, park administrators, or entities such as the National Recreation Association, remains debatable.

Findings of the survey of elementary school playgrounds indicated that equipment used by parents of those conducting the survey is still in use on a majority of playgrounds. This traditional equipment includes chinning bars, swings, overhead ladders, flat slides, fireman poles, balance beams, monkey bars, seesaws, geodesic domes, spring rockers, and merry-go-rounds. Single function equipment designed primarily for motor development, such as those listed above, comprised over 85 percent of total structures reported (Wortham, 1988a). The kindergarten-age child, who was included in the scope of Wortham's report, was often neglected in terms of appropriately scaled equipment and definitely in the area of developmental needs such as creative expression, dramatic play, social interaction, and building and construction play (Wortham, 1988b). Traditional equipment is still available, although linking play events together into improved complex multi-use structures has become prevalent in all major catalogs of equipment.

Whereas the market for public school equipment has been slow to change, the recent surge in building child care centers has created the most impetus for designing innovative equipment for young children. Landscape Structures estimates that by 1991, the preschool market will amount to at least 20 percent of their business (King, 1989). The best of these centers have positioned themselves in a child development and educational context rather than as baby-sitting services. Scaling down traditional play equipment has not met this need. More progressive manufacturers are responding with structures that encourage learning and creative activities. Moreover, safety guidelines disseminated by the U.S. Consumer Product Safety Commission (USCPSC, 1981) have shown many traditional structures to be unsafe. This report, along with child injury lawsuits and costs and requirements for liability insurance for private child care businesses, has forced manufacturers to initiate change. Even so, as reported in the preschool playground equipment survey, about 44 percent of equipment located on these playgrounds is comprised of swings and slides, the remainder being mostly traditional play events, including fireman poles and trapezes, which are inappropriate for the age group represented.

In addition to child care centers, Steve King, chairman of Landscape Structures, Inc., has identified other nontraditional markets for his products. They include corporations, hospitals, fast food chains, and large retail stores (King, 1989). These markets reflect child care needs for employed mothers, entertainment factors to make eating out at a fast food restaurant a more special event, and therapy both for mind and body in the context of hospitals.

The interview with major manufacturers in 1985 by *Parks and Recreation* magazine reflected public concerns and desires, including safety, relative to liability, durability (which includes minimal maintenance), colorful equipment, and total physical fitness. These pressures have affected the design of structures but have not directly affected play value as such. The major reasons for changes in innovative structures have come from research by interested investigators and more enlightened purchasers.

Research

Although the development of new materials and the availability of others, the parameters set forth by purchasers, and the creation of new markets for play equipment have all brought about change, the primary agent has been continuing research into play and safety concerns. The result of this research by educators, designers, the industry itself, government agencies, and professional organizations has been a change in philosophy toward play and child development and creation of standards to guide design and manufacturing.

In the United States, the most influential document affecting manufacturers has been *A Handbook for Public Playground Safety*, Volumes I and II, published by the U.S. Consumer Product Safety Commission in April 1981. This publication was offered as a guide rather than a standard and was the result of recommendations by the National Recreation and Park Association (draft standard, 1976) with assistance by the National Bureau of Standards in developing tests for various surfaces commonly used under play equipment. Although the bibliography for Volume I lists 53 wide-ranging books and articles on play and playgrounds published between 1965 and 1978, the focus of the handbook was exclusively on safety considerations in design, placement, and surfacing. The critical importance of safety problems in the design and construction of play structures and the importance of this one publication on facilitating and generating safety improvements cannot be overstated. Of the playground companies surveyed, Playworld Systems, Iron Mountain Forge, Big Toys, Quality Industries, and Landscape Structures/Mexico Forge, all refer to the USCPSC guidelines in one way or another.

Another standard, however, is used by Kompan and Game Time. Both companies carry the GS Safety Mark, which is issued by the German Ministry of Labor and Social Affairs. This mark indicates that an approved testing agency has examined and assessed the equipment in accordance with the Equipment Safety Law and that the equipment has been constructed in compliance with the accepted German rules of testing (Game Time, 1989). To date, the U.S. government has not developed a standard that by law must be followed.

Guidelines and recommendations on how children play and what constitutes the best environment to facilitate play have come from scholars and designers alike. Sutton-Smith (1985) reported that "research-oriented books in play across all fields from 1970 until the present [1985] number between 20 and 30, more than the total of such books from the preceding years of the twentieth century" (p. 10). This number can be expanded if books on the practical application of creating play environments and textbooks for education are included.

One of the more influential students of play for preschool children has been Jim Greenman, whose ideas are contained in his book, *Caring Spaces, Learning Places: Children's Environments That Work* (1988). Another contemporary book that considers an all-inclusive approach to planning for play and includes an emphasis on disabled children is *Play for All Guidelines* (1987) edited by Moore, Goltsman, and Iacofano. This book is in large part the result of input from educators, manufacturers, and designers obtained at the Stanford Conference organized by PLAE, Inc. in September 1986. The attendees of the conference were a good indication of the multiple fields and interests committed to improving play for children.

Manufacturers have also been helpful in informing the public of advancements in play design. Some took part in the Stanford Conference and have been in attendance or taken part in other presentations by professional organizations. Some catalogs include information that (although part of a marketing agenda) acts to educate the purchaser to the role equipment serves in the play environment. Designer Jay Beckwith created a Play Boosters Planning Kit for Mexico Forge in 1982 that included basic concerns of developmentally appropriate data on play in addition to layout devices for planning (Mexico Forge, 1982). Landscape Structures makes a form available to purchasers titled "Questions & Considerations When Developing a Master Plan of Your Outdoor Play Space" (1988, p. 2). The Children's Playgrounds catalog incorporates information on play value in a more informal discussion format (Children's Playgrounds,

1988), while Iron Mountain Forge includes a "Selection Process" chart to facilitate decision making as to age, handicap access, play events, and other equipment concerns (Iron Mountain Forge, 1989). Although by no means all-inclusive, such information is very useful in alerting the public to parameters for play not ordinarily a part of their awareness.

Play Value

The ultimate, inclusive goals of creating play environments cannot be realized simply by purchasing equipment and placing it in an outdoor area. The context of play and its concomitant ingredient of sensory, cognitive, social, and creative development require more. Just as buildings alone do not make a city, structures do not make a playground. Equipment, therefore, must be viewed as part of the total matrix of the play environment.

While playground equipment for preschool children has been part of the inventory of major manufacturers for years, the structures have been for the most part scaled-down facsimiles of larger pieces. Equipment typical of this type can be found in a 1973 catalog of the Recreation Equipment Corporation. The catalog includes a 5-foot diameter whirl with a solid platform, a 4-foot high galvanized slide, and toddler swings with marine plywood constructed swing seats. A tot swinging gate was also part of the inventory. Many of these pieces can still be found on playgrounds and in play equipment catalogs. They reflected what play researchers have termed traditional equipment.

During this same time period of the 1970s, manufacturers began to explore other options couching the traditional play events of climbing, sliding, and whirling about a center point in terms of theme contexts, either in their total form, or at least by name. Game Time (1976) offered its "Circurama," the titular equivalent of a three-ring circus with multicolored heads of animals and clowns added to an interconnected metal structure. Traditional play events were attached. Quality industries (1978), by now one of many companies producing wood structures, made use of names for otherwise unadorned connected play events such as "The Mother Lode Mine," "Golden Gate Bridge," "Fort Imagination," "Mississippi Riverboat," and numerous others.

This tendency toward the encouragement of dramatic play and socialization was extended by Miracle and Jamison with its "Storybook Village," where "Tiny tots can see their fairy tales come to life"

Five-foot diameter merry-go-round.

Four-foot-high portable slide.

Swinging gate.

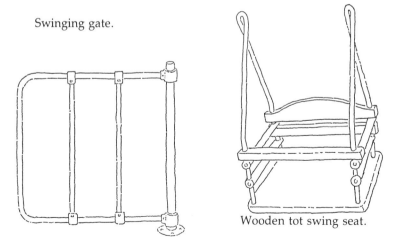

Wooden tot swing seat.

Figure 7.3. Typical equipment available in the 1970s for preschool age children.

(1976, p. 21). The complex included "Old Woman's Shoe," the "Cinderella Carriage," the "Gates of Camelot," and the "Castle Chute." With the addition of spring animals and a "superbug," the structures were essentially platforms for slides, fireman poles, and climbing events. Miracle also produced at this time its "Totland Pandora" that included a fiberglas mountain with slide, an "Elephant Slide," a playhouse, and a fiberglas turtle. Sand play was encouraged with a "Sand Crater," also constructed of fiberglas. Another product tied in to fiberglas technology during this period was the spring animal and the animal swing (Quality Industries, 1978; Game Time, 1976).

While the literature of play research in general increasingly called for more inclusive play possibilities (Moore, 1985), American manufacturers were continuing to produce structures that, with the exception of a theme or dramatic play association, remained traditional in their play event content. Though complex, linked structures characterized the designs for school-age children, preschool equipment remained as isolated play event structures or as one low platform with two or three activities attached.

During the 1980s, the more progressive companies availed themselves of current research in early childhood development and began expanding the play value of structures beyond a relatively superficial make-believe thematic manifestation, as well as creating play events that sought to encourage more than gross motor development. The reason for this change was apparently the growth in the market brought about by the growing child care industry.

In the realm of sensory, fine motor skill development and cognitive learning experiences, PlayDesigns and AdventureScapes have developed numerous panels that include games, dramatic play, color awareness, and other manipulative activity (Landscape Structures, 1988; Play Designs, 1990). Children's Playgrounds (1989) markets a structure called "Musical Hopskotch," which contains bells beneath foot-operated panels to create sound. The sandbox has grown from a simple container into a structural matrix of chutes, buckets on pulleys, and various table and shelf configurations to facilitate more creative activities (Children's Playgrounds, 1989; Kompan, 1989).

Grounds for Play, a small company producing custom wood structures, builds play houses with tube "telephone" connections, outdoor art easels, and a "Sensory Boat," which includes sensory surfaces, mirrors, rotating sound cylinders, and wheels to turn (Grounds for Play, 1989). All of these structures contribute to a richer experience for children at play.

On balance, the past ten years have seen the development of materials that have allowed manufacturers to enrich the play value of

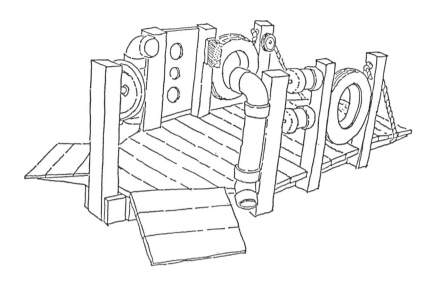

Figure 7.4. Sensory boat from Grounds for Play (designer prototype).

outdoor play equipment. These improvements have been encouraged by play research and by the growth of the child care industry. As long as they are augmented by landscaping, the creation of paths for walking and trike riding, an assortment of loose parts for free exploration and construction, and a consideration of multiple spatial experiences, as well as visual and auditory enrichment, then contemporary play structures for preschool children can be an important part of a true play environment.

References

Bruya, L., & Langendorfer, S. (1988). *Where our children play*. Reston, VA: American Alliance for Health, Physical Education, Recreation and Dance.

Children's Playgrounds, Inc. (1989). Equipment catalog. Cambridge, MA: Author.

Game Time (1976). Equipment catalog. Fort Payne, AL: Author.

Game Time (1988). Equipment catalog. Fort Payne, AL: Author.

Game Time (1989). Equipment catalog. Fort Payne, AL: Author.

Greenman, J. (1988). *Caring spaces, learning places: Children's environments that work*. Redmond, WA: Exchange Press.

Grounds for Play (1989). Equipment catalog. Arlington, TX: Author.

Iron Mountain Forge (1989). Equipment catalog. Farmington, MO: Author.

King, S. (November 6, 1989). Letter to author.

Kompan (1989). Equipment catalog. Windsor Locks, CT: Author.

Landscape Structures, Inc. (1988). *AdventureScapes preschool catalog.* Delano, MN: Author.

Mexico Forge. (1982). Play boosters planning list. Delano, MN: Author.

Miracle & Jamison (1976). *Bicentennial catalog.* Monett, MO: Miracle Recreation Equipment Co.

Moore, G.T. (1985). State of the art in play environments. In J. Frost & S. Sunderlin (Eds.), *When children play.* Wheaton, MD: Association for Childhood Education International.

Moore, G.T., Goltsman, S., & Iacofano, D. (Eds.). (1987). *Play for all guidelines.* Berkeley, CA: MIG Communications.

Parks and Recreation (1985). Trends in playground equipment: Interviews with four top manufacturers. *Parks and Recreation*, 20, 60–62.

Play Designs (1990). *Early childhood catalog.* New Berlin, PA: Author.

Quality Industries, Inc. (1978). *Playground equipment catalog no. 579*, Hillsdale, MI: Author.

Recreation Equipment Corporation (1973). *Playground equipment catalog no. 34.* Anderson, IN: Author.

Sutton-Smith, B. (1985). Play research: State of the art. In J. Frost & S. Sunderlin (Eds.), *When children play.* Wheaton, MD: Association for Childhood Education International.

U.S. Consumer Product Safety Commission (1981). *A handbook for public playground safety, Volume I: General guidelines for new and existing playgrounds.* Washington, DC: U.S. Government Printing Office.

Wortham, S.C. (1988a). Location, accessibility, and equipment on playgrounds. In L. Bruya & S. Langendorfer (Eds.), *Where our children play.* Reston, VA: American Alliance for Health, Physical Education, Recreation and Dance.

Wortham, S.C. (1988b). Development neglected on hand-me-down playgrounds. In L. Bruya & S. Langendorfer (Eds.), *Where our children play.* Reston, VA: American Alliance for Health, Physical Education, Recreation and Dance.

8

Maintaining Play Environments: Training, Checklists, and Documentation

Donna Thompson
Lawrence D. Bruya
Michael E. Crawford

The purpose of this chapter is to deal with assessment and risk management. While some literature has outlined legal concerns (Clement, 1989) and others have provided some assessment tools (Bruya & Beckwith, 1985, 1988; Moore, Goltsman, & Iacofano, 1987; Thompson & Bowers, 1989), including those in this volume, it is the intent of the writers of this chapter to: (a) provide a procedure for doing assessment, (b) outline several checklists that may be used for assessment, and (c) describe detailed processes for handling other risk management details.

The first section discusses ways to conduct a safety inspection. It highlights procedures to use to check for safe equipment configuration, emphasizes key aspects of safe installation, stresses checking maintenance of equipment and play zones, and provides information about evaluating specific equipment and design features. It is illustrated with figures of particular pieces of equipment and with details of the assessment procedure.

This general discussion of assessment procedures is followed by several detailed checklists with specific applications for (a) maintenance; (b) accessibility; (c) entrapment, entanglement, and protrusions; (d) fund raising; and (e) developmental benefits of playing on a play structure.

Last, the chapter develops the documentation of risk on preschool structures, discussing the (a) design process, (b) purchasing process, (c) installation process, (d) maintenance process, (e) repair process, (f) injury occurrence follow-up process, (g) safety program process, and (h) play structure curriculum. It is illustrated with a play structure documentation system for files and folders.

Readers will be introduced to ways of learning to do assessments, checklists to use, and a system to document the processes that the assessor has used. Readers can use the chapter to train administrators and safety personnel in order to provide a more appropriate risk management system.

How to Conduct a Safety Inspection

A builder will never be able to construct an injury free playground; no set of guidelines or method of constructing and installing equipment will totally prevent accidents. Children will always challenge themselves and take risks. However, professionals are obliged to avoid the creation of special risks and to ensure that the penalty for failed movement attempts or stunts is only a bruise or bump, rather than a serious injury or death. Although the U.S. Consumer Product Safety Commission (USCPSC, 1981) was careful to label its recommendations as guidelines rather than mandatory standards, the courts have tended to view its documents as the applicable standard for care for assessing reasonable conduct in cases involving playground injuries.

Any evaluation of a "safe" playground should include at least minimal guidelines. However, court findings of playground negligence have increasingly expanded beyond the USCPSC guidelines. Agencies and personnel responsible for policy and maintenance of playgrounds have been found culpable in cases of injury for a variety of reasons. In fact, some of the most recent litigation regarding playground injuries deals with undersurfaces and the environmental context of equipment installation (free from hazards such as tree branches or retaining walls, etc.) (Goldfarb, 1987). Thus, evaluation of a "safe" playground must consider not only (a) equipment features (as established by USCPSC) but also (b) configuration/design (are there adequate traffic paths and fall zone spaces?), (c) installation (is equipment firmly anchored and hazard free?), and (d) maintenance of the total play environment (are there any broken, missing, or worn parts or areas?). These aspects of playground safety are considered next.

Checking for Safe Equipment Configuration

Evaluating for a safe configuration or design includes looking at equipment adjacency, surroundings, and circulation characteristics. "Adjacency" refers to the relationship between equipment and other apparatus and/or play areas. A common problem with adjacency that should be checked is the so-called "dirty installation" where children can fall from one piece of equipment onto another instead of into a fall zone. AALR recommends a minimum of 10 feet distance between pieces of play equipment to avoid such dangers.

Related to adjacency is the concept of safe surroundings; the play zone itself must be hazard free. There should be no low tree branches in traffic pathways or in the internal play spaces of structures, and other man-made structures such as walls, fences, and buildings should not encroach upon the integrity of the play and traffic zones. Also, metal equipment, most notedly slide chutes, should be installed in shaded areas or directionally shielded from direct sunlight.

Circulation areas or play exclusivity zones vary depending on the type of equipment. Passive play equipment such as climbers don't require the same distance as more active apparatus such as spinners or swings. A safe yard will incorporate natural vegetation barriers into its design pathways that will steer traffic away from dangerous play areas such as swing bail-out zones and slide chute egress points. Yard designs that do not meet the criteria for safe equipment adjacency, surroundings, and circulation by their very design, increase the opportunity for serious injuries to occur (Burke, 1987). Agencies and personnel responsible for these designs can be held negligent for failing to address these design requirements.

Looking for Key Aspects of Safe Installation

In evaluating the safety of the installation of equipment, both the stability of the structures and component parts as well as the fall zone under and around the structure are of critical importance. First, the structural integrity of the apparatus should be considered when viewing from a distance. Is there any evidence of listing, sinking, bending, or warping of the equipment or any of its parts? Next, is the apparatus firmly anchored or seated into the ground? Does it move or sway under adult weight? What is the method of anchoring and are any of the anchor supports missing, broken, or protruding? Perhaps the most common problem with anchoring is the use of concrete footings to seat apparatus into the ground. Often the footings are left exposed above the ground and thus compromise the integrity of the fall zone. When the material around the fall zone area is brushed at the point of ground anchoring, the concrete footings or metal anchor parts should not be exposed. If they are visible, then the entire structure should be reseated.

The fall zone under and around the apparatus must contain an adequate safety surface (at least 6 inches of sand or a surface which meets the USCPSC 200g impact requirement) that extends an adequate distance from the play structure (generally a circumference of at least one and one-half the height of the structure) and is held in place by either a natural or man-made containment barrier. It is important to measure the depth of the fall zone material in several places to check for uniformity of coverage. Equipment installed without a fall zone that meets these criteria does not meet the USPCSC recommendations for an adequate safety surface. Such installations greatly increase the likelihood of slight injuries becoming serious ones (Donovan, 1987).

Maintenance of Equipment and Play Zones

A number of daily checks should be done, particularly during the active use season of a play yard. If the agency does not have a policy or procedure for checking the yard for garbage or debris, animal feces, or vandalism and for checking and ensuring adequate depth and uniformity of the fall zone surfaces, it is likely that other aspects of yard maintenance are similarly neglected. Agencies should document and keep records of their maintenance activities (dates and receipts of specific repairs, retrofits, etc.) as evidence of their concern for the play environment (Wallach, 1988).

Evaluating the condition of the playground includes looking at specific equipment features, fall zones, and circulation pathways. A safely maintained yard will contain equipment that is in good repair and working order. Check first for the more frequent and obvious safety problems resulting from poor maintenance: (a) loose screws, bolts, or nuts; (b) broken and/or missing rails, steps, seats, handles, or pedals; (c) worn or rusted chains, handsets, or connecting hardwood; (d) worn or frayed ropes, webbing, netting, or cables; (e) splintered or rotting wood; (f) worn bearings or mechanisms in moving parts; and (g) inadequate lubrication of moving parts or needed repainting of a structure.

Last, check the maintenance of fall zones. Focus principally on the adequacy of the undersurface. Check the depth around all structures. Are raking or additional fill needed? Have materials been compacted down or carried away over time? This inspection should include close review of all anchor points within the play space to ensure that footers or metal anchor parts have not become exposed over time through erosion of the surface. Finally, check the circulation pathways for worn surfaces (pay particular attention to carpet or astroturf-like materials, if used) and the condition of all retaining walls, barriers, or vegetation surrounding play equipment to ensure that they are still functional and safe.

Evaluating Specific Designs and Features

Evaluating equipment design is more complicated in the preschool environment than for other types of playgrounds due to the propensity of homebuilt structures. Many well-intentioned parents or day care providers have spent a weekend or two constructing some very dangerous homemade play structures. Other owners have hired the local community college industrial arts class who have built structurally sound equipment, but not according to USCPSC guidelines or other safety guidelines. There is also a tendency for providers to use equipment on their playground that is designed for home use, such as the traditional Sears or J. C. Penney multi-apparatus A-frame that is assembled from parts. Because the equipment is manufactured for home use, it does not fall under the USCPSC guidelines, which are intended to regulate public and commercial industry products only. Therefore, the consumer cannot be sure whether or not this equipment fulfills all safety design standards. Another additional complication of design is that many preschool yards have acquired equipment discarded from elementary schools or drive-in theaters. The majority of this equipment is age inappropriate. It is built on a scale too large for preschoolers to move on safely. The height, distance between grips and rungs, and dimensions of grips and rungs are the wrong size.

Regardless of the origin of the equipment present, there are some generic design features to consider during the evaluation of playgrounds. First, search for sharp edges or protrusions by running a cloth towel or gloved hand across the inside of components to help reveal these problems. Next, look for head entrapment spaces or openings in which a child could get caught. Generally any space between 4½ inches and 9 inches provides this opportunity. Related to this are finger entrapment spaces. Open pipes, cable reel holes, or floor spaces on climbing platforms provide opportunities for traumatic amputation of fingers. On moving apparatus, look for crush and pinch point features, including open hooks, loose connections between parts, and unshielded chains used for grips or suspension.

It is important to determine whether any toxic materials have been used, particularly for homebuilt structures. Wooden play structures built from old railroad ties and telephone poles could include creosote and pentachlorophenol. Any oozing or staining substance emanating from these materials should be considered suspect (Simpson, 1988). Also, many industrial paints contain lead and arsenic. If any commercial or industrial paint has been used, the contents of that paint should be clarified by analysis. Materials using lead paint should be removed from the playground. To avoid toxicity, lead paint should not be used.

When evaluating size or height of equipment and the desired dimensions or features of specific types of playground equipment, the USCPSC guidelines do provide a great deal of specificity in some instances, particularly the majority of so-called traditional individual pieces such as slides, swings, and merry-go-rounds. However, some types of playground equipment are more novel and are not specifically addressed, such as tree houses, forts, tunnels, fireman's poles, and balance equipment. Only the more generic aspects of the guidelines can be used in inspecting such structures for safety.

The accompanying series of eight figures incorporate many of the specific USCPSC guidelines that can be used as a measure of minimum safety compliance. Note that they incorporate specific details from the USCPSC guidelines (when available) regarding the equipment features; they also include detail from the four areas of playground safety reviewed in this chapter: installation, configuration, maintenance, and design. Much of the content is influenced by the AALR Committee on Play equipment survey checklist (see Appendix D), as well as other independent research efforts within the field (Guddemi, 1987; Goldfarb, 1987; Simpson, 1988). The figures may be used as field protocol to conduct a safety inspection; information relative to configuration and installation of equipment is located underneath the equipment depicted. Information regarding maintenance and design concerns surrounds the equipment in a halo which should be read from left to right.

Many authorities do not recommend structures on preschool yards in excess of 6 to 8 feet, or higher than the standing vertical reach of the tallest child using the equipment. The USCPSC guidelines were not specifically constructed with preschoolers in mind, and therefore do not speak to the notion of excessive height for the age group. Also, wherever novel equipment is present, such as tree houses, the evaluator must fall back on the more generic aspects of installation, configuration, design, and maintenance and use guidelines presented here in order to conduct a safety evaluation.

The evaluator should use the following items when conducting the evaluation: a protractor (to measure angles of component parts for tight V entrapment potential), a ruler or yardstick (to measure depth of fall zone surfaces), a long tape measure (to determine height of apparatus, as well as dimensions of fall zones), a camera to record any dangerous or hazardous aspects requiring immediate action, and a clipboard with the AALR assessment tool and the inspection checklists contained in this book.

AALR Playstructure Checklists

The checklists on pages 119–135 can be used in the assessment process; each checks a particular concept about playground equipment. The various maintenance checklists help assess how well the equipment is cared for. The accessibility checklist helps determine whether or not the play area is prepared for all children or children with special needs. The entrapment and protrusions checklist helps to evaluate the likelihood that equipment will cause head or limb entrapment, entanglement of clothing, and injury from protrusions such as bolts. The fundraising checklist includes a schedule and suggestions for use of items to consider when centers are ready to raise capital for the play area. The documentation system checklist provides a way to manage risk. Together with the figures (pages 110–118) and tables in this chapter, these worksheets (pages 119–135) provide the reader with material to use to provide a safer play area for children.

(Text continues on page 136)

Figure 8.1. Balance equipment safety inspection.

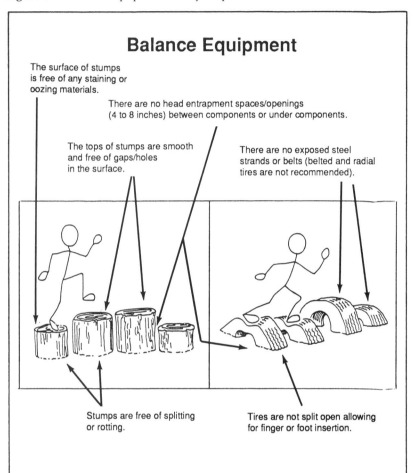

Balance Equipment

The surface of stumps
is free of any staining or
oozing materials.

There are no head entrapment spaces/openings
(4 to 8 inches) between components or under components.

The tops of stumps are smooth
and free of gaps/holes
in the surface.

There are no exposed steel
strands or belts (belted and radial
tires are not recommended).

Stumps are free of splitting
or rotting.

Tires are not split open allowing
for finger or foot insertion.

There is no evidence of standing water present
under or around components.

Each component is firmly anchored to the ground.

A safety surface of at least 6 inches of sand or a surface fulfilling the 200g force impact criteria
of the USCPSC surrounds the entire installation and extends 1 1/2 times as far as the height
of the tallest component plus the height of the tallest child using the apparatus and is held
in place by a natural or man-made containment barrier.

The use zone is free of debris/portable toys/obstacles/shrubs.

At least 10 feet separates independent installations to afford multidirectional player traffic.

Figure 8.2. Climbing poles safety inspection.

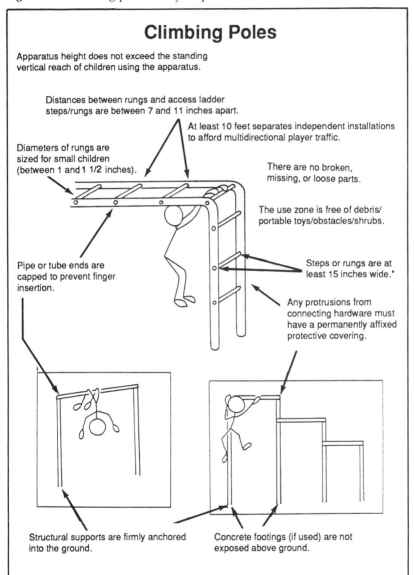

Climbing Poles

Apparatus height does not exceed the standing vertical reach of children using the apparatus.

Distances between rungs and access ladder steps/rungs are between 7 and 11 inches apart.

At least 10 feet separates independent installations to afford multidirectional player traffic.

Diameters of rungs are sized for small children (between 1 and 1 1/2 inches).

There are no broken, missing, or loose parts.

The use zone is free of debris/ portable toys/obstacles/shrubs.

Pipe or tube ends are capped to prevent finger insertion.

Steps or rungs are at least 15 inches wide.*

Any protrusions from connecting hardware must have a permanently affixed protective covering.

Structural supports are firmly anchored into the ground.

Concrete footings (if used) are not exposed above ground.

A safety surface of at least 6 inches of sand or a surface fulfilling the 200g force impact criterion of the USCPSC surrounds the apparatus and extends 1 1/2 times as far as the structure is high and is held in place by a natural or man-made containment barrier.

*A growing number of manufacturers are omitting ladder rungs for access to horizontal ladders because of the risk of children falling onto them. They also provide easy access to the top of the horizontal ladder which should be used from the underneathside only.

Figure 8.3. Climbing structures safety inspection.

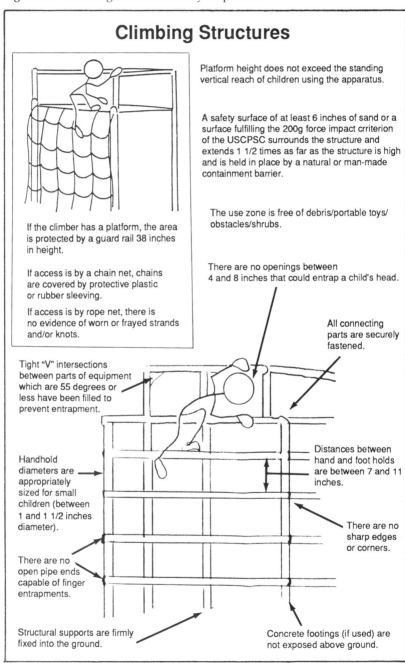

Climbing Structures

Platform height does not exceed the standing vertical reach of children using the apparatus.

A safety surface of at least 6 inches of sand or a surface fulfilling the 200g force impact crriterion of the USCPSC surrounds the structure and extends 1 1/2 times as far as the structure is high and is held in place by a natural or man-made containment barrier.

The use zone is free of debris/portable toys/ obstacles/shrubs.

If the climber has a platform, the area is protected by a guard rail 38 inches in height.

If access is by a chain net, chains are covered by protective plastic or rubber sleeving.

If access is by rope net, there is no evidence of worn or frayed strands and/or knots.

There are no openings between 4 and 8 inches that could entrap a child's head.

All connecting parts are securely fastened.

Tight "V" intersections between parts of equipment which are 55 degrees or less have been filled to prevent entrapment.

Handhold diameters are appropriately sized for small children (between 1 and 1 1/2 inches diameter).

Distances between hand and foot holds are between 7 and 11 inches.

There are no sharp edges or corners.

There are no open pipe ends capable of finger entrapments.

Structural supports are firmly fixed into the ground.

Concrete footings (if used) are not exposed above ground.

Figure 8.4. Rotating equipment safety inspection.

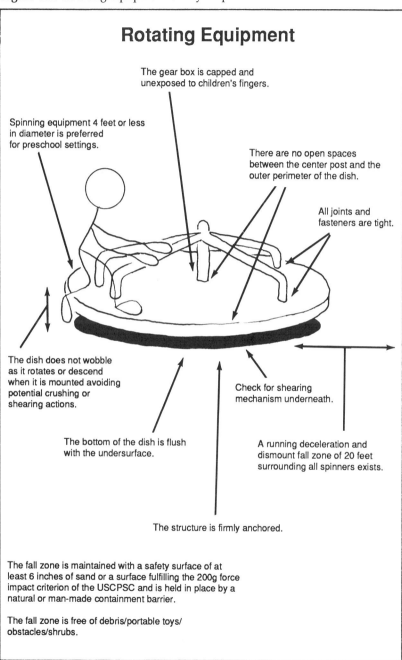

Rotating Equipment

The gear box is capped and unexposed to children's fingers.

Spinning equipment 4 feet or less in diameter is preferred for preschool settings.

There are no open spaces between the center post and the outer perimeter of the dish.

All joints and fasteners are tight.

The dish does not wobble as it rotates or descend when it is mounted avoiding potential crushing or shearing actions.

Check for shearing mechanism underneath.

The bottom of the dish is flush with the undersurface.

A running deceleration and dismount fall zone of 20 feet surrounding all spinners exists.

The structure is firmly anchored.

The fall zone is maintained with a safety surface of at least 6 inches of sand or a surface fulfilling the 200g force impact criterion of the USCPSC and is held in place by a natural or man-made containment barrier.

The fall zone is free of debris/portable toys/obstacles/shrubs.

Figure 8.5. Seesaw structures safety inspection.

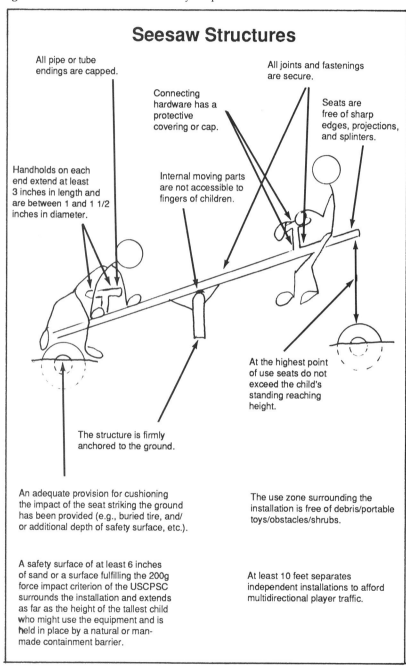

Seesaw Structures

All pipe or tube endings are capped.

All joints and fastenings are secure.

Connecting hardware has a protective covering or cap.

Seats are free of sharp edges, projections, and splinters.

Handholds on each end extend at least 3 inches in length and are between 1 and 1 1/2 inches in diameter.

Internal moving parts are not accessible to fingers of children.

At the highest point of use seats do not exceed the child's standing reaching height.

The structure is firmly anchored to the ground.

An adequate provision for cushioning the impact of the seat striking the ground has been provided (e.g., buried tire, and/ or additional depth of safety surface, etc.).

The use zone surrounding the installation is free of debris/portable toys/obstacles/shrubs.

A safety surface of at least 6 inches of sand or a surface fulfilling the 200g force impact criterion of the USCPSC surrounds the installation and extends as far as the height of the tallest child who might use the equipment and is held in place by a natural or man-made containment barrier.

At least 10 feet separates independent installations to afford multidirectional player traffic.

Figure 8.6. Slides safety inspection.

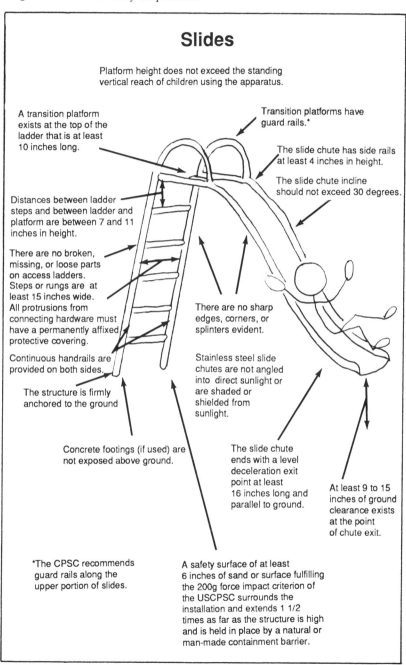

Slides

Platform height does not exceed the standing vertical reach of children using the apparatus.

A transition platform exists at the top of the ladder that is at least 10 inches long.

Transition platforms have guard rails.*

The slide chute has side rails at least 4 inches in height.

The slide chute incline should not exceed 30 degrees.

Distances between ladder steps and between ladder and platform are between 7 and 11 inches in height.

There are no broken, missing, or loose parts on access ladders. Steps or rungs are at least 15 inches wide. All protrusions from connecting hardware must have a permanently affixed protective covering.

Continuous handrails are provided on both sides.

The structure is firmly anchored to the ground

There are no sharp edges, corners, or splinters evident.

Stainless steel slide chutes are not angled into direct sunlight or are shaded or shielded from sunlight.

Concrete footings (if used) are not exposed above ground.

The slide chute ends with a level deceleration exit point at least 16 inches long and parallel to ground.

At least 9 to 15 inches of ground clearance exists at the point of chute exit.

*The CPSC recommends guard rails along the upper portion of slides.

A safety surface of at least 6 inches of sand or surface fulfilling the 200g force impact criterion of the USCPSC surrounds the installation and extends 1 1/2 times as far as the structure is high and is held in place by a natural or man-made containment barrier.

Figure 8.6. Slides safety inspection, continued.

Slides, continued

The method of climbing used does not exceed a slope greater than the examples below.

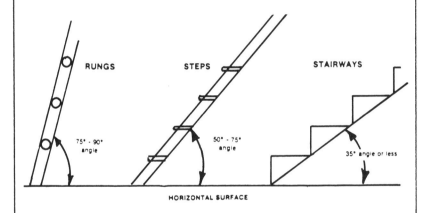

RUNGS

75° - 90° angle

STEPS

50° - 75° angle

STAIRWAYS

35° angle or less

HORIZONTAL SURFACE

The use zone surrounding the installation is free of debris/portable toys/obstacles/shrubs.

At least 10 feet separates independent installations to afford multidirectional player traffic.

Figure 8.7. Spring rocking equipment safety inspection.

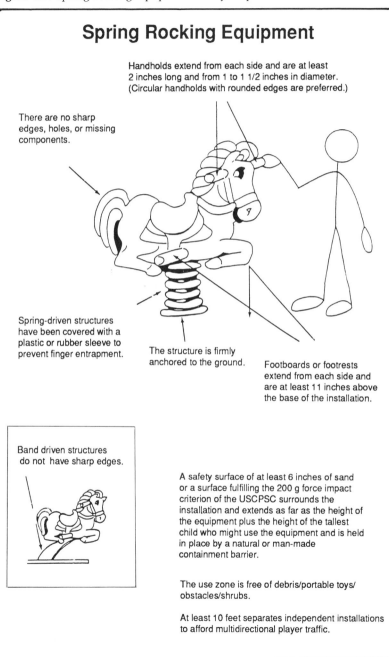

Spring Rocking Equipment

Handholds extend from each side and are at least
2 inches long and from 1 to 1 1/2 inches in diameter.
(Circular handholds with rounded edges are preferred.)

There are no sharp
edges, holes, or missing
components.

Spring-driven structures
have been covered with a
plastic or rubber sleeve to
prevent finger entrapment.

The structure is firmly
anchored to the ground.

Footboards or footrests
extend from each side and
are at least 11 inches above
the base of the installation.

Band driven structures
do not have sharp edges.

A safety surface of at least 6 inches of sand
or a surface fulfilling the 200 g force impact
criterion of the USCPSC surrounds the
installation and extends as far as the height of
the equipment plus the height of the tallest
child who might use the equipment and is held
in place by a natural or man-made
containment barrier.

The use zone is free of debris/portable toys/
obstacles/shrubs.

At least 10 feet separates independent installations
to afford multidirectional player traffic.

Figure 8.8. Swings safety inspection.

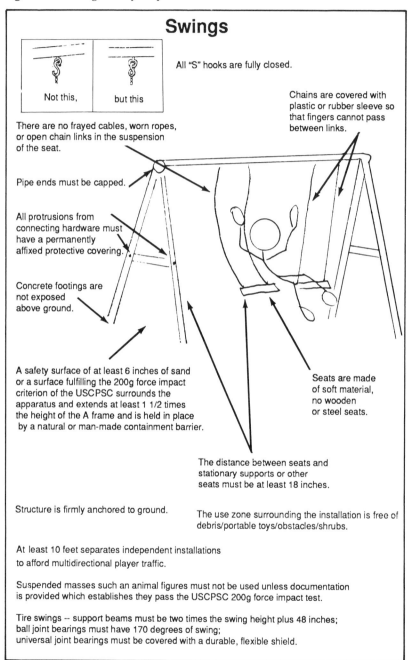

Swings

All "S" hooks are fully closed.

Not this,   but this

There are no frayed cables, worn ropes, or open chain links in the suspension of the seat.

Chains are covered with plastic or rubber sleeve so that fingers cannot pass between links.

Pipe ends must be capped.

All protrusions from connecting hardware must have a permanently affixed protective covering.

Concrete footings are not exposed above ground.

A safety surface of at least 6 inches of sand or a surface fulfilling the 200g force impact criterion of the USCPSC surrounds the apparatus and extends at least 1 1/2 times the height of the A frame and is held in place by a natural or man-made containment barrier.

Seats are made of soft material, no wooden or steel seats.

The distance between seats and stationary supports or other seats must be at least 18 inches.

Structure is firmly anchored to ground.

The use zone surrounding the installation is free of debris/portable toys/obstacles/shrubs.

At least 10 feet separates independent installations to afford multidirectional player traffic.

Suspended masses such an animal figures must not be used unless documentation is provided which establishes they pass the USCPSC 200g force impact test.

Tire swings -- support beams must be two times the swing height plus 48 inches; ball joint bearings must have 170 degrees of swing; universal joint bearings must be covered with a durable, flexible shield.

AALR Play Structure Checklist
© 1990 AAHPERD-AALR-COP

Surfacing, Location and Accessibility, Size and Placement, and Storage Areas Maintenance Worksheet

D. Thompson, University of Northern Iowa

● Surfacing

Are surfaces under the structure where falls are most likely of a resilient material (force-absorbing material)?

Are composite loose surfaces at least 6″ in depth at the shallowest point under equipment of 4′ or less?

Are composite loose surfaces deeper than 6″ under structures higher than 4′? (depth should be proportional to height)

Are under-structure surfaces made of concrete, asphalt, or packed dirt? (should be removed, or covered with resilient material)

Is composite loose surfacing replenished on a regular basis?

Is composite loose surfacing surrounded by containment barriers?

Are containment barriers at least 6″ higher than the composite loose surfacing?

Are containment barriers surrounded by a 5′ maintenance zone?

Does the maintenance zone contain material to allow settling and clean up of child carried composite loose surfacing?

Containment barriers should be visible enough to ensure against trips.

● Locations and Accessibility

Does a 4′ fence surround the playground?

Are the fence posts secured in the ground?

Does the fence have a gate for access? Does the gate latch?

Do the gate hinges show evidence of grease indicating maintenance at least twice per year?

● Size and Placement of Equipment

Are individual pieces of equipment at least 10′ apart?

Are concrete footings for each piece of equipment showing?

Is equipment placed to avoid crossing traffic patterns which could lead to injury?

Is equipment for infants or toddlers placed in a separate area?

Are the areas for infants and toddlers and for older children separated by a fence or barrier which effectively prevents crossover?

● Storage Areas

Are storage areas adjacent to the play area?

Are storage areas kept locked?

AALR Play Structure Checklist
© 1990 AAHPERD-AALR-COP

Swing Maintenance Worksheet

D. Thompson, University of Northern Iowa

● To and Fro Swings

Are swing seats soft material like plastic or rubber? (all metal or wooden seats should be removed)

Are swings for tots and swings for older children hung on separate structures?

Is there a barrier in front of or behind the action of the swings to prevent running into a moving swing?

Are all supports securely fastened in the ground?

Are all footings covered?

Are rough edges exposed to children?

Are all metal surfaces painted with unleaded paint?

Are all swing chains covered to prevent pinches?

Are moving parts of the swing lubricated according to manufacturer's specifications?

Are all nuts and bolts tight?

Is composite loose surfacing under the structure in depths of at least 6″ or more?

Is composite loose surfacing replenished on a regular basis?

Is composite loose surfacing surrounded by containment barriers?

Are containment barriers at least 6″ higher than the composite loose surfacing?

Are containment barriers surrounded by a 5′ maintenance zone?

Does the maintenance zone contain material to allow settling and easy clean up of carried composite loose surfacing from under the structure?

Are containment barriers visible enough to ensure against trips?

● Tire Swings

Is the fulcrum or center point on the swing in the center of the horizontal beam?

Are the vertical uprights placed away from the structure at a distance equal to or greater than the radius of the swing arc?

Is the swivel moving assembly lubricated?

Is the swivel moving assembly wearing through its support?

● Tot Swings

Are all sides of each tot swing structurally safe?

Can all hooks which close the seats to the sides be securely latched?

AALR Play Structure Checklist
© 1990 AAHPERD-AALR-COP

Sliding Equipment Maintenance Worksheet

D. Thompson, University of Northern Iowa

● Slides, General

Are there missing or broken parts?

Are there sharp corners, edges, or projections?

Are all footings firmly underground?

Are single wide slides replaced with double wide slides?

Is the slide surface smooth?

Does the slide surface need to be painted?

In slides over 4', does the bottom of the slide form an exit chute which decreases in angle from the rest of the slide surface?

Does the overall height of the slide exceed the total of 2.5 times the tallest child in the group?

Are composite loose surfaces deeper than 6" under structures higher than 4'? (depth should be proportional to the height of the structure)

Are understructure surfaces made of concrete, asphalt, or packed dirt? (these should be removed immediately, or covered with a resilient material)

Is composite loose surfacing replenished on a regular basis?

Is composite loose surfacing surrounded by containment barriers?

  Are containment barriers at least 6" higher than the composite loose surfacing?

  Are containment barriers surrounded by a 5' maintenance zone?

  Does the maintenance zone contain material to allow settling and easy clean up of child carried composite loose surfacing from under the structure?

Containment barriers should be visible enough to ensure against trips.

● Hill Slides

Does the hill slide have dirt under and around it so the slide surface is supported and secure?

● Spiral Slides

Is some part of the child visible throughout the descent? (remove slides where children disappear from view during descent)

● Tunnel Slides

Is some part of the child visible throughout the descent? (remove slides where children disappear from view during descent)

AALR Play Structure Checklist
© 1990 AAHPERD-AALR-COP

Climbing Equipment Maintenance Worksheet

D. Thompson, University of Northern Iowa

● General Climbing Equipment

Are all support structures securely anchored in the ground?
Are all footings covered?
Are surfaces under the structure where falls are most likely of a resilient material (force-absorbing material)?
Are composite loose surfaces at least 6" in depth at the shallowest point under equipment of 4' or less?
Is composite loose surfacing replenished on a regular basis?
Are all nuts and bolts securely fastened?
Are all open holes closed (e.g., at the end of pipes)?
Are spaces which could entrap hands or fingers removed?
Is the structure free of sharp corners, edges, and protrusions?
Are structures higher than 2.5 times as high as the tallest player is tall? (these should be removed)
Are all platforms 4' or higher enclosed with guard rails?
Does the structure have openings between 4.5" and 9"? Redesign these parts to be less than 4.5" or greater than 9". (For younger preschool children, these dimensions may need to be reduced.)

● Chain/Rope

Are chains covered to eliminate pinch points?
Are chain links worn or showing wear? (replace)
Are ropes frayed or showing wear? (replace)
Are parts which connect rope to the structure worn? (replace)
Is assembly which attaches chain/rope to the structure lubricated regularly?

● Horizontal Ladders

Are all footings cemented under the ground at least 6"?
Is there at least 8" of ground cover under the structure to protect against falls?

● Stairways

Are all stairway bolts fastened securely, including those which are used to attach it to the structure?

● Geodesic Domes

Are all stairway bolts fastened securely?
Are all nuts and bolts fastened securely?
Is there at least 8″ of ground cover under the geodesic dome to
protect against falls?

● Climbing Poles

Are all pole footings cemented under the ground at least 6″?
Is any connection at the top of the pole fastened securely?
Is there at least 8″ of ground cover under the pole to protect against
falls?

● Balance Beams

Are all balance beam footings cemented under the ground at least
6″?
Are there protrusions at the connecting points? (remove them)
Are all rough edges sanded smooth?
Is there at least 8″ of ground cover under the balance beam to
protect against falls?

● Chinning Bars

Are all chinning bar footings cemented under the ground at least
6″?
Are all nuts and bolts fastened securely?
Are all horizontal bars perpendicular to the uprights?
Is there at least 8″ of ground cover under the chinning bars to
protect against falls?

● Parallel Bars

Are all parallel bar footings cemented under the ground at least 6″?
Are all nuts and bolts fastened securely?
Is there at least 8″ of ground cover under the parallel bars to
protect against falls?

● Bridges

Are all bridge footings cemented under the ground at least 6″?
Are all nuts and bolts fastened securely?
Are bridge pinch points covered?
Is there at least 8″ of ground cover under the bridge to protect
against falls?

AALR Play Structure Checklist
© 1990 AAHPERD-AALR-COP

Rotating, Spring Rocking, and Seesaw Maintenance Worksheet

D. Thompson, University of Northern Iowa

● Merry-go-round, Swinging Gates

Is the support structure level and firmly secured in the ground?
Are all joints and fasteners secured?
Is the structure free from all sharp corners and edges?
Are all open spaces in the center of the structure between the
    center post and the outer perimeter covered?
Are all moving parts lubricated at least once a year?
Does the structure have moving parts (usually underneath) which
    create a shearing action that could sever or crush body parts?
    (all structures that have a shearing action should be removed)
Is the gear box covered?
Is there a 20' cleared running space surrounding the structure to be
    used for getting off?
Are composite loose surfaces at least 6" deep under the structure?
Is composite loose surfacing replenished on a regular basis?
Is composite loose surfacing surrounded by containment barriers?
    Are containment barriers at least 6" higher than the composite
        loose surfacing?
    Are containment barriers surrounded by a 5' maintenance zone?
    Does the maintenance zone contain material to allow settling and
        easy clean up of child carried composite loose surfacing from
        under the structure?
Containment barriers should be visible enough to ensure against trips.

● Spring Rocking Equipment

Is the support structure firmly secured in the ground?
Are all joints and fasteners secured?
Are there sharp corners, edges, or projections?
Are composite loose surfaces at least 6" deep under the structure?
Is composite loose surfacing replenished on a regular basis?
Is composite loose surfacing surrounded by containment barriers?
    Are containment barriers at least 6" higher than the composite
        loose surfacing?
    Are containment barriers surrounded by a 5' maintenance zone?
    Does the maintenance zone contain material to allow settling and
        easy clean up of child carried composite loose surfacing from
        under the structure?
Containment barriers should be visible enough to ensure against trips.

● Seesaw Equipment

Is the support structure firmly secured in the ground?
Are all joints and fasteners secured?
Are there sharp corners, edges, or projections?
Are all nuts and bolts countersunk?
Are all moving parts lubricated at least once a year?
Are moving parts covered?
Is there a cushioning surface (e.g., tire) under each end of the
    seesaw where it would normally come in contact with the
    ground?
Is the overall height of the seesaw at the top of the arc less than
    4'?
Are all hand holds 3" in length?
Are composite loose surfaces at least 6" deep under the structure?
Is composite loose surfacing replenished on a regular basis?
Is composite loose surfacing surrounded by containment barriers?
    Are containment barriers at least 6" higher than the composite
        loose surfacing?
    Are containment barriers surrounded by a 5' maintenance zone?
    Does the maintenance zone contain material to allow settling and
        easy clean up of child-carried composite loose surfacing from
        under the structure?
Containment barriers should be visible enough to ensure against trips.

AALR Play Structure Checklist
© 1990 AAHPERD-AALR-COP

Sand and Water Play Maintenance Worksheet

D. Thompson, University of Northern Iowa

● Designated Sand Play Area

Is the sand play area clean and free of debris?
Is adequate drainage provided to prevent collection of water?
Are sand play area boundary joints and fasteners secured?
Is the sand play area structure free from all sharp corners and edges?
Is sand replenished on a regular basis?
Is there an elevated sand play area for wheel chair access (e.g., sand table)?
Is the sand play area covered when not in use to prevent access to animals?
Is adult seating provided near the sand play area?

● Designated Water Play Area

Is the water play area located next to the sand play area to ensure that sand and water can be combined?
Are water play areas cleaned regularly according to relevant health department specifications?
Do spray heads have lime or water mineral build-ups on them?
  Is there regular maintenance to remove these build-ups?
Are movable parts for water clues or water wheels lubricated regularly?
Are all standing water areas fenced and gated to secure the area when inadequately supervised?
Is the water play area structure free from all sharp corners and edges?
Is there an elevated water play area for wheel chair access (e.g., water table)?
Is the water play area clean and free of debris?
Is adequate drainage provided to prevent unwanted collection of water and/or end of the play period drainage?
Is adult seating provided near the water play area?

AALR Play Structure Checklist
© 1990 AAHPERD-AALR-COP

Signs, Trees, and Pathways Maintenance Worksheet

D. Thompson, University of Northern Iowa

● Signs

Is there an overview map for the play structure configuration?
Are smaller signs provided as a part of the structure?
Are all signs both written word and graphically presented?
Are all signs bilingual?
Are there indications of accessibility on the signs?
Are phone numbers provided on the signs in case of emergency?
Are degrees of difficulty indicated on the sign?
Does at least one sign indicate the prohibition of animals on the play structure?
Do the signs include a caution for potential injury which may occur during play?
Do signs give information which provide ideas to expand exploration?

● Trees and Shade Structures

Do trees prevent wind from the prevailing direction?
Are live trees used for shade within the limits of the play structure borders?
Is shade available to shield structures (e.g., slide surface, sand area)?
Is there evidence of raking and removing leaves from the site?
Are trees trimmed and maintained?
Are there tree houses in the trees? Are tree houses securely fastened?
Is adult seating provided?
Is a drinking fountain provided near the play structure?
  Is the fountain head and base cleaned daily?
  Is the fountain prepared for winter?
  Are there sharp corners, edges, or projections?

● Pathways

Do pathways discourage the formation of waiting lines?
Are hard surface pathways free from weeds and other growth?
Are pathways wide enough for widest wheel toy?
Do pathways for wheel toys have at least one intersection?
Do pathways on the structure have at least one intersection?
Do structure pathways lead to areas spacious enough for child planning of play patterns?

AALR Play Structure Checklist
© 1990 AAHPERD-AALR-COP

Playhouse, Garden, and Manipulatives Maintenance Worksheet

D. Thompson, University of Northern Iowa

● Playhouse

Are all joints securely fastened?
Are all surfaces nonabrasive and free from sharp corners, edges, or projections?
Are all surfaces painted or treated with nonlead, nonharmful materials?
Are play houses open enough to allow easy visual and quick access by an adult play leader?
Does the playhouse have enough room for a table and chairs?
Are playhouses in trees (treehouse) securely fastened on major large branches?

● Wheel/Riding Toys

Are nuts and bolts on wheel toys tightened monthly?
Are moving parts on wheel toys lubricated regularly (at least every six months)?
Are additional instructions from the manufacturer for maintenance followed?
Are all surfaces nonabrasive and free from sharp corners, edges, or projections?
Are all surfaces painted or treated with nonlead, nonharmful materials?

● Gardens

Is the garden weeded regularly?
Are organic materials (e.g., leaves) mulched?

● Manipulatives

Are wooden blocks and other manipulatives free of sharp corners, edges, or projections?
Are tools, buckets, and other loose parts available for play?
Are manipulatives evaluated and upgraded on a monthly basis?
Are moving parts on smaller wheel toys lubricated regularly?

AALR Play Structure Checklist
© 1990 AAHPERD-AALR-COP

Accessibility for All Populations Worksheet

Donna Thompson, University of Northern Iowa

● Visual Disabilities

Are railings or ropes provided as cues to pathways on the structure?
Are all ground surfaces smooth?
Are structural surfaces free of trip hazards?
Are tactile cues provided as a part of the structure?
Are auditory cues (e.g., cassette players) provided to guide play?

● Auditory Disabilities

Are there signs in the general vicinity to provide information concerning the use of the play structure?
Are there signs on the structure to provide information concerning play event usage?

● Wheelchair Disabilities

Are extra wide doors and/or gates provided to accommodate wheelchairs?
Are ramps to accommodate wheelchairs available for use?
Do ramps have railings so players can get to events on the structure?
Are ramps available to allow commuting from one event to the next?
Are wheelchair swings provided for use?
Can entrance ramps to swings be lowered and secured?
Is a bench swing available which has one side that swings down to allow entrance?
Is there a ramp to provide access to the sand area?
Is there a sand table available which allows access by a wheelchair?
Is there a water table available which allows access by a wheelchair?
Is a firm surface provided to allow easy access to the play structure from other places on the playground?

● Developmental Disabilities

Is there provision for children who are younger?

Continued

● Reaction Time Disabilities

Is there equipment provided that does not require quick judgments?
Are there large spaces between swings and swing structures?

● Children on Crutches

Is a firm surface provided to allow easy access to the play structure
from other places on the playground?
Are there places provided for storage of the crutches?

● Children with Braces

Is a firm surface provided to allow easy access to the play structure
from other places on the playground?
Is the area free from debris?

● Children with Little Arm Strength

Are ropes with knots provided so children can pull themselves
along surfaces?
Is equipment provided at lower levels of the structure which allows
children to pull themselves through?
Are handles, handrails, and knobs shaped to provide easy
operation?

AALR Play Structure Checklist
© 1990 AAHPERD-AALR-COP

Playground Entrapment and Protrusions Worksheet

Donna Thompson, University of Northern Iowa

- ## Fences
  Are the tops of chain link fences covered?
  Are nuts and bolts countersunk? On the sides? Underneath?

- ## Decks
  Are nuts and bolts countersunk? On the sides? Underneath?
  Are railing slats less than 4" and more than 9" apart?
  Are all railing slats running in the vertical direction?

- ## Slides
  Are nuts and bolts countersunk? On the sides? Underneath?
  Are horizontal structural supports attached greater than 55 degrees?
  Is the top of the slide bed close to the platform to avoid entrapment?

- ## Climbers
  Are horizontal rungs between 7" and 11" apart?
  Are nuts and bolts countersunk? On the sides? Underneath?
  Are horizontal bars attached greater than 55 degrees?

- ## Swings
  Are horizontal structural supports attached greater than 55 degrees?
  Are nuts and bolts countersunk? On the sides? Underneath?

- ## Balancing Equipment
  Are nuts and bolts countersunk? On the sides? Underneath?

- ## Rotating Equipment
  Are nuts and bolts countersunk? On the sides? Underneath?
  Are horizontal structural supports attached greater than 55 degrees?

Continued

- ## Spring Rocking
  Are nuts and bolts countersunk? On the sides? Underneath?

- ## Seesaw Equipment
  Are nuts and bolts countersunk? On the sides? Underneath?
  Is the pivot point covered or secured to keep fingers out?

- ## Designated Sand Areas
  Are nuts and bolts countersunk? On the sides? Underneath?

- ## Signs
  Are nuts and bolt fasteners countersunk? On the sides?
    Underneath?
  Are signs placed to ensure that players will not bump their heads?

- ## Trees
  Are trees trimmed to 7' above the ground?

- ## Pathways
  Are pathways smooth to avoid trip hazards?

AALR Play Structure Checklist
© 1990 AAHPERD-AALR-COP

Playground Fundraising Schedule Worksheet

D. Thompson, University of Northern Iowa

• Step 1

Plan the playground structure.
Send structure ideas and rationale to manufacturers for design specification.
equipment   surfacing   installation   maintenance

• Step 2

Determine cost upper limit for total project.
Determine cost of equipment.   Determine cost of surfacing.
Determine cost of installation.
Compare total project cost with upper limit. Resolve differences.

• Step 3

Adjust design to fit total project cost upper limit.
Resubmit structure design to manufacturers for critique and cost estimates.
Repeat steps 1, 2, 3 as frequently as necessary.

• Step 4

Select manufacturer.
Determine payment schedule with manufacturer.

• Step 5

Elect fundraising chairperson and list responsibilities.
Brainstorm fundraising ideas.
selling pizzas   magazine subscriptions   t-shirts
writing grant proposals   writing foundation proposals
convincing board members to designate funds for the playground
convincing service club memberships to donate funds for the playground
convincing parents to donate x number of $ per square foot of the playground
seeking matching funds from select sources

• Step 6

Determine timeline for each procedure.

• Step 7

Chart donations.

AALR Play Structure Checklist
© 1989 AAHPERD-AALR-COP

Documentation System to Manage Risk: Files and Folders

Lawrence D. Bruya, Washington State University

STEPS TO DEVELOP A PLAYSTRUCTURE FACILITY

• Design Process

Are the qualifications of the designer on file?
Are the parameters under which the design was developed on file?
Is proof of adherence to design parameters on file?
Is a rationale for why the design is safe on file?

• Purchasing Process

Is information in the file concerning who made the decision to purchase the structure?
Are the name, address, phone number, and comments made by a second expert designer on file?
Is there evidence of educators', parents', maintenance personnel's and children's reviews of the design in the file?

• Installation Process

Are the name, address, phone number, and contractual agreements with the installer in the file?
Are the specifications for installation in the file?
Are all records of installation inspection in the file?
Is evidence of installation inspection training seminars in the file?
Is evidence of any design changes made during installation in the file?
Are guidelines for signing-off on the structure in the file?
Is there evidence of final signing-off in the file?

STEPS TO DEVELOP ON-SITE MONITORING FOR SAFETY

• Inspection Process

Is the inspection form used for regular inspection in the file?
Is evidence in the file of inspection training seminars for inspectors?
Is there evidence in the file of policy related to setting regular inspections?

Is a record of all inspection dates and forms kept in the file?

● Maintenance Process

Is a designer-suggested structure maintenance schedule in the file?
Is there evidence of a regular maintenance schedule?
Is there a record of a safety officer assignment in the file?
Is there evidence of work orders for maintenance in the file?
Is there evidence of a work order follow-up procedure in the file?

● Repair Process

Is there evidence in the file of work orders drafted by the safety officer?
Is there evidence in the file, i.e., a training program, of the capability of the work crews to repair the structure adequately?
Is there evidence in the file of a regular process to follow up work order repairs to ensure that the problem does not reoccur?
Is there evidence of a return to regular maintenance after repairs?

STEPS TO DEVELOP A PEOPLE-TO-PEOPLE SAFETY SYSTEM

● Safety Program

Is there evidence in the file of the involvement of the children in establishing safety rules?
Is there evidence in the file of integrated curriculum in the school for discussion of safety on the play structure?
Is there evidence in the file of student-prepared school safety newsletter or magazine?
Is there evidence in the file of parent, school administrator, and teacher support of the safety program?
Is a copy of the warning letter sent home to each school child's parent in the file?
Is a copy in the file of all signs posted on, or adjacent to, the play structure (verbal and graphic instructions).

● Playstructure Curriculum

Is a copy in the file of the curriculum used with the structure?
Is an indication kept in the file of children being trained to select appropriate skill activities at the advanced, normal, and remedial levels of activity?
Is there evidence kept in the file of instructing children in the manner in which to safely select skill activities on the structure?

● Injury Occurrence System

Is a record of interviews with injured child, witnesses, and adult supervisors on site at the time of injury in the file?
Is a record kept in the file indicating contact with the parents of the injured child?

Documenting Risk on Preschool Play Structures

Recently, hospital emergency room records have been monitored to determine the type and severity of injury to children who play on structures in play settings (USCPSC, 1979; University of Iowa, 1973). It is now evident that many of the injuries children experience are more serious than the scrapes, cuts, and abrasions that are associated with normal, everyday play. Records indicate that breaks, concussions, and sometimes even death occur from falls and/or caught clothing. The problem of falls has been specifically addressed through the recommendation for safety surfaces under structures (National Recreation Association, 1931; Butler, 1958; National Recreation and Park Association, 1976; USCPSC, 1981).

The provision of surfaces and structural designs that will provide the greatest protection from severe occurrences of injury has been addressed by several authors (Beckwith, 1988; Bowers, 1988). At the same time, designers and researchers are aware that the structures must continue to provide novel and complex play settings that are likely to hold the interest of children through challenges (Bruya, 1985a, 1985b).

The administrator of a preschool with outdoor play structures is aware that suggested guidelines and standards are evolving intended to increase safety (PLAE, 1990; Bruya, 1988). It is no longer possible to "plant" a structure on the playground at a preschool and assume that the needs of children are met.

Instead, it is necessary to consider play structures as unique within the total preschool play facility and address the issue of safety in a reasoned way (Frost & Klein, 1979). Recent literature has provided some processes for that approach (Bruya & Beckwith, 1985). Usually, this consists of a series of procedures which include: (a) the steps leading to development of play structures, (b) the safety steps for onsite monitoring of play structures, and (c) the steps for people-to-people interaction between those who use and those who monitor the play structures.

Steps for the Development of Play Structures

The preschool administrator's first and most important consideration for a play structure should be its safety. This concern does not eliminate the need to consider the developmental or educational benefits that the structures provide, but instead is the first in a list of important concerns. Nothing can more quickly negate the perceived good provided in a preschool play setting than a severe injury or death of a child. Thus, it is extremely important that safety be reasonably and logically handled.

When developing a safe play structure, it is necessary that certain processes be addressed methodically, one at a time. These include design, purchase, and installation. Then, each must be documented well if the administrator is to provide proof that it was reasonably considered (Bruya & Beckwith, 1988).

Design Process. The strength of the design of a play structure is determined by the understanding of safety and the developmental needs of children for which the structures are designed. This awareness is based on the qualifications of the designer relative to: (a) child development; (b) safety; (c) need for novelty, complexity, and challenge; (d) materials; and (e) the likelihood of injury occurrence. When attempting to provide the best for children in the preschool, it is not enough to pick and choose from marketplace designs. The qualifications of the designer must also be understood in order to make judgments concerning the probable worth of the selected structural design (Bruya & Beckwith, 1985).

In addition, it is important that the team or group of people who develop the preschool facility possess a clear picture of the parameters the design must fit. These include ages of the players, the need for expressive activity and role playing, and the need for vigorous activity. Other parameters such as the size of the space and topography are also important (Chu & Topps, 1979).

Equally important is a clear picture of ways the parameters were met. This logical and step-by-step process should include documentation of processes and procedures used to clearly deal with each parameter. Then it is possible to develop a rationale for the safety of the particular design and structures. If a structure is a unit purchased from a company, a rationale for safety should be retained in the file. All questions concerning safety can be addressed from the planning stage through construction of the play structure to a case of litigation related to an injury, if necessary.

A quick, efficient way to ensure adherence to careful consideration and monitoring of design for play structures is to answer questions listed in Table 8.1. As a reminder, a list of questions helps the administrator focus on the most important issues.

TABLE 8.1
The Design Process

Questions concerning the design should be addressed and materials kept
on file.
    Are the qualifications of the designer on file?
    Are the parameters under which the design was developed on file?
    Is a rationale for why the design is safe on file?

Purchasing Process. If a commercial unit is selected, once the
design has been agreed upon, the purchasing process can be undertaken. Usually, the decision is best made for purchase if a group of
experts has taken the opportunity to review the design. These experts
include other preschool educators, maintenance persons, safety experts, custodial staff, parents, child users, developmental specialists,
and playground experts.

Probably, the most important aspect of the expert review is the
opinion of a second designer. By using a second designer to review
the work of the first designer, a cross validation of the safety and
developmental features associated with the play structure is gained.

The review process using all or many of the review experts listed
above should be a formalized process (Bayless & Adams, 1985).
Signatures and times of review should be recorded, as well as
suggestions for improvement or verification comments which were
made upon review.

A quick and efficient way to ensure adherence to a purchasing

TABLE 8.2
The Purchasing Process

Questions concerning the purchasing process should be answered and
materials kept on file.
    Is the information in the file concerning who made the decision to
purchase the structure?
    Are the name, address, phone number, and comments made by a
second designer on file?
    Is there evidence of a design review phase?
    Is there evidence that educators, parents, maintenance personnel, and
children reviewed the design?

---

process for the play structure is to answer questions listed in Table
8.2. Such a list can help an administrator focus on the most important
issues.

Installation Process. Installation signals the beginning of the realization of an onsite facility. All energies concerning installation should be focused on high quality work and monitoring the process. Last minute changes to the structure during installation can significantly change the liability designation of the decision maker if an injury should occur on the equipment (Beckwith, 1983). All materials related to installation should be kept on file until the structure is removed from the playground.

Important concerns for the file include contractual agreements, specifications, and installation inspection forms. Other materials which will reflect competent processes to ensure proper installation include inspection training seminar materials and guidelines for signing off on the acceptance of a newly installed structure (Bruya & Beckwith, 1988). These materials should be recorded in the file.

A quick and efficient way to ensure adherence to a predesigned installation process is to answer questions listed in Table 8.3. These suggestions help the administrator focus on important benchmarks for installation.

TABLE 8.3
The Installation Process

Questions concerning the installation process should be answered and materials kept on file.

Are the name, address, phone number, and contractual agreements with the installer on file?

Are all records of installation inspection on file?

Is evidence of installation inspection training seminars in the file?

Is evidence of design changes made during installation in the file?

Are guidelines for signing off on the structure in the file?

Is there evidence of final signing off in the file?

Safety Steps for Onsite Monitoring.

Once the structure is on site and ready to use, the responsibility to monitor and ensure against injury becomes that of the supervisors, administrators, and teachers who oversee the children who use the structure. This means that personnel associated with the preschool must assume responsibility for: (a) regular inspection, (b) maintenance, and (c) repair. Each must be documented well if an administrator is to provide proof that all reasonable precautions were taken to ensure the safety of the children who play on the structure.

Inspection Process. Inspection is an ongoing process from the installation of the structure on the preschool site through its removal due to age or wear. Inspections should be regular and based on a standardized process usually exemplified by a uniform inspection form (Beckwith, 1988). Several form are available, including the ones in this chapter, the assessment form in Appendix D, and the Play for All Inspection List (PLAE, 1990).

All inspectors should be trained in uniform procedures, with records to verify such training kept in the file. Inspection policies that dictate frequency, responsibility, and ongoing record keeping should also be recorded in the file. The inspection process may be the most important of all the monitoring functions (Twardus, 1985) for protection against severe loss, both injury related and financial.

A quick, efficient way to ensure adherence to a strong inspection process is to answer a series of questions noted in Table 8.4. That list of questions assists the administrator in focusing attention on important concerns for inspection.

TABLE 8.4
The Inspection Process

Questions concerning the inspection process should be answered and materials kept on file.
   Is the inspection form used for regular inspection recorded in the file?
   Is evidence in the file of inspection training seminars for inspectors?
   Is evidence in the file of policy related to setting regular inspections?
   Are records of all inspection dates and forms kept in the file?

Maintenance Process. Maintenance grows out of the awareness that constant use by children will eventually loosen and/or excessively wear parts of structures. The designer and/or play structure company from which materials were purchased will usually provide a list of items and associated timelines that should be used for maintenance schedules. As a result, it is easier for the preschool administrator to designate and/or train a maintenance person to care for the structures at the center. Usually, that designated person is titled "safety officer" (Seattle School District, 1984). That person's responsibility is to ensure regular inspection checks, develop and submit work orders, and follow up on needed maintenance.

A quick and efficient way to assure adherence to a maintenance process is to answer questions listed in Table 8.5. These and others that the administrator feels are important will help focus attention on legitimate concerns.

TABLE 8.5
The Maintenance Process

Questions concerning the maintenance process should be answered and
materials kept on file.

Is a suggested maintenance schedule for structures in the file?
Is there evidence of using a regular maintenance schedule?
Is there a record of a safety officer assignment in the file?
Is there evidence of work orders for maintenance in the file?
Is there evidence of a work order follow-up procedure in the file?
After a worn or broken part is located, is a work order evident?

Repair Process. The repair process is used following a work order
drafted as a result of an inspection that located a worn or broken part.
All work orders sent to personnel who actually make repairs should
be kept in a file used as a holding area for unresolved repairs. This
type of tiered filing system in which work orders are kept by the
safety officer in a holding file and then moved to a completed repair
file employs a stepwise process to ensure that repairs are made.

Even if repairs must be major, rather than simply-made corrections,
the assumption is that repairs must be made. In some instances, and
with selected equipment, this may require special training for repair
personnel. For major repairs, the best source for specific training is
the manufacturer or installer.

The process to move work order repairs from the holding file to the
completed file requires a follow-up process. Basically, this process
requires a quick inspection of the repair to ensure that the repair was
made properly. Records should be kept to indicate that the process is
complete and that normal maintenance procedures can be reinstated
(Bruya, 1985b).

An efficient way to help administrators focus on the repair process
is to answer questions listed in Table 8.6. These and others similar to
them are likely to produce a reasoned approach to repair.

TABLE 8.6
The Repair Process

Questions concerning the maintenance process should be answered and
with all records kept on file.

Is there evidence in the file of work orders drafted by the safety officer?
Is there evidence in the file of the capability of the work crews to repair
the structure adequately, e.g., a training program?
Is there evidence in the file of a regular process to follow up work order
repairs to ensure that the problem does not reoccur?
Is there evidence of a return to the regular maintenance and inspection
process?

Supervision

The process that accounts for the greatest prevention of injury on the structures may be supervision (Thompson, 1989). This includes people-to-people interaction. Usually this system involves (a) a safety program process, (b) a curriculum to be used with the structure, and (c) a record of injury occurrence follow-up process.

Safety Program Process. The first process which is a part of the people-to-people safety system is designed to ensure the greatest probability of understanding the best use of the structure and the rules that may increase the likelihood of safe play. Generally, it is best if the children themselves are included in establishing safety rules (Warrell, 1988). This is usually most easily accomplished if discussion takes place during attempts to integrate curriculum areas or learning centers and safety (Lowe, 1988).

Integrated curriculum may even lead logically to a newsletter or work sheets to be used with children, explaining safety procedures to use on the play structure (Warrell, 1988). Finally, and maybe most important, is communication with parents and other adult caregivers. This is accomplished through letters sent home and signage on the preschool play structure site (Morton, 1989). All attempts at education through the people-to-people safety program should be recorded in a file.

A quick and easy way to ensure adherence to a safety program process to increase the likelihood of safe play is to answer questions listed in Table 8.7.

TABLE 8.7
The Safety Program Process

Questions concerning the safety program process should be answered and materials kept on file.

Is there evidence in the file of the involvement of children in developing safety rules?

Is there evidence in the file of integrated curriculum in the school used for the discussion of safety on the play structure?

Is there evidence in the file of a safety newsletter?

Is there a copy in the file of parent, administrator, and teacher support for the safety program?

Is a copy of the warning letter sent home to parents in the right order?

Is a copy in the file of all signs used on the playground?

Play Structure Curriculum. As suggested, a curriculum designed for use with play structures may help children use the equipment

(Sommerfield & Dunn, 1988). If a curriculum is used, a copy should be in the file. Frequently, curricula include levels of participation (Schoolyard Big Toys, 1980; Quality, 1989) and suggested ways in which children can be led to select most appropriate responses (Bruya & Sommerfield, 1987).

One way to ensure monitoring of the curriculum process on the play structure is to consider, answer, and record information related to questions outlined in Table 8.8. Answering these questions ensures the administrator's attention and focus on legitimate preschool play structure curriculum concerns.

TABLE 8.8
The Play Structure Curriculum

Questions concerning the play structure curriculum process should be answered and kept on file.

Is a copy of the curriculum used with the structure kept in the file?

Is an indication kept in the file of instructing children in the manner in which appropriate skill activities are selected to be used on the structures?

Is there evidence in the file of instructing children in the manner in which safe play will occur?

Injury Occurrence Follow-Up Process. In the process listed about injuries of injured parties, witnesses and supervisors take information to determine probable cause and circumstances surrounding the injury occurrence. This information can then be recorded and used when contacting or during a follow-up conversation with parents of injured children to determine their status relative to a return to full health. These conversations with caregivers are important to parents' perceptions of their child's care, as well as monitoring recovery and status of threatened parental action.

A quick and efficient way to ensure adherence to an injury occurrence follow-up process is to answer questions in Table 8.9. These items focus attention on injury occurrence and follow-up concerns.

TABLE 8.9
The Injury Occurrence Follow-Up Process

Questions concerning the injury occurrence follow-up process should be answered and kept on file.

Is there a record of interviews held with the injured child, witnesses, and adult supervisors on site at the time of injury in the file?

Is a record kept in the file indicating contact with the parents of the injured child?

A Play Structure Documentation System: Files and Folders

Included in the Committee on Play presentations at the National AAHPERD convention in 1989 was a presentation on a documentation system for managing risk on play structures. A checklist was explained describing a series of files and folders used to document occurrences related to play structures (see pages 134–135). This checklist provides administrators a way to monitor play structures. A process similar to the one outlined here is likely to assure sound management of risks associated with injury during play on structures.

References

Bayless, M. A., & Adams, S. H. (February 1985). A liability checklist. JOPERD, 49.

Beckwith, J. (May, 1983). Playgrounds for the twenty-first century. Cities & Villages, 21(5), 22–26.

Beckwith, J. (1988). Playground equipment: A designer's perspective. In L. D. Bruya (Ed.), Play spaces for children: A new beginning (pp. 49–102). Reston, VA: American Alliance for Health, Physical Education, Recreation and Dance.

Bruya, L. D. (1985a). Design characteristics used in playgrounds for children. In. J. L. Frost & S. Sunderlin (Eds.), When children play (pp. 115–120). Wheaton, MD: Association for Childhood Education International.

Bruya, L. D. (April, 1985b). Comprehensive risk management for play environments. Paper presented to Illinois Parks and Recreation Association, Chicago, IL.

Bruya, L. D. (Ed.). (1988). Play spaces for children: A new beginning. Reston, VA: American Alliance for Health, Physical Education, Recreation and Dance.

Bruya, L. D., & Beckwith, J. (Winter, 1985). Due process: Reducing exposure to liability suits and the management of risk associated with children's play areas. Children's Environments Quarterly, 2(4), 29–35.

Bruya, L. D., & Beckwith, J. (1988). A system to manage the risk of lawsuit. In L. D. Bruya (Ed.), Play spaces for children: A new beginning (pp. 218–239). Reston, VA: American Alliance for Heath, Physical Education, Recreation and Dance.

Bruya, L. D., & Sommerfield, D. (Eds.). (1987). Project OLE: An essential elements curriculum for use in the outdoor learning environment. El Paso, TX: Ysleta Independent School District.

Burke, W. J. (September, 1987). Designing safer playgrounds. *Parks and Recreation*, 34–38.

Butler, G. D. (1958). *Recreation areas: Their design and equipment* (2nd ed.). New York: Ronald Press.

Chu, B., & Topps, A. (1979). *A guide to creative playground development.* Ontario, Canada: Ministry of Culture and Recreation, Special Services Branch.

Clement, A. (1989). Litigation and playgrounds. In D. Thompson & L. Bowers (Eds.), *Where our children play: Community park playground equipment.* Reston, VA: American Alliance for Health, Physical Education, Recreation and Dance.

Donovon, J. P. (September, 1987). Playground surfacing: What are your choices? *Parks and Recreation*, 34–38.

Frost, J. L., & Klein, B. L. (1979). *Children's play and playgrounds.* Boston: Allyn and Bacon, Inc.

Goldfarb, A. (1987). These doctors make house calls to your playground. *Parks and Recreation*, 44–46.

Guddemi, M. P. (October, 1987). Play/playgrounds/safety. *Dimensions*, 15–18.

Lowe, P. (1988). Developing responsibility of children for playground safety. In L. D. Bruya (Ed.), *Play spaces for children: A new beginning.* Reston, VA: American Alliance for Health, Physical Education, Recreation and Dance.

Morton, R. (September, 1989). Updating playground safety. *School and College*, 19–22.

National Recreation Association. (1931). *Report of committee on standards in playground apparatus* (Bulletin No. 2170). New York: National Recreation Association.

National Recreation and Park Association. (1976). *Proposed safety standards for public playground equipment.* Arlington, VA: National Recreation and Park Association.

Moore, R. C., Goltsman, S. M., & Iacofano, D. S. (1987). *Play for all guidelines.* Berkeley, CA: MIG Communications.

PLAE, Inc. (1990). Play for all inspection list. Berkeley, CA: PLAE.

Quality. (Circa 1989). *Curriculum for the play structure.* Hillsdale, MI: Quality Industries, Inc.

Seattle School District. (1984). Recommendations based on the high risk study. Unpublished memorandum. Seattle, WA: Seattle Public Schools, Athletic Department.

Schoolyard Big Toys. (Circa 1980). *Hang-ups*. Tacoma, WA: Northwest Design Products, Inc.

Simpson, N. B. (October, 1988). Playgrounds: Safety and fun by design. *Parks and Recreation*, 30–33.

Sommerfield, D., & Dunn, C. (1988). Project OLE: Outdoor learning environment for children. In L. D. Bruya (Ed.). *Play spaces for children* (pp. 166–176). Washington, DC: American Alliance for Health, Physical Education, Recreation and Dance.

Thompson, D. (Spring, 1989). School playgrounds: Plan to improve safety. *Principal* (The Oregon Elementary), 23–24.

Thompson, D., & Bowers, L. (Eds.). (1989). *Where our children play: Community park playground equipment*. Reston, VA: American Alliance for Health, Physical Education, Recreation and Dance.

Twardus, B. (1985). Seattle Public Schools memorandum: Safety guidelines. Unpublished manuscript, Seattle Public Schools, Athletic Department.

University of Iowa, Accident Prevention Section. (October, 1973). *Public playground equipment: Product investigation report* (No. FAA 73–6). Iowa City, IA: Institute of Agricultural Medicine.

U.S. Consumer Product Safety Commission. (March, 1979). *Hazards analysis: Playground equipment*. Washington, DC: U.S. Government Printing Office.

U.S. Consumer Product Safety Commission. (1981). *A handbook for public playground safety: Vol. II: Technical guidelines for equipment and surfacing*. Washington, DC: U.S. Government Printing Office.

Wallach, F. (October, 1988). Are we teaching playground abuse? *Parks and Recreation*, 34–36.

Warrell, E. (1988). A system to establish playground safety in the school. In L. D. Bruya (Ed.), *Play spaces for children: A new beginning* (pp. 139–164). Reston, VA: American Alliance for Health, Physical Education, Recreation and Dance.

9

Promoting Perceptual-Motor Development in Young Children's Play

Tom Jambor

Children develop perceptual-motor skills through natural, spontaneous interactions within the environment in which they live. They seek out stimulation and physically explore, discover, and evaluate the environment in relation to themselves. It is through this active exploration that children develop the foundation of skills necessary for building the more integral and abstract dimensions of their expanding world. Basic to these skills that enable children to deal directly and effectively with the concrete and physical realities in their environment is perceptual-motor development.

But, what is perceptual-motor development? How does it affect the total development of the child? What is the relationship of perceptual-motor development to children's play? How can we enhance the outdoor environments in which young children play from what we know about perceptual-motor development? These questions are attended to in this chapter and help provide another foundation block upon which the reader can build a more complete understanding of how young children use play as a vehicle for individual growth, development, and learning within appropriate outdoor play settings.

What Is Perceptual-Motor Development?

From birth the child learns how to interact with the environment through the perceptual and motor processes. Although each is a separate process the two are usually interconnected to reveal their close interrelatedness to the overall process of human behavior. The hyphen that links perceptual to motor implies an interdependency between the development of perceptual abilities and the development of motor abilities (Gallahue, Werner, & Luedke, 1972). As viewed by Williams (1983), "perceptual-motor development is that part of a child's development that is concerned with changes in the movement behavior, changes that represent improvement in sensory-perceptual motor development and reafference processes that underlie such behavior" (p. 9).

In essence, all of our behavior can be considered as a series of perceptual actions followed by a series of motor actions (Gallahue, Werner, & Luedke, 1972). Simply stated it works this way:

1. Our behavior is touched off by the input of a basic stimulus—either touch, taste, sound, smell, or sight.

2. That sensory input then travels to the brain by way of neural channels.

3. The brain collects, organizes, and stores this sensory information to mix and match as new information continually arrives.

4. Based on the sensory information stored, a decision for action upon the environment is carried back down those neural channels and an action response is initiated.

5. The reaction to the response is then fed back to the individual as to its success or appropriateness.

6. Motor response feedback, thus, allows for a change in perception, enabling the individual to try out new responses.

7. As the feedback cycle continues, it ensures that the perceptual and motor learning processes are working together.

Thus, as perceptual-motor development proceeds, the child develops increased capacity for handling more complex quantities of sensory input. What we observe behaviorally in the child is an improved capacity on the part of the child to carry out more skillful, complex, and adaptive motor behavior (Williams, 1971).

Sensory Components

The developmental process of perceptual-motor abilities in young children depends on an interfacing of maturation and experience. While the child's innate maturation pursues a fixed, sequential course, we, as facilitators of the child's environment, can influence the experience factor by providing children with multisensory perceptual experiences that will help them become better information sorters (Gallahue, 1976). These experiences, in turn, affect the rate and quality of maturation.

Learning experiences begin as sensory-motor, lead to perceptual-motor, and are essential to later functioning. Visual perception as well as auditory and tactile discrimination are basic information processes that need to be nurtured. For perceptual acuity to increase, physical experiences within the environment must be provided. These learning opportunities, or a lack of them, will greatly influence the sophistication of each child's perceptual modalities (Gallahue, Werner, & Luedke, 1972).

Maturation is a natural continuum process, but the progressional provisions of experience that we can provide children throughout childhood enable them to acquire and refine successive levels of skills and abilities. If we fail to provide developmentally appropriate experiences for children during the early formative years we are likely to retard or inhibit the acquisition of motor and perceptual skills and abilities in later years. If we want children to have greater motor control, we must provide them with experiences involving texture, shape, color, distance, direction, speed, size, etc. so they can improve their capacity to perceive increasingly more complex types and amounts of information (Gallahue, Werner, & Luedke, 1972). For outdoor play this means that as a child's perceptual-motor control becomes more refined, that child will be able to throw more accurately, run more effectively, balance more efficiently, and climb more skillfully.

Perceptual-motor abilities can be promoted through kinesthetic and sensory mode experiences. Kinesthetic sensitivity in the environment is gained through movement and physical interaction within the realm of the child's spatial and temporal (time) structures (Gallahue, 1976). The specific perceptual-motor qualities within each structure are considered extremely important to develop and reinforce if we are going to enhance children's knowledge of their spatial and temporal worlds. Gallahue aptly summarizes these qualities:

Body awareness refers to the developing capacity of young children to accurately discriminate among their body parts. The ability to differentiate among one's body parts and to gain a greater understanding of the nature of the body occurs in three areas:

1. *The knowledge of the body parts*—being able to accurately locate the numerous parts of the body on oneself and on others.

2. *The knowledge of what the body parts can do*—developing the abilities to recognize the component parts of a given act and the body's actual potential for performing it.

3. *The knowledge of how to make the body more efficient*—recognizing the body parts for a particular motor act and the actual performance of a movement task.

Spatial awareness is a basic component of perceptual-motor development that may be divided into two categories:

1. *The knowledge of how much space the body occupies.*
2. *The ability to project the body effectively into external space.*

Children first learn to orient themselves subjectively in space and then proceed ever so carefully to venture out into unfamiliar surroundings in which subjective clues are useless. With practice and experience children progress from their egocentric world of locating everything in external space relative to themselves (egocentric localization) to the development of an objective frame of reference (objective localization).

Directional awareness gives dimension to objects in space (e.g., left-right, up-down, top-bottom, in-out, and front-back) and is commonly divided into two categories:

1. *Laterality*—refers to an internal awareness or feel for the various dimensions of the body with regard to their location and direction. Children who have adequately developed the concept of laterality do not need to rely on external cues (e.g., tying a ribbon around children's wrists to help remind them which is their left and which is their right hand) for determining direction.

2. *Directionality*—is an external projection of laterality. It gives dimension to objects in space. It is important to parents and teachers because it is a basic component in learning how to read. Children who do not have fully established directionality will often encounter difficulties in discriminating between various letters of the alphabet (e.g., b, d and p, q) or the reversal of entire words (e.g., cat/tac, bad/dab). Difficulty in the top-bottom dimension and writing or seeing words upside down are associated with the inability to project direction into external space.

While children try to make sense of their spatial world through body, spatial, and directional awareness experiences, they are also trying to develop an adequate temporal structure. Both spatial and temporal structures are developed and refined simultaneously, based on children's maturation and experiences. Children must learn how to function well in both the space and the time dimension. One cannot develop to its fullest potential without the other.

Temporal awareness is concerned with the development of an adequate time structure in children and is intricately related to the coordinated interaction of various muscular systems and sensory modalities. The terms "eye-hand coordination" and "eye-foot coordination" reflect the interrelationship of these processes. The individual with a well-developed time dimension is the one we refer to as "coordinated," while the one who has not fully established this is often called "clumsy" or "awkward." Everything that we do possesses an element of time. There is always a beginning point and an end point.

Within the child's temporal structure are rhythm, synchrony, and sequence. Gallahue (1976) indicates rhythm as the most important and basic variable for developing a stable temporal world. He emphasizes that rhythm is most important to any coordinated performance and that it is "the synchronous recurrence of events related in such a manner that they form recognizable patterns. Rhythmic movement involves the synchronous sequencing of events in time" (p. 99).

Since there is a rhythmic element or pattern appropriate to all calculated movement it is important that facilitating adults attend to this relationship during children's movement/physical action periods. While all the sensory modalities can be encouraged and reinforced through specific movement activities, it is through the auditory sense that the child first starts to make temporal discriminations. Young children should, therefore, be provided with daily activities that pair auditory rhythmic patterns with movement performance. For example, providing music with marching, running, jumping, and throwing activities, or to general movement periods can greatly enhance rhythmic movement ability. This blend helps children to integrate and pace their physical movement as well as to add enjoyment and stimulation to their actions. Suggested playground activities that will help foster kinesthetic and sensory development areas are provided later in this chapter.

Perceptual-Motor Development and Learning

The term "perceptual-motor" began to flourish in the sixties as an outgrowth of concern for children with learning disabilities. As educators realized that children with reading problems could be helped and that some barriers that prevented learning could be removed through motor activities, schools started to integrate motor activities into their curriculum as an approach to improving perception (Hanson, 1973). Curriculum objectives began to focus on visual and auditory perception, space orientation, tactile experience, kinesthetic awareness, and motor skill development to build learning skills and to strengthen learning potential in young children. Strategies for curriculum development zeroed in on progressions of developmental activities that fit individual needs and abilities and provided for individual successes (Hanson, 1973). What we now refer to in terms of what is "developmentally appropriate" is an outgrowth of three decades of concern for optimal potentials for children's growth, development, and learning.

Some Theoretical Relationships

Several maturational theorists have, over the years, been prominent in tying together the related components of maturation, experience, adaptation, and growth to represent their rendition of human development. Each theory has implications for perceptual-motor development (Gallahue, 1976) and is briefly discussed below.

Freud's (1962) psychosexual approach to human behavior centers on the progressive development of stages that generate a sequence of change over the maturing child's erogenous zones. Successful maturation at, and movement through, each successive stage relies significantly on both motor activity and physical sensation.

Erikson (1963) takes a psychosocial approach stressing a stage continuum of societal factors, rather than hereditary factors, that help facilitate change in children's development. For Erikson, motor development is seen as an extremely important foundation block for the development of the total child. The stage-related crises that all children are likely to deal with could be positively influenced by successful movement experiences and supportive societal systems.

Gesell's (1945) theory strongly supports the physical and motor aspects of children's behavior. His research reinforces the need to develop a thorough foundation of basic movement skills. The level of performance of these skills is a good indicator of social and emotional growth patterns in young children.

Havighurst (1952) sees children's development as continual interaction between physical maturation and the cultural pressure imposed to function effectively in society. His theoretical model of development accentuates "teachable moments," when the body is developmentally ready and when the child's social world starts making demands for task completion and success. Physical activity, movement, and play are heavily stressed for optimal perceptual-motor development.

During the 1960s a greater emphasis was placed on the relationship between cognitive ability and perceptual-motor functioning. The often controversial theories of Kephart (1971) and Delacato (1959) emerged during this time. Both took the basic position that cognitive development and ability could be enhanced through movement, but each explained his position in quite different ways. While both theories have been peppered with criticism because of a lack of scientific substantiation (e.g., Belka & Williams, 1979), both have maintained a following that still has an impact on contemporary educational theory (Payne & Isaacs, 1987).

Kephart believed children with learning difficulties suffered from inadequate sensory integration (the most crucial step in the perceptual-motor process) of immediate stimuli with stimuli already mentally cataloged; he is given credit for starting the emphasis on movement that educators now look to as help for improving children's academic performance (Payne & Isaacs, 1987). For Kephart, perception and cognition develop from a motor base and sequentially progress through seven developmental stages that provide the child with increasingly efficient information processing strategies. While normal functioning children automatically proceed smoothly through these stages, children with learning difficulties encounter a breakdown of the progression and either stop progressing altogether or are greatly delayed. When this occurs, according to Kephart, the child must be returned to the earliest stage of difficulty and "trained" to move through subsequent stages via activities that enhance both cognitive and motor functioning—temporal and spatial awareness, form perception, eye-hand coordination, laterality, directionality, and balance (Payne & Isaacs, 1987). Kephart strongly suggests the need to focus on prevention tactics to alleviate the potential for remediation and recommends that to decrease the possibility of a child skipping or not completing a stage, *all* children should be subjected to perceptual-motor activities—especially during the very formative, impressionable preschool years (Haywood, 1986).

It is now widely acknowledged that if such perceptual-motor training is going to be an effective treatment program it must be started as early as possible during early childhood and continue over a period of years rather than just a few months (Williams, 1984). Thus, play environments that provide for the perceptual and motor functioning needs of children through the preschool years could, with assistance from knowledgeable play facilitators, enhance perceptual-motor development not only for special needs children but for *all* children.

Delacato (1959) also stressed the importance of movement in the early years, indicating the need for infants to experience and perfect certain movements in order to decrease the possibility of cognitive problems later on in life. Delacato, though, used his theoretical approach primarily as a remediation tactic and believed that many cognitive problems (especially those associated with reading) could be corrected by going back to the early movement behavior that was thought to be impaired or left out. To counter a lost experience during infancy the child had to experience or reexperience that infant movement through a process called "patterning" (Payne & Isaacs, 1987). While there are still some strong allies of Delacato's theory and practice, many experts in the field (Seefeldt, 1974; Cratty, 1979; Williams, 1983) have concluded that his techniques are unsubstantiated and very questionable.

Although both Kephart's and Delacato's theories have been widely criticized, their perceptual-motor programs may still be an important *indirect* channel through which academic concepts can be introduced, reinforced, and developed (Gallahue, 1982, 1984). Payne and Isaacs (1987) state, "when academic concepts are creatively interspersed throughout a movement activity, movement may be an excellent medium through which reading, math, social studies, or problem-solving concepts can be facilitated" (p. 81). Moffitt (1973) further reinforces the close relationship between perceptual-motor development and school achievement, indicating that motor activities such as throwing and catching a ball, hammering a nail, throwing an object at a target, pushing someone on a swing or tire, and pulling a wagon all make important contributions to developing hand-eye coordination, which in turn promotes overall perceptual-motor development, which in turn increases the likelihood of work efficiency at school tasks and academic achievement.

No aspect of development seems complete without reference to Jean Piaget, who felt that perceptual-motor development was intricately interrelated with the perceptual and cognitive dimensions of development. His sensory-motor and preoperational stages are also known as the sensory-motor intelligence period, a time when the foundation for future development of higher order cognitive functions is set. Piaget's data reveal that:

> the young child develops from being the kind of organism that operates on and within his environment primarily via concrete, sensory-motor-based processes, into one who approaches adaptation to his environment on a more representational, abstract or conceptual basis. Thus, the child, as he grows and develops, learns to solve problems and to adapt to his environment first by simply "acting or behaving" in the environment and then observing the consequences of his behavior, and later by thinking about and analyzing the conditions that contribute to the formulation of solutions to these problems. (Williams, 1983, p. 14)

It was the growing popularity of Piaget's work in the 1960s and his references to the extreme importance of movement as an information-gathering vehicle for children to learn about themselves and their world that brought emphasis to the importance of movement in the development of both psychomotor and cognitive aspects of the child's behavior (Gallahue, 1976). Hence, this created an opportunity for educators to further justify the design of perceptual-motor curriculum to enhance children's cognitive abilities.

Perceptual-Motor Development and Play

Play is the child's primary nourishment for healthy growth, development, and learning. A child's minimum daily requirement, though, is unknown. But what has been well established over the past three decades is that play does promote and enhance all areas of development. A single play experience can effectively interface all areas of growth simultaneously—that is, play doesn't promote one area of development apart from the others. When children play they are always in motion, learning about their bodies and subsequent movement capabilities. As they observe, practice, and perfect successive motor-skill increments they also facilitate cognitive, social, and emotional growth.

Through play the preprimary-age child develops a wide variety of basic locomotor, manipulative, and stability abilities. During the *first two years* of life the child's play is dominated by practice and exploratory actions. The newborn has fundamental grasping movements and possesses motor reflexes that respond to environmentally induced stimuli. Infants gradually gain control over their body parts and progress from prone position wiggles to creeping and crawling. Near the end of their first year children have mastered pulling themselves up into a standing position, coordinated their actions to stay standing, and are taking their first steps alone (Johnson, Christie, & Yawkey, 1987).

During this period of fundamental gross motor development small motor coordination and strength also rapidly take shape. Children's hand skills during the first year quickly progress from the inability to grasp objects during the first month, to picking things up and coordinating the thumb-finger "pincer" movement by mid-year, to skillfully moving objects back and forth between hands and placing them with intent as the first year closes out. Informal manipulation of objects and practice behavior becomes the focus of children's play. Their exploration of objects and curiosity of cause and effect relationships allows children to acquire knowledge about themselves and control events within their immediate world (Johnson, Christie, & Yawkey, 1987). This is a time of sensory-motor interaction, where the infant acts upon visual, auditory, and tactile experience. An appropriate play environment provides and encourages grasping, feeling, watching, listening, and general exploratory opportunities. Samplings of texture, sound, shape, and color help children relate their senses to their immediate world.

During the second year children are literally off and running. As toddlers, they are immersed in play with objects and people, easily coordinating large muscle mobility with small muscle dexterity. During this development period crawling, rolling, and walking patterns become more complex and experimental. Jumping and climbing are added to the large motor repertoire and are practiced. As children mature, so must their play environment. Provisions must, therefore, be made to accommodate an array of developing motor needs, as well as provide an integration of continued auditory, visual, and tactile experiences. During this time, perceptual judgments and motor responses are also becoming refined through play, preparing the child for the more complex motor skills and higher-order thought processes that quickly emerge and need to be nurtured during the following preschool years.

The *preschoolers'* development of autonomy and initiative greatly contributes to their sense of expanding curiosity, their need to explore, and their active nature. Motor/physical skills and motor play behaviors (e.g., running, jumping, climbing, throwing, and trike riding) become more refined and articulated and are enjoyed for their own sake and for the simple pleasure of personal accomplishment (Gallahue, 1976). Play is the medium that can best enhance children's feelings of a positive self. Gallahue states, "If [children] have a stable and positive self-concept, the gradual gain in greater control over their musculature is a smooth one. The timid, cautious, and measured movements of the 2- and 3-year-old gradually give way to the confident, eager, and often reckless abandon of the 4- and 5-year-old. Preschoolers' vivid imaginations make it possible for them to jump from great heights, climb high mountains, leap over raging rivers, and run 'faster' than an assorted variety of wild beasts" (p. 39).

As the preschool years come to an end we see motor play becoming even more articulated, physical, and varied. Games of chase evolve from incidental running and climbing; jumping rope and forms of acrobatics extend from basic hopping, skipping, running, and climbing; and random physical skills and coordination ability channel into both informal and formal athletic activities.

A special subcategory of motor play also emerges at this time —"play fighting." Play fighting is not considered real fighting and is described in the literature (in more socially acceptable terms) as "rough-and tumble play" (Pellegrini & Perlmutter, 1986). In this form of play, "children engage in a form of make-believe in which their body parts and actions of themselves and others take on a symbolic significance which becomes the 'object' of play" (Johnson, Christie, & Yawkey, 1987, p. 61). Play fighting, or rough-and-tumble play, is an interesting vehicle that brings all avenues of development into the play situation. While the child physically encounters and challenges other children and the surrounding environment, the child engages in social communication and pretense action, is confronted with decision-making and problem-solving situations, and learns to control impulses and to discriminate between negative and positive feelings to allow for appropriate participation within the play group (Pellegrini & Perlmutter, 1986).

Some teachers of young children regard this form of play negatively, suggesting that play fighting may turn into real fighting and that it symbolizes violent acts of aggression. But data indicate that play fighting does not lead to statistically significant negative behavior and may indeed have developmental value (Pellegrini & Perlmutter, 1986). This developmental value was first recognized by Karl Groos almost 100 years ago and presented in his books on the play of animals (1896) and the play of man (1899) (Millar, 1968). Still often regarded as valid, Groos's "play is practice" theory is based on Darwin's principle of natural selection. As an evolution process, natural selection favors those animals that can adapt to the changing environment through inherited instincts that are flexible enough to bend with and benefit from experience gained. Central to and most persuasive for the practice theory of play is the notion that play fighting establishes relationships, tests the environment, and helps the species prepare for life encounters (Millar, 1968). Groos felt that those favored during the evolution process "must practice and perfect their incomplete heredity skills before a serious need to exercise them arises. They must play. Play is the generalized impulse to practice instincts. The more adaptable and intelligent a species is, the more it needs a period of protected infancy and childhood for the practice gained in play" (Millar, 1968, p. 19).

As the most adaptable and intelligent of earth's species it is our responsibility to protect children's rightful heritage to play, and to both encourage and enhance opportunities for practice activities that optimize their perceptual and motor skills within the context of total development. It is our responsibility to create developmentally appropriate play environments that provide these opportunities.

The Outdoor Play Environment

The outdoor play environment deserves serious consideration and commitment if young children are going to have well-developed perceptual-motor skills. It must be remembered that the first responses of young children are motor responses, that "meaningful-

Figure 9.1. As children explore the environment they are able to challenge their physical selves.

ness" is imposed on perceptual stimulation through movement and physical interaction with their environment, and that this match of perceptual and motor information enables the child to establish a stable spatial world and develop responses adaptable to various movement situations (Gallahue, 1982). Research studies being conducted by Haubenstricker and Seefeldt underscore the importance of motor needs, indicating that children who have poorly developed large motor skills at age five will probably never, even with remedial intervention, develop efficient motor skills (Hildebrand, 1990). The preschool outdoor play setting, then, appears to be an essential environment for providing opportunities to foster these skills.

The following perceptual-motor categories list suggested outdoor play activities that can help foster kinesthetic and sensory development (Hildebrand, 1990; Haywood, 1986; Storage & Bowers, 1983; Gallahue, 1976). In reviewing these activities, keep in mind that in addition to suggested play structures and motor enhancing materials, fall areas must have "soft" surfaces, general safety conditions must be met, and children must be assisted and supervised by accountable adults. These points will be dealt with in other chapters of this text.

Locomotion

- Rolling in various directions on flat and sloped grassy areas with arms in different positions
- Creeping, crawling, and walking on or across textured surfaces (to increase sensory input)
- Crawling through "space-holes": barrels, open-ended boxes, single mounted tires, tire tunnels, low playhouse windows
- Crawling across a wide plank
- Climbing on hills, ramps, stairs, platform levels, connected tire formations, rope nets, ladders, multipurpose structures, low limb tree branches, overhead and multidirectional ropes
- Stepping up on graduated levels: platforms, logs, tires, stumps, large wide blocks
- Jumping/bouncing on flat spring boards, large flexible horizontal tires, inner-tubes, mattresses (trampolines are considered dangerous and not recommended)
- Jumping from varying heights: tires, wooden platforms, stone/ earth ledges, stumps, spring boards
- Hurdling over "natural" objects, objects prepared by adults (e.g., a horizontal bamboo pole between two adjustable vertical support points)
- Hopping in place with both feet, then with one foot at a time; hopping, back and forth over lines, between rungs of a wooden ladder on the ground

- Running and walking across bridges, up and down natural slopes and man-made ramps, in open grassy areas
- Chasing and "tag" games that utilize most play apparatus and available space
- Crossing "hand-over-hand" on overhead ladder
- Pumping a swing
- Pulling or pushing a wagon
- Wheel toys that coordinate alternate pumping and steering with feet and hands; obstacle course routes that challenge the coordination of perceptual and motor skills

Many of these actions and activities, as well as those that follow, can be controlled and enhanced by listening for music cues for stopping, starting, and intensity of action.

Balance

- Standing and balancing (both feet, then only one) on walking beam, vertical in-ground tire, moving bridge, suspended horizontal rope with overhead hand support; close eyes for added sensation
- Walking various heights, widths, and spans of wooden beams, vertical in-ground tires, large diameter rope and fire hose (with overhead hand supports to keep upright)
- Walking on wide beams with arms extended holding a weighted object in one hand or both
- Walking on a line or thin diameter rope configuration on ground
- Walking with one foot on and one off a ground level beam, on a curb edge, on an edge of a ladder lying on ground, around the edge of a large diameter horizontal tire
- Following the leader on a spontaneous or preplanned obstacle course throughout playground

Body and Space Perception

- Large mirror area for viewing self, specific body parts, and experimenting with ways these parts can function
- Identifying body parts and relating them to a function of movement activity
- Responding to requests to use a body part(s) on climbing or balancing apparatus
- Coordinating body parts to perform physical feats of strength and agility in play spaces and on equipment
- Using arm and leg movements to create "snow/sand angels"
- Pushing someone on a swing

- Fitting into spaces: boxes, large tire opening, wagon, playhouse, play boat or car, across a bridge span, on a swivel tire, at top of a slide (number and size relationship concept)
- Coordinating running and movement activities within a limited space
- Climbing "on," "under," "around," "through," etc.; going to the left or to the right (body-objects relationships and directionality)
- Any activity requiring movement in space!

Figure 9.2. Balancing and jumping from various heights coordinate perceptual and motor responses.

Rhythm and Temporal Awareness

- Recurring rhythm: swing (standard infant and strap seats, suspended tire or rope, swivel tire, vestibular platform, porch style); rocking boats, etc.; wheel toys
- Methodic, rhythmic bouncing on large tires, inner-tubes, spring boards
- Jumping over stationary rope or one swung in a quarter arc to a rhythmic beat
- Galloping, marching through playground to music, with rhythm instruments, or hand claps
- Accelerating and decelerating physical movement to given tempo
- Running up or down diagonal ramps and hills
- Tossing, catching, kicking, dodging objects (e.g., various size balls, beanbags, balloons)

Rebound and Airborne Movement

- Bouncing on spring boards, mattresses, large flexible tires, inner-tubes (music varies the variety and tempo of action)
- Jumping onto a mattress, or into sand, pea gravel, or other resilient ground base from varying heights
- Hanging by hands or legs from climbers, chinning bars, low tree branches, etc.
- Swinging on vertical rope; pushing off of objects to continue or vary movement

Projection and Reception Movement

- Rolling large balls to others or at a target
- Throwing soft balls (e.g., nerf ball) at a target (e.g., mounted vertical tire), through a hoop (e.g., bottomless peach baskets nailed at various heights on tree trunks)
- Trapping a ball rolled between legs while sitting
- Catching a large ball with open arms
- Chasing and "catching" soap bubbles
- Kicking a large stationary ball
- Kicking a slowly moving ball; change speeds to increase challenge; allow for random use throughout playground
- Striking a plastic ball with a plastic bat: tossed by adult; from a waist high "tee"; on the ground, golf style
- Keeping balloons in the air with hands or plastic bat, wand, etc.
- Swinging/punching/kicking at suspended bag filled with paper, soft rubber pieces, etc.

Figure 9.3. Interlinking combinations of wood, rope, tires, and fire hose offer alternative textures that stimulate the senses and promote motor responses.

Conclusion

As children crawl, roll, run, jump, and generally move in space, they must be given needed opportunities to make necessary ongoing modifications and adjustments to stabilize balance, distance and depth orientation, and general movement patterns (Moffitt, 1971).

When children have developed coordination, confidence, and self-control in their motor activity, their sense of competence and accomplishment is carried over to other areas of development. "When a child is able to achieve mastery of his body and direct it for his purposes, he develops an image of himself as a learner and a doer. This concept of self, in turn, becomes a vital force in both acquisition of knowledge and personality development" (Moffitt, 1971, p. 2). Good perceptual-motor development promotes social interaction with peers, formal and informal athletic successes, reasoning and judgment decisions, and academic development and achievement.

The most natural medium to enhance perceptual-motor skills is play. Play allows children to reach out, grasp, and interact with the environment through movement and through the use of all their senses. A well-designed and challenging outdoor play environment can assist the play function by providing an array of activities that encourage children to use a variety of motor patterns that test themselves in meaningful ways.

As providers for future generations, we have the capacity to either hinder or enhance a child's potential for optimal development. It is our responsibility to provide developmentally appropriate environments within which children can grow, develop, and learn. For perceptual-motor development, that environment is the child's outdoor play setting.

References

Belka, P., & Williams, H. (1979). Prediction of later cognitive behavior from early school perceptual-motor, perceptual, and cognitive performance. *Perceptual and Motor Skills, 49,* 131–141.

Cratty, B. J. (1979). *Perceptual and motor development in infants and children.* Englewood Cliffs, NJ: Prentice-Hall.

Delacato, C. H. (1959). *Treatment and prevention of reading problems.* Springfield, IL: Thomas.

Erikson, E. (1963). *Children and society.* New York: Norton.

Freud, S. (1962). *The ego and the id.* New York: Norton.

Gallahue, D. L. (1976). *Motor development and movement experiences for young children (3–7).* New York: Wiley & Sons.

Gallahue, D. L. (1982). *Understanding motor development in children.* New York: Wiley.

Gallahue, D. L. (1984). Effects of perceptual-motor training on development in children. Presentation at the National Conference of the American Alliance for Health, Physical Education, Recreation and Dance, Anaheim, CA.

Gallahue, D. L., Werner, P. H., & Luedke, G. C. (1972). *A conceptual approach to moving and learning.* New York: Wiley.

Gesell, A. (1945). *The embryology of behavior.* New York: Harper.

Hanson, M. (1973). Directions and thrusts. *Instructor,* January, 2–3.

Havighurst, R. (1952). *Developmental tasks and education.* New York: Longmans, Green and Co.

Haywood, K. M. (1986). *Life span motor development.* Champaign, IL: Human Kinetics.

Hildebrand, V. (1990). *Guiding young children.* New York: Macmillan.

Johnson, J. E., Christie, J. F., & Yawkey, T. D. (1987). *Play and early childhood development.* Glenview, IL: Scott, Foresman and Co.

Kephart, N. C. (1971). *The slow learner in the classroom.* Columbus, OH: Merrill.

Millar, S. (1968). *The psychology of play.* Baltimore, MD: Penguin Books.

Moffitt, M. (1971). Play as a medium for learning. Proceedings, Region East Perceptual Motor Conference. American Alliance for Health, Physical Education, Recreation and Dance, Washington, DC.

Moffitt, M. (1973). Physical play—it's vital! *Instruction,* January, 5–7.

Payne, V. G., & Isaacs, L. D. (1987). *Human motor development.* Mountain View, CA.: Mayfield.

Pellegrini, A., & Perlmutter, J. (1986, April). *The developmental and educational significance of children's rough-and-tumble play.* San Francisco: CA: American Education Research Association.

Seefeldt, V. (1974). Perceptual-motor program. In J. H. Wilmore (Ed.), *Exercise and sports sciences reviews*, Vol. 2. New York: Academic Press.

Storage, T. W., & Bowers, L. E. (1983). Playgrounds of the future. *Parks and Recreation,* April, 32–35.

Williams, H. G. (1971). Perceptual-motor development in children: Information and processing capacities of the young child. Proceedings, Region East Perceptual Motor Conference. American Alliance for Health, Physical Education, Recreation and Dance, Washington, DC.

Williams, H. G. (1983). *Perceptual and motor development.* Englewood Cliffs, NJ: Prentice-Hall.

Williams, H. G. (1984). Problems in research in perceptual-motor development. Presentation at the National Conference of the American Alliance for Health, Physical Education, Recreation and Dance, Anaheim, CA.

10

The Role of Adults in
Children's Play

Thomas D. Yawkey

On any given day, as you walk around a day care center or
kindergarten, you see infants, toddlers, and older children doing
activities. In addition to the usual work activities, you find them
building with lumber or blocks, filling and emptying large and small
containers with water, mud, stones, or sand, pushing and pulling
wheel toys, and dramatizing mother at work or Aunt Veronica talking
to Uncle Joe. These younger and older children are engaged in play
activities and more than likely using play materials.

Regardless of whether you may view these activities as cognitive
play (e.g., functional repetitions of independent motor movements to
rule governed games) or as social play (e.g., solitary to group settings)
(Rubin & Howe, 1985), these children are playing. And they may be
playing outdoors or indoors. Play is a spontaneous activity, is fun and
pleasurable. Play is purposeless "in the sense that it is engaged in for

The author's research and writing on young bilingual children's communication,
cognition, and play is, in part, supported by Title VII (Academic Excellence) Project
PIAGET under grant number G008710679 from the Office of Bilingual Education and
Minority Languages' Affairs, United States Department of Education. The author's
views and opinions expressed herein do not represent those of the funding agency.

the sake of the activity itself" (Beers & Wehman, 1985, p. 405). Also, play is rather serious because of the high level of intensity at which children play, and it is self-initiated (Beers & Wehman). Finally, play has context representing physical setting (e.g., outdoor, indoor materials) and social theme (e.g., "building a house"), and has activity (e.g., motor, verbal, and/or mental) (Trostle & Yawkey, 1990). Play, comprising these seven characteristics, becomes a dynamic and necessary structure of children's development and learning.

Children play with toy materials and objects as part of their physical environment. Viewed as the setting, the physical environment of play objects and materials including toys is necessary for and influences children's development (Piaget, 1962). As examples, Bradley's (1985) and Wachs's (1978) findings show that the presence or availability of play materials and books shows moderate to substantial correlations with infants', toddlers', and older children's scores on mental development indices. Bowers' results (Chapter 3, p. 19) show great availability of play houses, cars, truck, and boats at centers in the United States for maximizing children's growth potential. Here, the sensorial and physical characteristics of play materials and objects are salient contributors to children's development.

In addition to the physical environment, children's play is part of their social environment. As younger and older children play something or with somebody, the social environment of peers and adults is correlated with and influences their development (Piaget, 1962). In support, the findings of several of the play tutoring studies where adults co-play and guide children's dramatic and sociodramatic play show that social or interactional feedback with adults in play increases preschoolers' problem-solving capacities (e.g., Sylva, Bruner, & Genova, 1976), language abilities (e.g., Smilansky, 1968), and reading readiness growth (Yawkey, 1980, 1990). The interactional feedback in play between children, peers, and adults influences children's growth on various social, cognitive, and academic measures.

Using the context of the social and physical environments, this chapter begins by examining the value or significance of the adult in child's play. Next, we describe various roles that adults perform in child's play as they maximize physical and social environmental contingencies for children's development. Finally, several considerations for adult planning of child's play are addressed.

Value of the Adult in Child's Play

In the previous section, we identified the core characteristics of play and explained briefly several impacts that play has on children's development relative to physical and social settings. A salient factor threading play, children, and environments is the adult and the values or benefits of the adult's support and involvement in children's play.

In working with young children, infancy through kindergarten levels, adults as teachers, group leaders, and parents in classrooms, playgrounds, other recreational areas and in homes intervene to meet needs. In the process of intervening, adults develop and modify strategies, activities, materials, services, and techniques in order to maximize children's potential (Fallen & Umansky, 1985). Further, the values of adults in child's play assume that intervention, in varying degrees and dimensions, is a basic understanding and accepted principle of classroom, playground, or home.

Accordingly, the value or rationale of adult intervention rests on the benefits of play intervention, for maximizing children's development and competence and understanding associated factors such as rapport with children. In addition, we explain several limitations of adult intervention.

For the Child's Development

The adult in child's play benefits children's development along several growth continua: imitative role play, pretend play with physical objects, pretend play with actions and situations, and persistence in play (Smilansky, 1968).

Imitative Play. The first benefit of adult involvement in child's play is recognizing the need, at minimum, and increasing the opportunities, at maximum, for the children's imitative play for developmental purposes. In imitative play, younger children model adults, significant family members, and other nurturing individuals. Older children, in addition, use imitative play to show roles of super heroes (e.g., "Ninja turtles," "Robocop"), heroines (e.g., "She-Ra," "Counselor Troy"), supervillians (e.g., "Joker," "Shredder"), and significant others outside the family.

Adults provide play opportunities for imitative play so children can imitate, practice, and develop roles. Whether imitating "Mommy," "Daddy," "Mrs. Burns"—the kindly next-door-neighbor, or supervillians, imitative play helps them identify with and understand the adult world. Young children actually build these roles in a figurative way as they play; older children enter and plan for their roles prior to their play and expand them spontaneously as they enact them.

Imitating adult roles gives younger and older children opportunities to handle situations and thereby share the "envied" power and authority of significant adults in their lives. Further, imitative play permits children to relive and play back previous experiences, as well as "live" anticipated future experiences. As children live these experiences, imitative play becomes a vehicle to separate "fear" and "anxiety" from these past or anticipated future events and helps them better understand and cope with them (e.g., going to the doctor's for immunizations prior to school entry) (Piaget, 1962). Finally, we can gauge children's understanding of self and self in group settings by whether they imitate individuals inside or outside the family (or creatively interrelate both) and by the quality and quantity of the perspective taken in imitative play.

Object Play. A second value or benefit of the adult in child's play for children's development is through pretend play with physical objects (Smilansky, 1968). Through adult support by involvement in child's play, children increase their capacities to operate in the symbol world by substituting toys, unstructured objects and materials, sounds, and verbal statements for real or pretend objects. From movement actions of pounding, rolling, or bouncing objects as functional play of younger children to substituting real objects for other objects as in sociodramatic play of older children, symbolic representation emerges, develops, and is practiced. As a result of symbolic representation, children initially enter the symbol world where their play objects are subject to the requirements of their play. For example, younger children, two to three years old, require highly structured and realistic objects to spark their play; Barbie dolls with detailed accessories and realistic miniature cars with movable doors and trunks are required (McLoyd, 1983). Older children, four through seven, tend to use toys and play materials that are low in realism and less structured because they can symbolize and substitute any object for the "desired," pretend one in their play (Johnson, Christie, & Yawkey, 1987).

Social Play. The third benefit of adult involvement and support of child's play is children's development of pretend actions and situations (Smilansky, 1986). In play, children substitute verbal expressions and dialogue for physical actions and situations. An older child in playing "swimmer," for example, says "I swam from one end of the YMCA pool to the other and leaped from the water!" A younger child says the same thing in a figurative sense, but at the same time moves the hands rapidly to show swimming actions. Short verbal descriptions with accompanying physical actions and movements serve to clarify, anchor and give meaning to pretend play.

This pretend play with verbal dialogue and physical actions takes the place of reality, for children can modify and change personal or object identity for pretend ones. Thus, pretend play with actions and situations provides young children with direct, personal means of communication. As they expand their play, pretend play statements and verbalizations for real experiences become increasingly important and critical as play and social growth approach more complex levels of symbolic play and games with rules.

Persistence. The final component of children's development that is maximized by adult support and involvement in play is children's persistence (Smilansky, 1968). Persistence shows the ability to remain with a role in play for increasingly longer periods of time. Although dramatic play of fours and fives is brief and they jump from one role to another with little or no transitions, Smilansky notes that children in this age range should be able to remain with a single or related role for a minimum of five minutes. For older children of five to eight who elaborate their roles, Smilansky notes that they should be able to persist with a role or related roles for a minimum of ten minutes.

When adults support or involve themselves in children's play, persistence of younger and older children in play increases dramatically and significantly. Johnson, Christie, and Yawkey (1987, p. 25), for support, cite the findings of Dunn and Woodring (1977) and Sylva, Roy, and Painter (1980), which show that children play significantly longer when adults are involved in their play compared to when they play alone or "when they played only with their peers." Persistence at play shows ability to focus and concentrate on tasks, and this persistence is vital to school achievement and classroom successes.

For the Child's Competence

The support and involvement the adult provides child's play also benefits children's language and intellectual competencies. From the point of view of encouraging language competencies, the child in play is immersed in a sea of words, statements, and other verbalizations. With continued involvement with play, the preschool and kindergarten child in just a nine-month period of 15 minutes daily increases significantly the number of words and new combinations of words and average length of sentences (Smilansky, 1968). Through adult support of play, children show increasing complexity of language structures such as Troy, a four-year-old moving a block in "running" fashion and saying, "The big brown dog runs down the street with cars and doesn't get hurt!" Spontaneous use of language labeling for objects, actions, and situations is relative to higher levels of dramatic play behavior (Freyberg, 1983).

In addition, adults desiring to increase language and interaction of preschoolers might limit the number of play materials that children select from and use in play. The findings of Bjorklund (1979) show increases occur in social language among toddlers when the number of play materials is reduced. Similarly, reducing the amount of space in which the children play tends to increase significantly the amount of dramatic play (Peck & Goldman, 1978). Dramatic play makes possible the use of the child's own experience, background, and thinking and provides practice and recall as children grow toward greater language maturity.

Intellectual competencies also flourish and are nurtured by dramatic play by "compelling" children to act at mental levels higher than their chronological ages. Dramatic play provides children with insight into their own behavior and requires mental integration of situations, events, and play materials. As children use a "Campbell soup box as a car complete with sounds" or represent people or situations as others, they must show flexibility of mental thought and problem solving. Here, they visualize how one set of objects and situations already experienced can be used in place of others not directly experienced. The capacities to analyze, synthesize, formulate, and internalize through dramatic play are all key processes for intellectual competencies. In support, Vygotsky (1976) notes that a responsive environment of play materials nurtures intellectual competencies when play materials are used toward goals in dramatic play.

In addition, Arnold (1968) identifies several intellectual competencies that are direct outcomes of dramatic play. These include:

qualitative relationships—hot/cold, color and texture differences
quantitative relationships—big/small, many/few, thin/thick
spatial relationships—far/near, square/round
observation of sequences—seasons, meals of the day
response to given directions—comprehension of instruction
labeling—names of people, animals, objects, etc.

sequential directions—production of a sequence of actions
flow of events—school activities
flow of processes—cow—milk
flow of words—building a house, bridge, etc.
description of events—what, when, where, why, when, and how

The more the adult supports dramatic play, the greater opportunities children have of developing these intellectual competencies and internalizing them, and the greater potential there is for these competencies to transfer to schooling situations.

For Approval and Rapport

The value of adult involvement in children's play benefits children in other ways. These associated benefits are approval and rapport (Johnson, Christie, & Yawkey, 1987, p. 23–25).

Adult involvement and support of child's play in classrooms and recreational areas are signals to children that adults approve of their play. By standing in close proximity to their play or becoming involved in it, adults say to children that their play has value and is worthwhile.

Many times children hear a different message about play when adults say, for example, "Go play, don't bother me!" This message about play is a different signal to children than adult approval of play. This says to children that their play and play activities are valueless and worthless, while the former one implies that their play activities are valuable and worthy of both adult and child time. Johnson, Christie, and Yawkey (1987) stress that "An effective way to help these children realize that make-believe is acceptable is for the teacher to join in children's play and model pretend behaviors" (p. 24).

Another related benefit of adult involvement is rapport. "Participating in children's play is an excellent way for parents and teachers to build rapport with children" (Johnson, Christie, & Yawkey, p. 24). By building rapport through child's play, adults better understand children's developmental levels, achievements, feelings, and attitudes. With these understandings, adults can more clearly and meaningfully communicate with children and establish concrete relations. Through rapport, adults show they are willing to work with children in meaningful ways rather than from positions of superiority and authority (Johnson, Christie, & Yawkey, 1987).

Some Limitations

Although the benefits of supporting and becoming involved with child's play are positive and significant for children and adults,

Johnson, Christie, and Yawkey (1987) note some limitations or cautions. These limitations focus on the amount of adult participation in child's play. Great amounts of involvement and over extended periods of time may reduce children's concentration and persistence and actually shorten their dramatic play episodes (p. 26).

Through observation of child's play, the adult needs to determine the appropriate amounts of intervention and the proper time for intervening in play. Adult sensitivity for amount and timing of intervention produces greater dividends for the child's development, competence, approval, and rapport through children's play activities.

In sum, adult support and involvement in child's play has many values and benefits for the child's development, including increased imitative play and persistence at play and fostering language and intellectual competencies. In addition, these rewards of adult involvement imply adult approval of child's play and rapport with children. Limitations of involvement focus on the amount and timing of adult intervention and suggest the need for adult sensitivity and observation prior to involvement.

Having examined the value of adult involvement and support of child's play and several limitations associated with it, we now address the roles in which adults become involved constructively in child's play. These roles are numerous, multifaceted, varied, and cover preparatory guidelines, discovery strategies, and direct play teaching.

Adult Roles as Preparatory Guidelines for Child's Play

Prior to actual involvement in child's play, adults need to plan for their involvement and for children's dramatic play. Johnson, Christie, and Yawkey (1987, p. 26–29) cite four preparatory guidelines developed by Griffing (1983) in helping adults with their planning: (a) time, (b) space, (c) materials, and (d) preparatory experiences.

Time

In planning for child's play, time is needed for children to develop ideas, gather materials, discuss roles, and improvise for meaningful dramatic play episodes. An appropriate amount of time is also required to permit children to develop persistence in their play episode and play-related tasks. Johnson, Christie, and Yawkey (1987, p. 26) note that although "the exact amount of time required varies, depending on the child's age and play skills," 30- to 50-minute free play periods are appropriate for three- and four-year-old and kindergarten children (cf. Griffing, 1983). For monolingual and bilingual preschoolers and kindergarteners in full day programs, Peters, Neisworth, and Yawkey (1985, p. 34) and Yawkey (1990) recommend 60-minute free play periods.

This amount of time is also required for massed experiences in play activities (Peters, Neisworth, & Yawkey, 1985). Ample time helps children develop, use, and generalize concepts through many varieties of play activities and experiences in individual and group settings. Large blocks of play time are more beneficial to young children than short, segmented blocks of time (Peters, Neisworth, & Yawkey). Because play time in many school and recreational programs is sacrificed for "academic" time, "it is preferable to schedule several lengthy play periods per week than to have short (10- to 15-minute) play periods per day" (Johnson, Christie, & Yawkey, 1987, p. 27).

Space

After the element of time, space consideration is the next preparatory guideline for adult involvement and support of child's play. Ample space for child's play includes arrangement and use of materials and group size of children participating in play activities.

Numerous studies present findings on the arrangement and use of space for young children and the impact on their behavior. The amount of physical space for play in classrooms and recreational areas influences children's interaction and play activity. As a result of decreasing space using movable partitions, interaction among children and adults, aggressive behavior between children, and parallel and onlooker play increase (Smith & Connolly, 1976, 1980). In addition, dramatic play and interaction among children increase when classrooms are partitioned into play areas having low adult-child ratios (Smith & Connolly, 1980). Adults in supporting play should tailor the amount of space available to children to types of play activities, thereby creating more optimal play and interactional conditions. Further, the findings suggest that large open classrooms may not be as conducive or responsive to dramatic play and interaction as previously thought (Featherstone, 1974).

In increasing or decreasing space, preschool children, in turn, adjust their use of space. Preiser (1972) found that as space in free play areas changes, young children change their use of the area and their proximity to play materials. Children's self-initiated changes in space utilization play suggest that space and arrangement of material not only affect the child but "let him know indirectly who he is supposed to be (or at least who we think he is) and how he is supposed to learn" (Getzels, 1975, p. 12). Pfluger and Zola (1974), in an interesting study of children's use of space, permitted preschoolers to rearrange materials and furniture in their classroom. The results showed that young children rearranged movable furniture against the walls, creating a large open area in the classroom to conduct art and construction play activities. Moreover, the children's levels of dramatic play increased in their new arrangement, as well as their uses of the truck, housekeeping, and block play areas.

Another aspect of space arrangement and use focuses on understanding how environments designed for differing types of play might affect play activities of preschoolers and kindergarteners. With equal amount of time for play in various types of play environments, Vandenberg (1981) showed that associative play was used most often in the "gross motor room" and parallel and solitary play in the "fine motor room." The "gross motor room" with its tumbling mats and sliding boards encouraged large group size, clustering, and associative play, whereas the "fine motor room" with its crayons, paper, and scissors fostered small and individual groups and more solitary and parallel play.

In a different study, Black, Freeman, and Montgomery (1975) compared differing types of play environments on play behaviors and interactions of handicapped preschoolers. The handicapped children showed differing types and levels of play in different play environments. In the stark play environment, without play materials, more solitary and repetitive play was shown, whereas a play environment with regular materials elicited greater gross motor and imitative play modeling. Further, play materials that are easily accessible to children and at their eye levels foster dramatic play (Hare & Hare, 1977).

Ample space also means examining the group size of children participating in play activities in classrooms and recreational areas. As an aspect of the adult's role in child's play, group size appears to have an impact on the quality and quantity of children's play and play activities. When preschoolers move from six to eight children per group (holding the amount of square feet constant per group), children in groups of eight compared to six showed significantly greater amounts of group play activity, aggression, and anger (Loo, 1972; Loo & Kennelly, 1979). Further, when group size is changed while maintaining constancy of materials and classroom size, normal children explored the boundaries of the classroom while handicapped children's social interaction decreased and their aggression increased (Hutt & Varzey, 1966).

Thus, increasing the group size of preschoolers with the same amounts of physical space modifies their play behaviors, activities, and personality. Adults in supporting child's play can monitor group size and change the number of children per group depending on the required play activity and desired quality of interaction.

Materials

A third preparatory guideline for the adult's role in child's play is the need for quantity and quality of play materials in classrooms and recreational areas. Aguilar (1985) recommends a range of play materials and equipment for young children's play endeavors. With variety of play, toys, and equipment, children's developmental and physical needs are met, a greater "match" emerges between their play materials and their abilities and they show greater success and problem-solving ability. The adult in support of play should make efforts to ensure a range of play materials available to children.

In order to ensure a range of play materials, Yawkey and Trostle (1982) recommend that adults systematically include four types of play materials in classrooms and recreational areas. These types rest on the intent or purpose of the commercial manufacturer in making them, although the intent of the play materials within each type may vary by children's use.

One type is instructional play materials, which support the teaching of various academic skills such as one-to-one correspondence, alphabet letters, part-to-whole relations, and so forth. Examples include nesting toys, puzzles, and stacking materials. The second type is constructional materials characterized for their many uses. These play materials are used repeatedly and in many divergent ways. This group includes various small and large wooden, plastic, and cardboard blocks. The results of the 1989 survey of play materials in 349 preschool centers in 31 states show a great need for increasing the quantity of constructional materials such as wooden blocks found in these centers. Other examples of constructional materials include Tinkertoys, transformers, and Lincoln Logs.

A third type is real materials, and this type has no defined shape. They are found naturally and abundantly in the physical milieu and take the shape of their containers. Examples include sand, navy beans, mud, gravel, water, and clay. Various adult clothing used in dramatic play fits into this category. The final type of play material is toys. Toys are manufactured to represent replicas of real or fantasy life. This type has many subgroups which include, for example, housekeeping toys such as miniature dolls, plates, cups, and saucers. Other subgroups are transportation toys, for example, cars, busses, spaceships, and passenger jetliners, and animal and people toys, such as teddy bears, cuddly cats, soldiers, and space monsters. Findings of the national survey reported by Bowers in Chapter 3 show that over half of the 349 preschool centers surveyed have toy trucks, cars, other small replicas, and wheel toys. Surveying the children's play area to ensure the inclusion of representatives from each of the four groups helps determine whether there are ranges of materials necessary for sound play environments.

Further, adults can survey existing materials in the environment for the types of play modes that the objects facilitate and encourage. Based on such a survey, adults plan for additional play objects and their uses. For example, some play materials are ideal for play activities such as social interaction and functional play, while others provide for dramatic or solitary play. Rubin (1977) found that house play, wheel toy play, and reading and number activities provided the highest levels of social play, whereas playdough, painting, and puzzles contributed the lowest levels of social play. Play activities such as role play and large muscle equipment with two or more children encouraged cooperating and helping each other in these play activities. From another perspective, Naylor (1985) found that children spend more time in play activities when two or more play modes and materials can be used together. Examples are tire slides and a fort in outside play environments, which serve as focal points for climbing, dramatic play, functional play, and social interaction.

Finally, and at a different level, adults can examine play materials from the perspective of movability (Aguilar, 1985; Naylor, 1985). In order to support play activities and ensure that they have learning potential, young children must be able to move the play materials and equipment. Movement of the body, fine and gross motor ability, and coordination ensure that children's learning potential and motivation are by-products of the play materials. (Rules for safety as part of play materials appear in Chapter 4.)

In support of child's play, this third basic guideline ensures that play materials show a range of objects for classroom and recreational areas, facilitate varied types of play, and have movability for learning and motivational potential.

Preparatory Experiences

The final basic guideline for adult support of child's play prior to children's actual play activities is preparatory experiences. Regardless of the type of play, whether dramatic and creative play, functional play, or games with rules, children need real and concrete experiences for them to play. Concrete experiences, as roots of play and learning, can be planned and implemented. In order to develop experiences that are used as "grist" for play activities, Trostle and Yawkey (1990) recommend field trips, walks, resource people, novel objects, books and television, and videotapes as sources of potential experiences. Field trips to a carnival, circus, or a railway station and books and videos about space travel, as examples, provide children with active experiences for their play activities and interaction. Adults should make every effort to prepare the children for play by planning and providing these necessary experiences fundamental to child's play.

Adult Roles as Discovery and Direct Play Teaching Strategies in Child's Play

In the previous section, we considered several procedures for helping adults begin and prepare for their support of child's play. In this section, we describe various strategies that involve the adult directly in the play activities of young children: free, prompted, and directed discovery (Peters, Neisworth, & Yawkey, 1985). In addition, there is direct play teaching (Fallen & Umansky, 1985).

Free Discovery

In free discovery, the young children explore, experiment with, and use play materials in their own way. They are free to choose these play objects over other play objects. Although usable in prompted and guided discovery, activity centers are ideal for free discovery. Children select, focus, persist at, and plan their own types of play in particular locations in classroom and recreational areas. For free discovery, findings from several studies show interesting relationships between play activities and activity centers.

Shure's (1963) findings show that play types vary as a function of different activity centers. Solitary play was the most common play type used in the block and game activity center. Highly complex social interaction occurred most frequently in the doll activity center where children in many cases interacted while holding the dolls. Constructional play occurred most frequently in the art and block activity centers. And the two most preferred of the five centers were the block and art activity areas.

Shapiro (1975) examined the effects of activity centers, physical space, and group size. Activity centers as well as classroom space affect children's play activities. Children's play at activity centers was highest in classrooms with 30 to 50 square feet per child and lowest with 30 or less feet and 50 or more feet per child. Apparently, onlooker play predominated in activity centers with classrooms having 30 or less square feet per child and exploratory play with 50 or more square feet per child.

Activity centers used in a free discovery mode contribute to children's play activities, and types of play and interaction vary among these centers.

Prompted Discovery

With prompted discovery, adults determine the play materials children use. Essentially, the play environment is structured by the materials and permits increasing opportunities for self-discovery and learning. For example, in an activity center, the adult places a large plastic water-filled tub and nearby two flat styrofoam pieces, cork, golf ball, two nails, and a small piece of flat metal. The adult encourages children to explore and become familiar with the objects and then they place them one at a time into the water. The children discover that some of the objects "float" while others "sink." In prompted discovery the adult: (a) structures the environment by determining the play materials that are used, (b) encourages the children to explore the materials to become familiar with them, (c) may indirectly prompt various uses of the objects, (d) may ask peer group members to model their actions and uses of the materials, (e) permits the children to use the materials in many ways, and (f) doesn't tell the children the main idea, skill, or concept.

In prompted discovery and a prepared play environment, adults encourage creative uses of materials by suggesting that these objects can represent other objects. These suggestions of "objects representing other objects" after initial exploration and use foster dramatic play (Rubin & Howe, 1985).

For prompted discovery, Beisel and Yawkey (1986), in a study of activity centers types of language used under adult absent and present situations, found some interesting results with adult involvement. Initially, the results showed that imaginative language significantly increased in the housekeeping center as regulatory language decreased. Regulatory language prompts the behavior of others, such as, "Give me water because I'm thirsty" (Beisel & Yawkey). Further, younger children's use of imaginative language increased significantly when adults used imaginative language in this activity center. This finding was not shown for older children. For purposes of prompted discovery, the types of play materials that foster particular kinds of play identified in this and other chapters are ideal for developing structured environments.

In addition, and for other types of activity centers for prompted discovery, Johnson, Christie, and Yawkey (1987, pp. 196–197) list several common types for preschoolers and kindergartners:

1. Art area—paints, easels, brushes, scissors, glue, wallpaper books, small pieces of wood and styrofoam, paper, felt pens, clay, and Play-doh.

2. Block area—unit blocks, large hollow blocks, and small replicas (vehicles, people, and animals).

3. Floor play area—large vehicles, bean bags, balls, Tinkertoys, and empty boxes.

4. Housekeeping area—replicas of kitchen furniture and appliances, small table and chairs, dishes and eating utensils, used adult furniture, dress-up clothes, dolls, doll beds, and baby strollers.

5. Music area—phonograph, cassette player, rhythm instruments, and autoharp.

6. Book area—books and rug.

7. Science area—animals in cages, aquarium, objects to sort and feel (shells, seeds, stones), magnifying glass, seeds to grow, ant farm, water table, and sand box.

8. Woodworking area—tools, nails, screws, wood, workbench, and vise.

For other examples of play materials and activity centers see Trostle and Yawkey (1990).

Directed Discovery

In play activities, directed discovery assists children to focus on relevant attributes of play materials and situations for purposes of developing meaningful understanding. The adult may use a number of play modes in directed discovery. The adult may decide to co-play with the children (Johnson, Christie, & Yawkey, 1987). Here, the adult enters directly into the play activity by pretending to be a character in the children's dramatic play.

Another play mode for adults in directed discovery is encouraging creative uses of play materials by suggesting that these objects can represent other objects and by questioning. Both help children elaborate and extend their play with objects and activities. Suggesting and questioning can be formated in several ways (Ellis, 1973).

Verbal prompts either as suggestions or questions are used to focus and increase the child's attending to and using the play materials and extending dramatic play. Examples include: "Show me how you feed the baby!" and "Is this block heavier than this one? How do you know?"

Physical prompts are also used by adults as they add extraneous play toys and materials to the play activities as children play. Examples are providing the child with another car to use in a garage already filled with cars and giving children Lincoln Logs to use with their set of unit blocks. These extraneous objects added to children's play activities can either relate to the ongoing activities or themes or be unrelated to them. An example of extraneous related objects is adding pots and pans after the children played with plastic spoons and baby dolls in their "housekeeping play." Pots and pans relate clearly to the dramatic play theme and play activity. Examples of extraneous unrelated play objects are giving children a paper bag to use in their building of elephant puzzles and handing children a paper clip as they are dramatizing "piloting airplanes."

With verbal and physical prompts, the children incorporate them in their play activities and dramatics. The length of time they play increases and the children develop problem-solving strategies to incorporate the prompts creatively in their play activities (Ellis, 1973).

Adult modeling can also be used in directed discovery for child's play (Fallen & Umansky, 1985). In play modeling, the adult demonstrates specific movements and/or verbal statements in play activities and children imitate and practice the same actions. Modeling is the basis for all young children's finger play activities and games (Yawkey, Dank, & Glosenger, 1986). It is used successfully with younger and older normal children (Bandura, 1969) and handicapped children (e.g., Baer, Peterson, & Sherman, 1967) to acquire meaningful learning through play and play activities.

Fallen and Umansky (1985) note that children also model play behaviors and activities for other children. In addition, modeling play materials and activities is useful in mainstream settings where handicapped and nonhandicapped are integrated (Beers & Wehman, 1985). Beers and Wehman, noting the findings of Knapczyk and Peterson (1975) and Devonney, Guralnick, and Rubin (1974), suggest the potentials of peer modeling for increasing cooperative and social play in handicapped children with modeling by nonhandicapped children.

Direct Play Teaching

In direct play teaching, adults train children to play using behavioral analytic methodologies. Beers and Wehman (1985, p. 429) say that direct teaching is "occasionally necessary," especially for severely handicapped children who exhibit "little spontaneous play." Direct play teaching includes the following routines: instructions, physical prompting and fading, task analysis and sequencing, reinforcer sampling, and consequence conditions. These routines are explained elsewhere in detail (see Beers & Wehman, 1985), but a brief overview of each routine provides additional adult roles in child's play especially with severely handicapped and other handicapped children.

Direct play teaching using instructions calls for the use of verbal cues and instructions using physical demonstrations and modeling followed by social reinforcers for appropriate responses such as hugging the child (Beers & Wehman). They are especially relevant for teaching games having rules. Physical prompting and fading is used to develop commands in play activities. Commands, for example, "jump," "drop the ball," "run," are taught by the adult manually guiding the child through successive steps in each of these commands followed by reinforcement for successfully accomplishing each step. Beers and Wehman (p. 430) recommend that fading of prompts must accompany manual guidance if the children are to internalize this learning.

Another example of direct play teaching is using task analysis and skill sequencing (Beers & Wehman). Here, the adult breaks down a play activity into small, manageable behaviors that comprise a particular activity such as "pulling a toy" or "riding a wagon" and sequences these behaviors from simple to more advanced toward mastering a particular play activity. Reinforcer sampling, as a direct play teaching routine, involves the adult demonstrating a new toy or play material to the handicapped child. Since novel play materials for the severely handicapped may not be motivating, the adult demonstration of the materials and toys pinpoints their attractive qualities because "their reinforcing value has not been established" (Beers & Wehman, p. 430).

Finally, consequence conditions emphasize the use of reinforcers to develop play activities. According to Beers and Wehman (1985), "the best reinforcers may be the toys, play materials and games used in play development" as well as "praise, attention and approval from peers, parents, teachers and others." However, they caution against the use of "edibles, points and pennies" because "initiated play behavior does not occur when under control of artificial reinforcers such as tokens and pennies" (p. 431). In a final cautioning note, Beers and Wehman believe "that only severely handicapped children will need many of these strategies. For many young handicapped children, the arrangement of toys and equipment along with occasional modeling is sufficient" (p. 431).

The adult in child's play has many choices of strategies to use in supporting and becoming involved in children's play and materials. They range from free discovery to direct play teaching.

Final Considerations for Adults in Child's Play

We discussed in the previous sections many adult roles in child's play. Basic preparatory guidelines, free discovery, prompted and directed discovery, and direct play teaching are all potential roles for adults working with young children. In helping adults choose which of the adult roles to use in child's play, Langley (1985, p. 105) outlines questions that focus on play materials and equipment and their responsiveness to the child.

1. Can the toy afford the child independent play experiences, or must a peer or adult always assist in toy play?
2. Is the activation mode appropriate for the motoric grading potential of the child (e.g., is the child sufficiently strong, flexible, or coordinated to operate the toy)?
3. Can the toy be adapted to better accommodate the child's auditory and visual acuity/efficiency, movement possibilities, postural control, and level of tactile/proprioceptive integration?
4. Can the toy enable the child to adjust his or her level of arousal and attending (e.g., can the toy be used to calm and organize an excitable or hyperirritable child or to alert the nonresponsive, lethargic child)?
5. Can the toy be adapted or positioned to allow the child to explore it and to obtain different tactual, visual, or auditory perspectives?
6. Will the toy minimize the effects of the child's handicapping condition(s)?

7. Will the toy allow for cognitive mastery or success in physical control (i.e., will the toy challenge but not frustrate)?

8. Will the child have to maintain contact (visual, physical, or auditory) with the toy in order for it to operate or for it to be enjoyed?

For additional considerations in helping the adult to decide on which adult roles to use in child's play, Langley (1985, p. 106) offers additional questions on how effectively play materials and toys contribute to and foster development.

1. Will the toy be appropriate for the developmental abilities of the child?

2. Will the toy be capable of eliciting a range of developmental skills so as to encourage the child to acquire more progressive behaviors while reinforcing targeted skills?

3. Will the toy afford the child experiences that are otherwise unattainable?

4. Will the toy enable the child to adapt to his or her everyday surroundings (i.e., will it elicit behaviors that will facilitate the child's control over his or her environment)?

5. Will the toy have the potential to elicit a variety of behaviors across a wide developmental spectrum?

6. Will the toy be used to elicit behaviors across developmental domains (e.g., cognitive, sensory motor, social)?

7. Will the toy be an effective agent for facilitating social and communicative interactions?

8. Will the toy facilitate concomitant and collateral developmental skills (e.g., will the toy develop head rotation although its primary function is to enhance visual awareness and localization)?

9. How much potential does the toy have for eliciting a variety of play behaviors?

10. Will the toy be useful in combination with other toys?

11. Will the toy accommodate to a variety of chronological and developmental levels?

12. Will the toy have the potential to be enjoyed simultaneously by more than one child or in a turn-taking situation?

13. Will the toy be effective across a variety of handicapping conditions?

14. In the selection of toys for a classroom or for specific instructional purposes, will there be a range and variety of toys available for eliciting targeted behaviors and for simultaneously matching the current cognitive, sensory, physical, and arousal level of the child or children?

Summary

This chapter emphasizes the adult's role in child's play. Globally, the adult's role in child's play spans children's play and materials in their physical and social environments. To the questions of "Why participate in child's play?" or "Why bother?" this chapter responds with numerous answers. These responses include fostering the child's development and competence and for approval and rapport. Child's play is of value in its own right and for related benefits to children and adults.

The varied roles of adults in child's play are basic guidelines preparatory to play, discovery play forms of free, prompted, and directed involvement, and direct play teaching. These adult roles are framed around considerations relating to responsiveness of play materials and toys to children and to their development.

References

Aguilar, F. E. (1985). Social and environmental barriers to playfulness. In J. L. Frost and S. Sunderlin (Eds.), *When children play: Proceedings of the international conference on play and play environments* (pp. 73–76). Wheaton, MD: Association for Childhood Education International.

Arnold, A. (1968). *Your child's play*. New York: Simon and Schuster Publishers.

Baer, D., Peterson, R., & Sherman, J. (1967). The development of imitation by reinforcing behavioral similarity to a model. *Journal of Experimental Analysis of Behavior, 10*, 405–416.

Bandura, A. (1969). *Principles of behavior modification*. New York: Holt, Rinehart & Winston Publishers.

Beers, C. S., & Wehman, P. (1985). Play skill development. In N. H. Fallen & W. Umansky, *Young children with special needs* (pp. 404–440). Columbus, OH: Charles E. Merrill Publishing Company.

Beisel, R. W., & Yawkey, T. D. (1986). *Imaginative language use of children in a housekeeping activity center in preschool settings*. Paper delivered at the Annual Meeting, American Educational Research Association, San Francisco.

Bjorklund, G. (1979). *The effects of toy quantity and qualitative category on toddlers' play*. Paper delivered at the Biannual Meeting, Society for Research in Child Development, San Francisco.

Black, M., Freeman, B.J., & Montgomery, J. (1975). Systematic observation of play behavior in autistic children. *Journal of Autism and Childhood Schizophrenia, 5*(4), 363–371.

Bradley, R. H. (1985). Social-cognitive development on toys. *Topics in Early Childhood Special Education, 5*(3), 11–30.

Devonney, C., Guralnick, M., & Rubin, H. (1974). Integrating handicapped and nonhandicapped preschool children: Effects on social play. *Childhood Education, 50*(6), 360–364.

Dunn, J., & Wooding, C. (1977). Play in the home and its implications for learning. In B. Tizard & D. Havey (Eds.), *Biology of play* (pp. 45–58). London: Heinemann Publishers.

Ellis, M. (1973). *Why people play.* Englewood Cliffs, NJ: Prentice Hall Publishers.

Fallen, N. H., & Umansky, W. (1985). *Young children with special needs.* Columbus, OH: Charles B. Merrill Publishers.

Featherstone, H. (1974). The use of settings in a heterogeneous preschool. *Young Children, 29*(3), 147–154.

Freyberg, J. T. (1983). Increasing the imaginative play of urban disadvantaged kindergarten children through systematic training. In J. L. Singer (Ed.), *The child's world of make-believe: Experimental studies of imaginary play* (pp. 104–130). New York: Academic Press.

Getzels, I. W. (1975). Images of the classroom and visions of the learners. In D. G. Thomas & B. D. Wright (Eds.), *Learning environments* (pp. 14–31). Chicago: University of Chicago Press.

Griffing, P. (1983). Encouraging dramatic play in early childhood. *Young Children, 38*(4), 13–22.

Hare, B., & Hare, J. (1977). *Teaching young exceptional children.* New York: Grune and Stratton Publishers.

Hutt, C., & Varzey, M. J. (1966). Differential effects of group density on social behaviors. *Nature, 209*(4), 1371–1372.

Johnson, J., Christie, J. F., & Yawkey, T. D. (1987). *Play and early childhood development.* Glenview, IL: Scott, Foresman and Company.

Knapczyk, D., & Peterson, N. (1975). *Social play interaction of retarded children in an integrated classroom environment.* Unpublished paper, Indiana University, Developmental Training Center, Bloomington.

Langley, M. B. (1985). Selecting, adapting, and applying toys as learning tools for handicapped children. *Topics in Early Childhood Special Education, 5*(3), 101–118.

Loo, C. (1972). The effects of spatial density on the social behavior of children. *Journal of Applied Social Psychology, 2,* 372–381.

Loo, C., & Kennelly, D. (1979). Social density: Its effects on behaviors and perceptions of preschoolers. *Environmental Psychology and Nonverbal Behavior, 3*(3), 131–146.

McLoyd, V. (1983). Effects of structure of play objects on the pretend play of low-income preschool children. *Child Development, 54,* 626–635.

Naylor, H. (1985). Design for outdoor play: An observational study. In J. L. Frost & S. Sunderlin (Eds.), *When children play: Proceedings of the international conference on play and play environments* (pp. 103–113). Wheaton, MD: Association for Childhood Education International.

Peck, J., & Goldman, R. (1978). *The behaviors of kindergarten children under selected conditions of the social and physical environment.* Paper delivered at the Annual Meeting, American Education Research Association, Toronto, Canada.

Peters, D. L., Neisworth, J. T., & Yawkey, T. D. (1985). *Early childhood education: From theory to practice.* Monterey, CA: Brooks/Cole Publishers.

Pfluger, L., & Zola, J. (1974). A room planned by children. In G. Coates (Ed.), *Alternative learning environments* (pp. 66–98). Stroudsburg, PA: Dowden, Hutchinson & Ross Publishers.

Piaget, J. (1962). *Play, dreams and imitation in childhood.* New York: W. W. Norton.

Preiser, W. F. (1972). Behavior of nursery school children under different spatial densities. *Man-Environment Systems, 2,* 247–250.

Rubin, K. (1977). Play behaviors of young children. *Young Children, 41*(6), 16–24.

Rubin, K. H., & Howe, N. (1985). Toys and play behaviors: An overview. *Topics in Early Childhood Special Education, 5*(3), 1–9.

Shapiro, S. (1975). Preschool ecology: A study of three environmental variables. *Reading Improvement, 12*(4), 236–241.

Shure, M. B. (1963). Psychological ecology of a nursery school. *Child Development, 34*(4), 979–992.

Smilansky, S. (1968). *The effects of sociodramatic play on disadvantaged preschool children.* New York: Wiley.

Smith, P. K., & Connolly, K. J. (1976). Social and aggressive behavior in preschool children as a function of crowding. *Social Science Information, 16,* 601–620.

Smith, P. K., & Connolly, K. J. (1980). *The ecology of preschool behavior.* New York: Cambridge University Press.

Sylva, K., Bruner, J., & Genova, P. (1976). The role of play in problem solving of children 3–5 years old. In J. Bruner & K. Sylva (Eds.), *Play.* New York: Basic Books.

Sylva, K., Roy, C., & Painter, M. (1980). *Childwatching at playgroup and nursery school.* Ypsilanti, MI: High/Scope Press.

Trostle, S. L., & Yawkey, T. D. (1990). *Integrated learning activities for young children.* Boston: Allyn and Bacon.

Vandenberg, B. (1981). Environmental and cognitive factors in play. *Journal of Experimental Child Psychology, 31,* 169–175.

Vygotsky, L. (1976). Play and its role in the mental development of the child. In J. S. Bruner, A. Jolly, & K. Sylva (Eds.), *Play: Its role in development and evolution* (pp. 537–554). New York: Basic Books.

Wachs, T. (1978). The relationship of infants' physical environment to their Binet performance at 2½ years. *International Journal of Behavioral Development, 1,* 51–65.

Yawkey, T. D. (1980). Effects of social relationships' curricula and sex differences on reading and imaginativeness in young children. *Alberta Journal of Educational Research, 26*(3), 159–168.

Yawkey, T. D. (1990). *Effects of Title VII Project PIAGET Academic Excellence Programs: A final report covering 1987–1990.* Office of Bilingual Education and Minority Languages Affairs, U.S. Department of Education. University Park, PA: Pennsylvania State University.

Yawkey, T. D., Dank, H. L., & Glosenger, F. L. (1986). *Playing inside and out: How to promote social growth and learning in young children including the developmentally delayed child.* Lancaster, PA: Technomic Publishing Company.

Yawkey, T. D., & Trostle, S. C. (1982). *Learning is child's play.* Provo, UT: Brigham Young University Press.

Figure 11.1. The adventure playground provides children with more opportunities to explore, construct, and pretend than the traditional or contemporary playground *(photo by Joe L. Frost)*.

11

Outdoor Play—What Happens Here?

Mary S. Rivkin

The lives of women and children too poor to be sent to the country can now be saved in thousands of instances by making them go to the Park. During a hot day in July last, I counted at one time in the Park eighteen separate groups, consisting of mothers with children, most under school age, taking picnic dinners brought from home. The practice is increasing under medical advice, especially when summer complaint is rife.[1]

—*Frederick Law Olmstead,*
writing about New York City
a century ago

Baby boomers are producing their own baby boom, and where will all the children play? If they live in new apartment buildings in big cities, the children may never have to leave home. Partly to comply with zoning regulations and partly to attract buyers with young children, developers are providing playrooms. . . .

---

[1]Cited by Davidoff, P. (1980, p. 143), from S. B. Sutton (Ed.), (1971, p. 94), *Civilizing American cities: A selection of Frederick Law Olmstead's writings on city landscapes.* Cambridge, MA: MIT Press.

One reason such playrooms are becoming popular is that some parents find public parks unpleasant and dangerous. Ellen Arthur, a resident of the Upper West Side of Manhattan, occasionally accompanies her 5-year-old daughter, Charlotte, and her son, Jeremy, 2, to Central Park or to Riverside Park. "There are so many homeless people and so many rats . . .," she said.

So most days they stay at home. . . . In the building's health club a classroom-sized space is reserved for children [where] Charlotte and Jeremy can roam in a plastic house, play basketball or skid bicycles across the vinyl floor.[2]

—*The New York Times*, 1990

When Olmstead, the designer of Central Park, commented on the benefit of the outdoors for young children, he represented a 19th century consciousness that industrialization and urbanization were altering, perhaps ineradicably, a historical relationship between humans and their environment, then called "nature." And while the "progress" that urbanization and industrialization represented was wonderful, the diminishing of the relationship to nature was deplorable, even dangerous, perhaps particularly to children.

A century later, Olmstead's carefully preserved remnant of nature is itself perceived as dangerous to young children.

These perceptions are perhaps extremes. Most of the outdoors for most people in most places of the world today is neither life-saving nor life-threatening. In North America, we generally value being outdoors. We relate healthiness to being outdoors. Many of us sacrifice considerable time and effort to maintain the small, single-species botanical enclaves of lawns, often so that children might have play places. Yet as Yi-Fu Tuan observes (1978, p. 7), being raised in "nature" is no guarantee of childhood health. Jeremy and Charlotte, with their inoculations, vitamins, consistent appropriate nourishment, watchful pediatricians, and attentive parents are far more likely to grow to adulthood without playing outdoors than a child born into a poor rural New Guinean family who plays outdoors almost exclusively.

So, is outdoor play necessary or desirable for children? Are there benefits to children in outdoor play not duplicable in indoor play? Some researchers have investigated these questions. In surveying the extant literature, I found little doubt that outdoor play is good for children, for a host of reasons, but deep concerns about quality of the

---

[2]Kahn, E. M. (Jan. 11, 1990). In the urban jungle, rooms for playing. *New York Times*, p. C1.

play. There are also concerns about research itself: What is the ecology of play when one is looking at "the outdoors"? How do you conceptualize the totality of the sky, wind, trees, streets, buildings, cars, fences, dirt, asphalt, people, and perhaps a swing set?

In the following, I will attempt to share what a reading of the literature shows about our understanding of outdoor play for young children.

There is no body of literature dealing directly with the benefits of outdoor play (Moore, 1986). Three points are relevant here. First, knowledge of outdoor play often can be inferred from anthropologists, who in documenting child rearing provide limited information on location (Whiting & Edwards, 1988). A recent series of studies by Bloch (1989), in fact, deals specifically with location of American and Senegalese two- to six-year-olds' activities.

Second, the outdoor play that has been most frequently studied is that of designated play spaces, that is, playgrounds. Two problems exist here. One, these playgrounds tend not to be used very much by children and also are designed by people who don't know very much about play (Wilkinson, 1980, pp. 14–15). Two, although play on preschool playgrounds has been studied in recent years (e.g., Henniger, 1985), and most preschools do know about play and attempt to have playgrounds that support play, these playgrounds lie within the fixed and geographically limited boundaries of "adult-managed" settings (Moore, 1986, p. 11). The wider range of children's outdoor play is invisible in these studies.

Finally, the research on children and the outdoors is, according to Yi-Fu Tuan, inherently difficult.

> To the Western scientist the study of children and the natural environment presents a special challenge in objectivity. The social scientist, whether he is aware of it or not, is embedded in the dominant values of his culture. In the Western world, "nature" is such a "value." (1978, p. 29).

Western culture with its manipulation and destruction of the natural environment is especially passionate about "nature."

We don't know much about how natural settings affect perceptual and conceptual development of children (Tuan, 1978, p. 30) but we intuit that they are important because, perception and culture aside, it

> remains true that the human body evolved biologically in close association with nature's animate and inanimate elements. Human beings are predisposed in their favor. A sense of kinship with nature is universal.

. . . Children the world over seem to enjoy playing with such basic earth substances as water, clay, and sand; they like to climb trees and slide down slopes. Nature . . . is a relatively unstructured environment in which children's carefree vigor can be allowed full play. (Tuan, 1978, p. 29)

The universality of children's liking for play outdoors is a start in studying the benefits of outdoor play.

To move from very young children's liking the outdoors to figuring out why children in particular like the outdoors, what in the outdoors they like, and what good it does them, requires some traveling, given the present state of knowledge about outdoor play. The knowledge we do have comes from several sources: developmental psychologists, educators, ethnographers, ethologists, anthropologists, and urban planners. I plan to review representative studies from each group and offer a critical look at their contributions. Piecing together a quilt of information about preschoolers and outdoor play necessitates a passel of inferential thinking, with which I hope you will be patient.

Benefits of Play: Developmental Research

Play has been widely studied in the last three decades, particularly by child developmentalists. Substantial reviews of the research exist in Rubin, Fein, and Vandenberg (1983) and, most recently, Johnson, Christie, and Yawkey (1987). And, despite the fact that our culture has tended to trivialize ("just playing") or dislike ("get serious!") play, the research "provides overwhelming evidence of the multiple benefits of play for the overall development of children" (Frost, 1988, p. 10). Johnson, Christie, and Yawkey (1987) advise that the play "optimal for development" in children is that which "reflects or slightly stretches the current social or cognitive abilities of the child" (p. 18). This Vygotskyian perspective is doubtlessly accurate, although it does subtly negate the role of pure pleasure in development, the pleasure Piaget observed in repetitive assimilative play done for the sheer joy of mastery. Pleasure may create in children, as it seems to do in us, a sense of well-being that in turn creates a receptivity for being "slightly stretched" and developed.

To be succinct, play enhances physical development (see Chapter 9), cognitive development (e.g., Piaget, 1962), social development (e.g., Garvey, 1977), and emotional development (e.g., Erikson, 1950). It also creates (Huizinga, 1950) and reproduces (Corsaro, 1985) culture.

Definitions of Play

Definitions of play trouble the precise-minded, but most contemporary writers agree that play is characterized by being fun and being freely chosen. King (1979) has sensitized us to the fact that only the player really knows if it is play. Her work with kindergarteners showed that what looked like play to an adult observer wasn't necessarily experienced as play. King's kindergarteners judged any teacher-directed activity to be "work." Nonetheless, most play research continues to take an adult perspective and assumes that most children's activities, especially during "free-play" time in nursery school or child-care settings, are play—even though it is clear that adults are managing these settings.

We don't know how much young children interpret adult management as adult direction. Some evidence suggests that in present playgrounds (where adult management is usually far less restrictive than indoors, because teachers often use outdoor playtime to recoup their own equanimity, build relationships with other adults, and give children "a break" from everything indoors), children think their activities are all play (Reifel, Briley, & Garza, 1986; Esfehani, 1989).

Developmentalists: Levels and Types of Play

Most of the studies that have established the value of play in children's development have been conducted indoors, especially in institutional settings (centers, preschools, kindergartens), although homes have also been used. To analyze play activities, levels of social play (Parten, 1932) and Smilansky's formulation of Piaget's levels of cognitive play (1968) have been widely used by play observers, especially when combined by Rubin, Maioni, and Hornung (1976). Some studies that look at outdoor play used these as well as a way of achieving comparability of indoor and outdoor play (Henniger, 1985; Bloch, 1989). In such studies the setting is a variable but is very lightly evaluated. Henniger, for instance, describes his setting as an inventory of materials and equipment.

> The outdoor environment contained a variety of fixed and movable equipment. Stationary equipment included a treehouse platform with slide and steps, a jungle gym, a sandbox, a concrete bike path, a water play area and a swing set. Movable equipment, rearranged and/or changed each week, consisted of a boat, a steering wheel mounted in a box, metal triangular climbing structures with ladders, a tepee-type climber, large wooden crates, metal barrels and an assortment of wooden boxes and tires. Storage facilities outdoors gave children ready

access to tricycles, numerous sand toys, water play materials, shovels, rakes, balls, chairs, ropes, traffic signs, and wagons. (1985, p. 145)

Bloch describes her settings even more lightly as Middlewestern middle-class suburbia and a Senegalese rural village of housing compounds. Tizard, Philps, and Plewis (1976) used social class as a variable comparing indoor and outdoor play and, again, the setting was lightly described as "six centers."

What Has Been Learned about Outdoor Play from Developmentalist Studies?

These studies tell us something about the outdoor play of preschoolers. Henniger's (1985) four- and five-year-old children exhibited more functional play outdoors than in, as much cooperative play outdoors as in, and more dramatic play outdoors than in. In the discussion, Henniger adds a more informative description about the setting—the adult-child ratio was low, and the teachers took "considerable time each week in planning and changing the materials and equipment placed" (p. 148) in both environments. He allows that these sociocultural factors may have influenced his results. His bottom line is that all kinds of play can occur both indoors and out, given proper facilitation, but that the additional space of outdoors is an advantage for enabling the active dramatic play created by boys. Outdoor dramatic play—by boys more than girls who prefer indoor dramatic play—was shown also by Sanders and Harper (1976). These authors in their conclusion acknowledged that environmental factors such as equipment were perhaps material.

Tizard, Philps, and Plewis (1976) also compared indoor and outdoor play to find that lower-class British children played more and at a higher social level outdoors than in. The authors speculated that the culture of the lower-class children was relevant and that being outdoors with relatively less adult interaction simulated home environments. Such children may play with less complexity inside, less from immaturity than cultural discontinuity (Slaughter & Dembrowski, 1989).

Bloch's (1989) studies of rural Senegalese two- to six-year-olds reflected a similar orientation to cultural factors. American middle-class two- to six-year-olds spent about 60 percent of their time inside their houses, rural Senegalese about 13 percent. Both groups of children played about the same portion of time (about 30 percent) and, interestingly, while American children had more gross motor play, "both groups were virtually identical in time spent in pretense, functional, constructive, exploratory, rough-and-tumble, and music/art-play" (pp. 139–140). Bloch's study is of note in that it captures children's play at home, in their yards, and neighborhoods, where presumably play environments reflect general culture rather than professionally biased efforts such as schools observed by Henniger exemplify.

An implication of the study is that young children of different cultures have basically the same play interests, but the location of the play is culturally determined. Relatively big American houses allow indoor play. Senegalese children generally only slept, waited, and had transition and social activities in their much smaller houses.

I have criticized each of these studies for looking at play with little regard to the features of the outdoor environment. By contrast is the report of a decade of observations and experiments at Pacific Oaks College play yard and classrooms, reported by Kritchevsky and Prescott (1977).

Carefully Designed and Planned Space

Kritchevsky and Prescott (1977) report in some detail how environments influence behavior and the monograph is summarized here. First, program goals are linked to spatial arrangements.

> For instance, one goal for a particular Head Start program may be to help young children learn to pay attention to teachers, not only as adults whose directions should be followed, but as warm, trustworthy sources of needed and useful play ideas, information and help. Under these circumstances, space should not encourage children to go off and manage on their own. The necessity and usefulness of teachers-as-resource might be maximized by limiting the number of easily available play ideas in the space and by increasing the ratio of teachers to children. (p. 7)

Furthermore, the play space is described by (a) both contents and the empty space around the contents and (b) how the parts function as a whole, "since it is apparently the total setting which children perceive and to which they respond" (p. 9). The contents are categorized into play units—"simple" units such as swings, "complex" units such as sand and digging equipment, or "super" units such as sand, digging equipment, and water (p. 11). Variety in what a child can do is a characteristic among units: a playground with 10 trikes, 3 wagons, and a climber would have 14 play units but a variety score of two—climbing and riding (p. 14). Amount to do per child is a ratio of play spaces per child, for example, a trike would provide one play space, a climber perhaps five (p. 15).

The placement of the units around a clear path with sufficient empty spaces is critical.

> Good organization is dependent on the presence of enough empty space and a broad, easily visible path. Both function to facilitate freedom of movement through the yard or room. Where there is a clear path throughout the space, (1) children on one unit cannot reach children on another unit; (2) teachers and children do not need to walk through play units and their necessary surrounding space to get from one place to another; (3) no play units are permanently hidden; and (4) there is no dead space. Good organization typically is found in space where the surface is no less than one-third and no more than one-half uncovered; larger numbers of children appear to require the greater amount of empty space to maintain ease of movement. (p. 23)

Poorly planned space can result in negative behavior that can counteract program goals: "Developing feelings of self-worth may be very difficult in a setting whose poor organization constantly invites the negative, disruptive behavior which teachers must restrict" (p. 24). Well-planned space will increase the chances of goal-related behavior and not create negative behavior; it will also free time for teachers and children that might otherwise be wasted in poor behavior or disciplinary actions (pp. 25–26).

Kritchevsky and Prescott's research also led them to recommend age-grading play spaces (p. 28) and to be watchful for arrangements and equipment that deceivingly please adults but distract or limit children (pp. 28–29). They also observed that socioeconomic and cultural factors influence use of space. For instance, middle-class children function better in larger spaces, while "relatively crowded and/or congested space was seen to support a high level of interest and involvement among segments of certain ethnic groups" (p. 35). "Warm family cultures" with historical or present experiences of congestion were suggested as an explanation (p. 35). Different children may " 'read' identical settings differently" (p. 35).

Kritchevsky and Prescott's monograph is important for preschool teachers and playground planners because of its detailed, observation-based approach to children's interactions with space. It is consistent with developmental research in considering that play is play wherever the location, but is an improvement on that research by describing major interactions of location with activity.

Types of Playgrounds Influence Play

Other research into the interaction of play with location is found in the writings of the last decade on identifiable types of playgrounds (e.g., Frost, 1988; Johnson, Christie, & Yawkey, 1987). "Traditional" playgrounds predominate in the United States—large metal structures (swings, slides, and climbers) on which children can exercise. "Contemporary" playgrounds account for most newly constructed playgrounds here, generally being linked wooden structures that allow climbing, swinging, sliding, swaying, and a variety of shelters or enclosures to facilitate dramatic play. "Adventure" playgrounds popular in Scandinavia and England provide a wealth of movable, unlinked materials and tools with which children can create their own play structures. The creative aspect holds a potential for injury, which seems to underlie the American avoidance of such playgrounds.

Hart and Sheehan (1986), comparing preschoolers' play on a traditional and a contemporary playground, found little difference in the verbal interactions, social play, and cognitive play engaged in by the children. The study was confined to two adjacent playgrounds with many elements in common, so it is possible that differences were not that salient for children.

Prima facie, the adventure playground provides children with more opportunities to explore, construct, and pretend than the traditional or contemporary playground.

While preschool teachers often put a touch of adventure in their playgrounds by adding loose materials (paints, boards, boxes, and hoses) to the extant structures, it is highly uncommon to find a thoroughgoing adventure playground for preschoolers in the United States. A description of such a playground for three- to six-year-olds on an Israeli kibbutz demonstrates the possibilities for enhanced play (Smith, 1985).

The "Workyard" of a Kibbutz Nursery School

By Smith's description, the "workyard" has an area set aside for large-scale motor play. The main part of the yard, though, has "metal pieces of all kinds" and a jerry-built shed containing "pillows, clothing, and old cloths." Piles of "cans, lumber, wheels, tires, and buckets" are along the side of the yard. Children have access to all the materials:

> Each child makes his own space in the yard. All you have to do is claim some interesting materials, pull them into an open area, play there for

a bit, and the territory is yours to keep for as long as you like. Children can build private places or they can work with a friend or group. Once a week, on Fridays, there is a clean up (nothing more threatening than tidying your construction and returning stray junk). The *ganenet* [teacher] rakes over the ground around and under the constructions. With that one exception, the buildings and groups of builders are the business of the children. (Smith, 1985, p. 20)

In the "workyard"—not "playground"—children build with real-world objects, such as machine parts, tractor tires, and discarded lumber. The materials are "sometimes heavy, long, rusty, even sharp. Handling them requires children to *look alive*, be self-aware, planful, even cautious, to become competent" (p. 22).

In the setting, Smith asserts that children learn the following concepts:

You can make the land yours.

Nothing need be wasted.

Out of nothing much can be made.

You can work alone, but it is possible to ask for help or join together.

If you think, if you try, if you imagine, if you study the environment, you will survive—and more.

Use your mind freely. You can do no damage and you can learn.

Though there is danger in the world, this is a safe environment.

Adults care—they offer materials so that you will learn, they trust you, they watch over what happens.

The first concept is an especially striking reflection of cultural values, as this workyard is in a West Bank kibbutz.

Smith contrasts the workyard with American playgrounds saying that Americans "think about children as softer, more vulnerable, and quite different from adults" and hence overprotect them with playgrounds of pony swings and climbing domes, rather than provide them with adult-world materials with which they could become competent, resourceful, and creative (p. 23).

Kritchevsky and Prescott's reminder that physical spaces ought to support program goals for children is relevant here. Frost in this volume and elsewhere (Frost, 1988) has argued eloquently for our taking lessons from the adventure playgrounds to make American playgrounds reflect goals far broader than physical exercise.

Moving from the literature of nondescribed playgrounds and thoughtfully designed ones with two variants, we now examine a study that reveals how a playground facilitates children's construction of their own social world.

A Preschool Playground—Incubator of a Constructed Social World

As the study of the kibbutz workyard reveals, play spaces designed by adults reflect societal values. A year-long ethnography of a preschool, including its playground, by Corsaro (1988) further shows that children at play not only reproduce the established social world but in their peer interaction *create* their own unique social world from which they derive their sense of self and society. Furthermore, some of this world can exist independently of adults' knowledge or supervision, particularly on a playground where adult interaction with children tends to be less than indoors.

The outdoors appears in Corsaro's study especially important to the development of peer culture. For one thing, of the play spaces that adults refrained from entering (partly because they were too big), most were outside; inside, the playhouses were the only child-dominated places, but outside the children controlled the sandpile, the climbing bars, and the climbing house—a raised platform with several routes of egress (p. 28). These peer-dominated places allowed for peer routines, for example, being "bad" by swearing (p. 260). Such routines are seen by Corsaro as stable elements of peer culture, ones that strengthen children's sense of who they are. He (p. 193) cites Goffman in *Asylums:* "Our sense of being a person can come from being drawn into a wider social unit: our sense of selfhood can arise through the little ways we resist the pull."[3] Corsaro writes of swearing as a "ritual that symbolizes one of children's most cherished desires: to defy and challenge adults, share the experience, and not be detected" (p. 199). So much for the sweet innocence implied by "Wendy houses"!

Second, the larger area allowed for more mobility and aggression, two behaviors valued by children that represent their ongoing effort to acquire control. Running and chasing routines are well-known staples of outdoor play (e.g., Smith & Connolly, 1972).

Third, the climbing areas permitted expression of a cherished theme of preschool play—"bigness." Children repeatedly climbed to the top of structures and notified the public of their "bigness." Being at the top of structures or inside play houses also allowed children to protect their play from invasion by others. Interestingly, Corsaro does not interpret the well-known phenomenon of children's resistance to

---

[3]Goffman, Erving. (1961). *Asylums.* Garden City, NY: Doubleday. p. 320.

interruption by others ("You can't play with us!") as selfishness; rather, he sees it as children's recognition of communal action. When children are young and just developing social skills, they need to protect what already exists (1985, p. 150).

Finally, Corsaro's playground, because it interfaced with the urban adult world in a way more typical of lower-class than middle-class suburban playgrounds (Kritchevsky & Prescott, 1977), provided children a chance to develop a uniquely empowering ritual: "Garbage Man." In this situation, the children who were outside would run to the fence to watch and cheer the garbage man emptying the dumpster near the nursery school. For the cheering, they received a wave and a honk.

> In this activity the children literally *reach out beyond* the physical boundaries of the nursery school to the adult world and transform a mundane everyday event (the collection of garbage) into a routine of peer culture which they jointly produce and enjoy. (Corsaro, 1985, p. 252)

Teachers at the school seemed to be just lightly aware of the existence of some interaction around the garbage man, which led Corsaro to further observe:

> And, at an even deeper level, the routine is significant because the children are *successful at procuring the participation of adults* (who wave and beep a horn) *in an event which the children create and control and of whose significance adults have only a surface recognition.* (1985, p. 252)

This function of outdoor play—interacting with, even slightly controlling, the adult world—is one I have not seen commented on elsewhere in the literature.

One other aspect of outdoor play that Corsaro observed was that "animal family role play always occurred outdoors," while human family role play was usually indoors (1985, p. 109). Animal family play was more physical, more aggressive, more mobile, and had less supervision of subordinates, for example, animal children were not as restricted as human children (1985, p. 110). The playground allowed mobility and aggression—those prized values—to be expressed in play in a way that indoor play did not.

Corsaro's study, *Friendship and Peer Culture in the Early Years,* was not focused on play. In fact, Corsaro took a minimalist Deweyian definition of play—"activities not performed for the sake of any result beyond their own production" (1985, p. 77), yet he repeatedly demonstrated that play is a primary means of producing friendship and peer culture. Nor did he focus on the playground, but my

Figure 11.2. Outdoors, the child controls the sandpile, and many other elements of the environment (*photo by Joe L. Frost*).

reading of his work is that in institutions (schools and centers) the playground is a premier incubator of peer culture, due to the collaboration of its structures, space, and the kinds of play permitted by adults and, in this case, its interface with the adult world. Young children's peer culture develops into school-age culture and beyond. Thus Corsaro's playground is every bit as noteworthy, though until now less appreciated, as the "playing fields of Eton."

Living Outdoors

Children who spend many hours on preschool playgrounds have been of interest to researchers (partly because of their availability for study), but they are not typical of the world's children. Most young children playing outdoors are at or very near their homes.

Indeed, our words "outdoors" and "outside" reflect the home-centeredness of our concept. The door and the sides of the dwelling are the reference points; what is related to them is not described by us otherwise. We may specify "yard" or "playground" or "field," but where are they? Outdoors. Etymologically, "being" shares its root with "dwelling" and "neighborhood."[4] We are building-centered, perhaps from our need for shelter in the climates of Western civilization.

Yet being "outside" the house or building can mean being in the whole other world. How are we to study young children's play in limitless spaces? Anthropologists and urban planners both provide some insights.

Young Children of the !Kung

An instructive contrast to the playgrounded children so far described are the hunter-gatherer !Kung children of the Kalahari bush. Draper (1976) reveals their living and playing space:

> For someone unaccustomed to the !Kung ways of building huts and laying out a village, it would be possible to walk within six meters of a village and never know it was there. Standing on the outskirts of a !Kung camp for the first time one thinks of birds' nests clinging with frail strength in the branches of bushes. The low, inconspicuous huts are built of branches and grass and so are entirely camouflaged. During most months of the year the people make no effort to clear away grass

---

[4]"Bheu" is the Old Germanic root from which are derived the English words "being," "dwelling," and "neighborhood." See Indo-European Roots in American Heritage Dictionary, p. 1509. Boston: Houghton Mifflin 1973.

and bushes from the periphery of the village to mark the disjunctive of the open bush with the settled village. People prefer to build their huts backed into the bush and facing into the center of the common village space.

The children living in these camps are limited in their range of movements. It is hardly an exaggeration to say they have almost no place aside from the village and near its periphery where they can go to be by themselves to play games or whatever. There is simply the cleared village space; and in back of each hut stretches the Kalahari bush which from a child's vantage point is vast, undifferentiated, and unsocialized. It was a surprise to me to see what little use children made of the bush hinterland. Older children use the bush beyond eyesight of the village to some extent, but children under about 10 years stayed close to home and most often were inside the village circle in close association with adults. (p. 201)

The !Kung family does not use a hut for living or privacy but primarily for sleep, to keep possessions dry, and to make its residence. Thus, virtually everything that "happens" is outdoors. "The village itself is a kind of big room" (p. 201). Adults and children are not separated; their activities intermingle, and adults are highly aware of the children at all times. Draper relates watching:

> One afternoon I watched for 2 hours while a father hammered and shaped the metal for several arrow points. During the period his son and his grandson (both under 4 years old) jostled him, sat on his legs, and attempted to pull the arrow heads from under the hammer. When the boys' fingers came close to the point of impact, he merely waited until the small hands were a little farther away before he resumed hammering. Although the man remonstrated with the boys (about once every 3 minutes), he did not become cross or chase the boys off; and they did not heed his warnings to quit interfering. Eventually, perhaps 50 minutes later, the boys moved off a few steps to join some teenagers lying in the shade. (p. 206)

Children play with one another as well, usually in multiage groups because each village has, perhaps, only 11 or 12 children, aged up to 14 (pp. 202–203). Shostak (1976), another observer of the !Kung, comments that generally "their games do not reflect a separate children's culture. They are usually imitations of adult activities: hunting, gathering, singing adult songs, trancing, playing house, and playing marriage" (p. 267). They do very little work, preschoolers virtually none, similar to American children (Whiting & Edwards, 1988, p. 68). Very young children, three and under, are on their mothers' backs a great deal, while the mothers gather food and perform other tasks. Weaning from the back and from the breast are major traumas in toddler life.

In contrast to the studies discussed previously, here is a play area not separated out by the adults for children's use. Here children and adults are in continuous contact, mutually aware of all activities. A major similarity between the kibbutz and !Kung play is the imitating of adult life; the clearest difference is in technology and materials.

In thinking about the play of !Kung children, it makes no sense to call it "outdoor." They live on the unadorned surface of the earth without being divided from it by asphalt or floors, or separated from the sky by roofs. They walk across the surface in search of food places, no permanent encampments to assert "here I am, here I dwell." Their bare skin connects to the air and ground, the soles of their feet always know what sand or stone or clay is beneath them. Wind, sun, rain, and shade are omnipresent. A baby or toddler is a little more insulated, sleeping on a cloth and being held with a cloth to the mother's body. They exist with their natural environment.

The !Kung children are not spending time outdoors on their way toward being a grownup in an office with windows that do not open. They are where they will be—those that survive to adulthood—in a continuous stream of life without separations between house/yard/ neighborhood / car / store / mall / park / camp / preschool / playgrounds/ schools/high school/job—separations that punctuate, stimulate, and agitate Western children's lives, giving meaning to the concepts of outdoors, indoors, and nature versus people.

Ethologists: Children's Instinctual Outdoor Behavior or the Nature in People

Before I move into discussing the work of urban planners/ecologists/ interdisciplinarians who currently struggle with the relationships between Western children and the outdoors, let me carry the vision of the !Kung toddler thoroughly immersed in the natural environment to an English urban park. Here imagine his mother sitting (shivering) on a bench and the 18- to 30-month-old moving around the area, at some distance from his mother but within mutual vision. He runs out a bit, points to the distance with one hand while looking back at her. She looks but doesn't respond, so he runs somewhere else and points again, again looking back. This pointing-checking behavior is the most common gesture and is directed only at the mother, although friendly strangers are occasionally talked to or shown things (Anderson, 1972). The ethologist J. W. Anderson observed this pattern in English toddlers and speculated that because mothers did not really know what the babies were pointing at (i.e., no clear and present danger or obvious attraction, as one mother said, her child was noticing the absence of birds in the trees), this behavior represented a universal attachment-related environmental scanning. A secure toddler will check his/her mother's perception of the big outdoor world; if she does not get excited (no response), everything must be all right. The pointing behavior is thus indicated to be a pan-human instructional survival strategy basic to a child's being safe in finding the outdoor world. It would be interesting to replicate the study in other cultures where perhaps "attachment" is not such an issue as in Western societies.

Anderson (1972) also observed another distinctive exploratory behavior in the outdoor setting. The toddlers frequently picked up objects, examined them, then dropped them and stomped on them. They never threw them. This intent exploration culminating in stomping and often crushing is more appropriate to outdoors than in. The toddlers also frequently scraped the ground with hand or foot, a behavior much more informative to the toddler outside, where rocks or dirt, sand, or leaves move, than inside on stationary floors.

A more general ethological study (Smith & Connolly, 1972) comparing indoor and outdoor play in three English nursery schools (settings not described) showed that two- to four-year-olds in their play yards compared to classrooms engaged in more running, moving play, laughing, smiling, rough-and-tumble play, and wandering alone doing nothing. They engaged in less stationary play, less staring, less sucking, and fewer aggressive behaviors. There were no differences in "social" (nonagonistic) behaviors. These findings are often reported in the literature and do not surprise any observer of traditional preschool playgrounds.

More Than Playgrounds: A Broad View of Outdoor Play

Studies that confine their focus to playgrounds, as do most of those reported above, even well-described playgrounds, are ultimately unsatisfactory because they provide limited information about children's play, most of which does not occur on playgrounds. Bloch (1989) showed that American and Senegalese preschoolers spent about 30 percent of their lives playing, virtually none of it on playgrounds. Other studies (Moore, 1986) have repeatedly confirmed that even older children who have more mobility than preschoolers spend only 15 percent of playtime on playgrounds. This is partly because playgrounds tend to bore children (Chace & Ishmael, 1980) and are inaccessible due to traffic or other perceived dangers.

Several studies have shown where young children tend to play. In Whiting and Edwards' cross-cultural study (1988), children were labeled "lap," "knee," and "yard" children, corresponding approximately to the more conventional infants, toddlers, and preschoolers. These labels convey the location of the children. "Yard" children, four- to five-year-olds, usually have some neighborhood freedom, particularly boys. Bloch's study (1989) corroborated the prevalence of yard play for under-sixes. It seems that nowhere are young children allowed to wander far from their houses. Moore (1978) cites a 1974 study by Coates and Bussard that quantified the range of children's movements in a moderate-density suburban planned unit development. The four- to five-year-olds were "bound in a compact home-base bubble extending about 50 feet from the front doors . . . and between 90 and 140 feet laterally" (Moore & Young, 1978, pp. 95–96).

Figure 11.3. Studies that confine their focus to playgrounds, even well-described ones, are ultimately unsatisfactory because they provide limited information about children's play, most of which does not occur on playgrounds (*photo by Joe L. Frost*).

Interdisciplinary Studies

Coates and Bussard represent an ecological approach to studying play espoused by urban planners and ecologists. Wilkinson wrote in 1980 that "planning for play is usually done by professionals from collateral disciplines (urban planning, landscape architecture, social work, etc.)" (pp. 14–15). There has been an attempt to understand fully how children experience the world beyond their houses. As Hart described his study of a small Vermont town, he said it was

> designed to describe the relationship of children to the landscape, focusing on their physical and experiential engagement with it from the door of their home to the fringes of their known world. This required the simultaneous study of those aspects of the child-environment relations commonly investigated separately: spatial activity, place use, spatial cognition, and place values and feelings. This work revealed the importance of parents' and children's feelings about danger and other negative forces in the environment influencing children's spatial ranges out of doors . . . how dramatically children's access to the environment varies not only in relation to children's ages and sex but also as a function of the degree of traffic, crime, type of housing, social fears and amount of time parents are able to spend at home. (Perez & Hart, 1980, pp. 252–253)

The ecological psychologist Paul Gump identifies the basic question of the ecological perspective to be "What goes on here?" (1989, p. 53) and suggests that efforts to prove theory by observing children's natural behavior have often dead-ended. We "need atheoretical, nonexperimental data in large doses . . . to answer questions about children's behavior in real life situations" (p. 37).

Gump points out some of the problems in describing the influence of settings in children's natural habitat. First, the environment needs to be unitized—a swimming pool is clearly a unit, but what about a field with a variety of terrain and ground cover? How children use a field in play would show the relevant units. What activities are required by a setting? What is the coercive pull? For instance, a slide would require active sliding/climbing, but it might also lend itself to quiet shaded sitting under. Does the setting call for cooperation or independent behavior? When units are identified and described they can be mapped to show the flow of behavior. Gump calls for studies which look at children actively "throughout their territorial ranges (not just studies in experiments or in convenient but limited natural areas such as nursery schools and playgrounds)" (p. 54). With such studies we can see how "variations in settings' action structures shape play behaviors and developments" (p. 55).

Robin C. Moore exemplifies the urban planning approach (Moore, 1980). His latest study, *Childhood's Domain* (1986), deals with the ecology of play among British eight- to twelve-year-olds. A basis for the study is the concept of "territorial range." A child has a "habitual" range right around home (where preschoolers are most of the time), the "frequented" range of less accessible places used more likely on weekends and holidays, and the "occasional" range exemplified by trips or vacations (pp. 17–18). Moore asserts that the range must be continually expanding for children in order to supply "new material for the continuing drama of a child's discovery of the world, without which the acquisition of competence and understanding would be impossible" (p. 93).

Moore and others (e.g., Perez & Hart, 1980; Fjelsted, 1980) are concerned that many urban and suburban settings restrict children's range far too much. Traffic is a major hazard to children, especially "yard" children, who are just beginning to venture beyond close supervision (Chace & Ishmael, 1980). Time is another constraint even for preschoolers; with schools, naps, meals, and nightfall, there "is simply not enough time to wander far from home" (Moore & Young, 1978, p. 94). Dangers perceived by parents and children also limit range. Although very young children everywhere have limited range, many latchkey children spend their afternoons locked inside their houses (Gambarino, 1989). Too many constraints on exploration may be highly adverse to development. Perez and Hart (1980) believe that "serious restriction of exploration will deny a child the ability to develop into a competent, happy individual and is to be avoided at all costs" (p. 256).

Recommendations for Improving Play Spaces for Children

The realization that playgrounds do not satisfy play requirements has led urban planners to offer suggestions for the total environment. Verwer (1980), for example, advocates that in play planning: (a) children and adults must be able to use the whole residential environment, not just the playgrounds and (b) all town planning should take play into account. In the planning, say Perez and Hart (1980), children's interpretations of the environment should be taken into account, because children categorize things differently from adults. Several uniquely child-originated categories from the Vermont study by Perez and Hart were "dirt for building," "climbing trees," and "long grass for hiding and building" (Perez & Hart, 1980, p. 268). Moore (1986) further suggests that carefully maintained play areas discourage play; thus, he advises, make plantings random, don't mow all the grass, and allow for sticks to be found, broken, and used in projects because a certain level of disorder invites play and doesn't look ruined by play (pp. 243–244).

Kritchevsky and Prescott (1977) caution against simply providing "nature" for young children because they do not view it the way adults do; children lack both the memories and concept of "nature" that stimulate adult appreciation. Furthermore, Tuan (1978) reminds us of Piaget's observations on young children's artificialism and animism; for example, they think clouds are from smokestacks and that the moon is following them. Tuan believes that nature "does not in itself inspire children to learn. . . . Children have to be taught by adult human beings" (p. 25). Planners need to shape the natural environment for young children.

Conclusion

The value of children's play is part of our historically developing consciousness of children. As Garbarino (1989) says, "The modern concept of children with 'free play' as its cornerstone, is a hard-won cultural achievement" (p. 18). Because outdoor play has been the freest of the free play, and thus potentially the most suited to the developing child's needs,[5] we ought to be both especially aware of contemporary encroachment on it and actively seeking to expand its range and opportunities.

Furthermore, insofar as playing outdoors is interfacing with nature, outdoor play serves to familiarize and affiliate children with what is coming to seem a vulnerable, fragile biosphere. Protecting the environment looks to be a long-term endeavor, which surely must be underlaid by knowledge and caring in today's children. Recognizing the value of outdoor play supports humanity's fundamental aims and interests—much as, on a smaller scale, children's affiliation with a particular piece of land is held as a cardinal tenet of the Zionist kibbutz.

Unconscious immersion in the outdoors—exemplified by the !Kung—is barred by our cultural inheritance of technology and literacy. Maybe Manhattan preschoolers like Jeremy and Charlotte do

---

[5]Personal conversation with Mary Tupper Dooly Webster, December 1989.

not need much exposure to the outdoors. But given our biological inheritance of having evolved within nature, it seems intuitively that our well-being requires outdoor play. Moore and Young (1978) say that this has not been proved, but if researchers, working closely with young children interacting with natural systems, can find evidence to support this intuition, then we may be able to help both children and nature together.

References

Anderson, J. W. (1972). Attachment behavior out of doors. In N. Blurton Jones (Ed.), *Ethological studies of child behavior* (pp. 199–215). Cambridge, England: Cambridge University Press.

Bloch, M. N. (1989). Young boys' and girls' play at home and in the community: A cultural-ecological framework. In M. N. Bloch & A. D. Pellegrini (Eds.), *The ecological context of children's play* (pp. 120–154). Norwood, NJ: Ablex Publishing Co.

Chace, E., & Ishmael, G. (1980). Outdoor play in housing areas. In P. F. Wilkinson (Ed.), *Innovation in play environments* (pp. 171–193). New York: St. Martin's Press.

Corsaro, W. A. (1985). *Friendship and peer culture in the early years.* Norwood, NJ: Ablex Publishing Corporation.

Corsaro, W. A. (1988). Children's conception and reaction to adult rules: The underlife of the nursery school. In G. Handel (Ed.), *Childhood socialization* (pp. 193–207). New York: Aldine de Gruyter.

Davidoff, P. (1980). Respect the child: Urban planning with the child in mind. In P. F. Wilkinson (Ed.), *Innovation in play environments* (pp. 141–151). New York: St. Martin's Press.

Draper, P. (1976). Social and economic constraints on child life among the !Kung. In R. B. Lee & I. DeVore (Eds.), *Kalahari hunter-gatherers: Studies of the !Kung San and their neighbors* (pp. 199–217). Cambridge, MA: Harvard University Press.

Erikson, E. H. (1950). *Childhood and society.* New York: Norton.

Esfehani, B. (1989). *Let's play/work: Four- and five-year-olds' perceptions of their school experiences.* Unpublished manuscript.

Fjelstad, B. (1980). "Standard" versus "adventure" playground. In. P. F. Wilkinson (Ed.), *Innovation in play environments* (pp. 34–44). New York: St. Martin's Press.

Frost, J. L. (1988). Child development and playgrounds. In L. D. Bruya (Ed.), *Play spaces for children: A new beginning* (pp. 3–28). Reston, VA: American Alliance for Health, Physical Education, Recreation and Dance.

Garbarino, J. (1989). An ecological perspective on the role of play in child development. In M. N. Bloch & A. D. Pellegrini (Eds.), *The ecological context of children's play* (pp. 16–34). Norwood, NJ: Ablex Publishing Co.

Garvey, C. (1977). *Play.* Cambridge, MA: Harvard University Press.

Gump, P. V. (1989). Ecological psychology and issues of play. In M. N. Bloch & A. D. Pellegrini (Eds.), *The ecological context of children's play* (pp. 35–56). Norwood, NJ: Ablex Publishing Co.

Hart, C. R., & Sheehan, R. (1986). Preschoolers' play behavior in outdoor environments: Effects of traditional and contemporary playgrounds. *American Educational Research Journal, 23* (4), 668–678.

Henniger, M. L. (1985). Preschool children's play behaviors in an indoor and outdoor environment. In J. L. Frost & S. Sunderlin (Eds.), *When children play* (pp. 145–149). Wheaton, MD: Association for Childhood Education International.

Huizinga, J. (1950). *Homo ludens: A study of the play element in culture.* London: Routledge & Kegan Paul.

Johnson, J. E., Christie, J. F., & Yawkey, T. D. (1987). *Play and early childhood development.* Glenview, IL: Scott Foresman.

King, N. R. (1979). Play: The kindergartener's perspective. *Elementary School Journal, 80,* 81–87.

Kritchevsky, S., & Prescott, E. (1977). *Planning environments for young children: Physical space* (2nd ed.). Washington, DC: National Association for the Education of Young Children.

Moore, R. C. (1980). Generating relevant urban childhood places: Learning from the "yard." In P. F. Wilkinson (Ed.), *Innovations in play environments* (pp. 45–75). New York: St. Martin's Press.

Moore, R. C. (1986). *Childhood's domain: Play and place in child development.* London: Croom Helm.

Moore, R. C., & Young, D. (1978). Childhood outdoors: Toward a social ecology of the landscape. In I. Altman & J. F. Wohlwill (Eds.), *Children and the environment.* New York: Plenum.

Parten, M. (1932). Social participation among preschool children. *Journal of Abnormal and Social Psychology, 27,* 243–269.

Piaget, J. (1962). *Play, dreams, and imitation in childhood.* New York: W. W. Norton.

Perez, C., & Hart, R. A. (1980). Beyond playgrounds: Planning for children's access to the environment. In P. F. Wilkinson (Ed.), *Innovation in play environments* (pp. 252–271). New York: St. Martin's.

Reifel, S., Briley, S., & Garza, M. (1986). Play at child care: Event knowledge at ages three to six. In K. Blanchard (Ed.), *The many faces of play* (pp. 80–89). Champaign, IL: Human Kinetics Press.

Rubin, K. H., Fein, G. G., & Vandenberg, B. (1983). Play. In P. H. Mussen (Ed.), *Handbook of child psychology: Vol 4, Socialization, personality, and social development* (4th ed., pp. 693–774). New York: John Wiley & Sons.

Rubin, K. H., Maioni, T. L., & Hornung, M. (1976). Free play behaviors in middle- and lower-class preschoolers: Parten and Piaget revisited. *Child Development, 47,* 414–419.

Sanders, K., & Harper, L. (1976). Free play fantasy behavior in preschool children: Relations among gender, age, season and location. *Child Development, 47,* 1182–1185.

Shostak, M. (1976). A !Kung woman's memories of childhood. In R. B. Lee & I. DeVore (Eds.), *Kalahari hunter-gatherers: Studies of the !Kung San and their neighbors* (pp. 246–277). Cambridge, MA: Harvard University Press.

Slaughter, D. T., & Dembrowski, J. (1989). Cultural continuities and discontinuities: Impact on social and pretend play. In N. M. Bloch & A. D. Pellegrini (Eds.), *The ecological context of children's play* (pp. 282–310). Norwood, NJ: Ablex Publishing Corporation.

Smilansky, S. (1968). *The effects of sociodramatic play on disadvantaged preschool children.* New York: Wiley.

Smith, N. R. (1985). The workyards of Sde Eliyahu: Places to learn resourcefulness. *Beginnings, 2* (2), 19–23.

Smith, P. K., & Connolly, K. (1972). Patterns of play and social interaction in preschool children. In N. Blurton Jones (Ed.), *Ethological studies of child behavior* (pp. 65–96). Cambridge, England: Cambridge University Press.

Tizard, B., Philps, J., & Plewis, I. (1976). Play in preschool centers —II. Effects on play of the child's social class and of the educational orientation of the center. *Journal of Child Psychology and Psychiatry, 17,* 265–274.

Tuan, Y. F. (1978). Children and the natural environment. In I. Altman & F. Wohlwill (Eds.), *Children and the environment.* New York: Plenum Press.

Verwer, D. (1980). Planning and designing residential environments with children in mind: A Dutch approach. In P. F. Wilkinson (Ed.), *Innovation in play environments* (pp. 152–170). New York: St. Martin's Press.

Whiting, B. B., & Edwards, C. P. (1988). *Children of different worlds.* Cambridge, MA: Harvard University Press.

Wilkinson, P. F. (Ed.). (1980). *Innovation in play environments.* New York: St. Martin's Press.

12

Magical Playscapes

James Talbot
Joe L. Frost '

The primary motive for writing this paper was the authors' dissatisfaction with current developments in play environment design and
development. Widespread misunderstanding of children's play has
resulted in a growing tendency to replace vibrant, enchanting,
natural, and magical playscapes with overly slick, technology in-
spired, manufactured structures. Further, the child's life is growing
increasingly structured and centered upon the achievement ethic in
the mistaken notion that what adults think is good for adults is also
good for children. Overly anxious parents and misguided bureaucrats
are robbing children of their right to play and, consequently, of their
sense of wonder and enchantment. We trust that this paper will
inspire designers, builders, and other implicated adults to reconsider
their involvement in children's play, to think back to the magical
places and events of their own past and look at play once again
through the eyes of the child.

As adults, we often drift back to magical moments of childhood.
We create works of art, build places, and present spectacles intended
to transport us into other worlds; we create realities and convey
impressions that are not completely understandable either to the
senses or to the intelligence. An instinctive desire for the mystical is

Reprinted from *Childhood Education*, 66, 11–19 by permission of the authors and the
Association for Childhood Education International, 11141 Georgia Avenue, Wheaton,
MD (copyright 1989 by ACEI).

universal; it is part of what makes us human. We have accumulated an astounding array of techniques to fulfill this need according to the tastes and technologies of the era.

At no time in life is a person more receptive to the magical than in childhood, when limits have not yet solidified and the mind is not yet bound by the physical and the rational. Indeed, leaps into the magical through symbolic, imaginative, make-believe, or pretend play are the child's chief means of transition from the concrete to the symbolic, from primitive to elaborate thought and action.

We all have fond memories of mysterious, enchanting, dreamlike places in our pasts, when we were one with the world, in love with life, suspended in an eternal present. It might have been during a special party, a foggy lamplit evening, or some brilliant, dewy, early morning sunrise. We recall the places that best supported or evoked that state of mind: the beach, a rose garden, a special park, Grandmother's yard, some state or national monument, a restaurant, a snowy meadow, a woods or creek or orchard. These are the places that enhanced us and lent sustenance to our highest selves.

Yet for a growing number of children these precious moments and places are all but lost to the trivialities and technologies of modern living. The natural, soft, sheltered places are giving way to concrete, steel, and machines; the tender moments with parents, grandparents, and close relations are being supplanted by a growing array of strangers; the magical playscapes, once created by the child, are now the domain of clever adult researchers, designers, and salespeople. In our own clumsy, short-sighted ways we are seriously attempting, yet often failing, to satisfy both a very basic need and an exalted purpose—the experience of the magical in childhood.

Design Guidelines

We can create *with* children playscapes that are fitting to the magical child *if we feel it is important enough.* But we must be willing to transcend the traditional and the scholarly and engage once again in the mystical, the enchanting, and the elusive. Toward this end we propose a modest outline that employs a range of design guidelines geared to the child's perspective.

Changes of Scale

Children's imaginations thrive on possibilities and resist limitations. For children, there really *are* giants up the beanstalk and leprechauns under the rose bush. The fantastic topographies and mini-worlds in storybooks don't just amuse children, they extend their capacities to imagine and dream. Alteration of scale forces us all to see the world more fully, freshly, closely. There seem to be three scales of operation which create novel responses in children and open the doors of the imagination: the miniature, the child-sized (which puts the child in relative primacy), and the colossal.

Miniature Scale—The Precious. Children of all ages delight in the diminutive (Poltarnees, 1986). The words "charm" and "charming" derive their original meaning and potency from smallness. The authority children possess over the destinies of toys and tiny landscapes offers a deep satisfaction, a type of personal power, a way of validating the self; they can enjoy a sense of omnipotence and sovereignty in a world that so often seems to render their lives ineffective. This is the beginning of their taking control of their lives and their world and balancing the helplessness they feel with real and imagined strengths. Consider the magic children sense when viewing a spiritual Christmas tree or nativity scene. Is it not, to a great extent, the character of the miniature that engages and transports them to other realms? Their fascination with model trains, dollhouses, model-building, insects, tiny animals, and figurines attests to a very special attraction to small cosmologies.

Taken to another degree of magnification, tiny becomes microscopic and new worlds open up. Children have a special fascination with the myopic. The world seen close up reveals yet new wonders at the cellular level. New patterns, structures, become evident. Many of these, such as a snowflake or the veins in a leaf, are reduced to mere geometries and abstractions. Perhaps they suggest to children some of the inner workings and energy patterns of the universe. Or maybe they can imagine themselves reduced, not just to doll-size, but all the way down to ant-size (or smaller), and involved in escapades in an entirely new world, where pebbles are boulders, and a cocoon is a bedroom. Whatever the scale, children gain a sense of perspective over miniatures. They return from their escapades among the small, having gained a new perspective, a new sense of shape, clarity, and interrelations, and more prepared to face an enormous and sometimes threatening "real world."

Child-Scaled—"Just my size!" Environments and objects built exactly to the scale of the child create many of the same effects as do miniature objects. Besides facilitating their daily actions in a world that is simply too big to function in easily, a child-sized place imparts a special message. It says "You are right just the way you are. You are catered to and cared for. You are important, and this world is for you, too." Notice how children respond to places like miniature golf courses, the small trains in parks, and objects downscaled for their use.

The Heroic, Colossal Scale. In a place of huge scale, adults and children are essentially reduced to equals, both having lost primacy, and both are compelled to see things with new eyes. There is also a sense of grandeur not normally attained in the everyday world, a feeling that one is walking in a realm created by a higher power. Besides having gigantically scaled objects or places in the playscape, consider as well the Japanese gardening practice of "captured views," a method used to help gain a vastness of scale. In "capturing a view," some landmark in the distance is framed by the judicious pruning of vegetation in the garden to become, in effect, part of it. Erecting a play tower might suggest a closer proximity with the vast worlds among the clouds. Even locating swings on a hillside with an expansive view would help augment that larger-than-life feeling.

The Suggestion of Other Beings

Humans have always enjoyed imagining they share the world with small versions of themselves: brownies, goblins, pixies, elves, leprechauns, hobbits, faeries, little animals that talk and act as we do. This notion has been convincingly perpetuated through children's literature and folk tales (Gulliver's Travels, Thumbelina, Alice in Wonderland).

On one hand, we're somehow less alone in a fully-peopled world. On another, we seem to have an instinctive distaste for an existence that is thoroughly mapped and defined. We welcome tales of ice people, talking trees, undersea kingdoms, Mad Hatters, Toons, and Star Wars animalettes. We feel joy in being a part of an existence in which the possibilities of being are endless. Children exhibit this joy every day in their make-believe play.

Kids themselves are little people in a too-big world, surrounded by huge creatures. The idea is comforting to them that there are smaller folk who, by their own wits, are leading independent lives. They feel a sense of power in relation to these tiny beings, and self-esteem through comparison and domination over them.

A sense of magic is felt in a place that shows obvious signs that such beings inhabit it. Children love visiting Santa's workshop and Easter wonderland. They never tire of watching the Wizard of Oz. These are the homes of magical creatures and therefore of expanded possibilities; anything can happen. Find a featureless wall in your

Figure 12.1. In our own clumsy, shortsighted ways we are seriously attempting, yet often failing, to satisfy both a very basic need and an exalted purpose —the experience of the magical in childhood (*photo by Joe Frost*).

playground and add or paint a hobbit homefront. Create a cozy garden setting framed by trees and flowering shrubs that defines a setting for children and adults to relive time-honored fairy tales through reading aloud and sharing stories. Storytime can become realtime when adults provide the freedom, space, and materials for children to relive their fantasies through make-believe play.

"Realness"

Children sense the difference between toys and real objects. In many situations, especially where size is not a problem, they prefer the real thing over the sham. Perhaps it has to do with physical attributes—a greater and more minute degree of its detail, its weight and heft, its strength and longevity, or its being constructed of denser materials. Or maybe it has to do with association—"this is the hammer my Dad uses"—that magically imparts attributes of the original user to the novice. Or perhaps its value, in terms of materials or time spent in creating it, gives it a quality that a mere copy can never have. It might also be its actual usefulness, that is, it will do more things better, longer, or easier.

For instance, a real fire engine in a playground will have a much more profound impact on the children than a climber made to remind children of one, especially if it has its original bell, hoses, gauges, chrome plating, tires, and other details still intact, since things that actually do something help so much to create its rich character. In fact, the more working or mechanical parts it actually has that children can either control or relate to, the better. This gives it a specialness that no copy can match, and by association with both its original purpose and its history, it endows the new users with special capabilities.

Archetypal Images

There is a collection of symbols and myths that, throughout the ages, has given life meaning and direction. These images and stories can be found in all cultures. Childhood is perhaps the time we are most open to them. Our fairy tales (with their glass slippers, dragons, and golden balls) and holidays (consider the Christmas tree and the Easter egg) abound with such symbolism. As a matter of fact, many children's stories are age-old myths handed down from generation to generation.

Childhood is a time before rational thinking has had a chance to crowd out these more subtle and profound thought processes. Observation reveals certain images almost universally common to children's art, images such as the ever-present sun, circles, trees, the house, and others. We could greatly enhance the range of experiences taking place in our playscapes by conscientiously incorporating some of these shapes, keeping in mind the preferences of the children and the beliefs of the surrounding community. Even if children do not understand initially why we're doing this, they will sense that such symbols are important. In time the meanings will surface.

Sense of "Placeness"

For a place to be magical there needs to be a certain denseness of atmosphere, a degree of containment that serves to separate off the rest of the world. Don't children often feel more at home in corner places than they do in the middle of an open, exposed location? There is a certain specialness that only boundaries can create. A garden surrounded by a low picket fence will have a different feeling from that same garden with no fence at all. The very term "outdoor room" connotes entirely different images from simply "the outdoors." These places need not be completely enclosed since children like to be aware of what is happening around them.

Placeness might also be enhanced by having a mood-setting focus, a heart of some kind. Consider such things as a statue, sundial, birdbath, Japanese lantern, ornate wind chime, stone or hewn-log bench, fireplace, hammock, or pool. Anything having meaning or usefulness that imbues the surroundings with ambience, and creates an atmosphere apart can make a special place little ones just enjoy being in. Try involving children in the creation of an amphitheater surrounded by plants and covered with trellising.

Open-endedness

Forms which are overdefined tend to dictate meaning, and this is the antithesis of the magical state of mind we are seeking. Shapes whose meanings are not so clearly defined or measurable to the eye, on the other hand, lend themselves to more than one interpretation—they can become more than one thing. Remember the old story about the child who spends more play time with the box than with the didactic and one-dimensional toy that came in it?

When an object or environment is open to many interpretations and uses, the child holds the power to tell it what it is to be or do, rather than it giving the child some preconceived "correct" way to perceive or act. Consider the amazingly differing functions of building blocks versus puzzles or coloring books.

Open-ended spaces and forms often have associative qualities that remind children of various areas of meaning, but leave much for them to fill in. A conical peak can become a castle, a mountain peak, or rocket; an unknown rounded shape might be a lizard, a dinosaur, or a dragon. The addition of a steering wheel or a low counter to almost any platform or play enclosure will greatly expand its dramatic potential.

Nature and the Elements

Gardens, woods, jungles, groves, and orchards have always been potent sources of enchantment. An increase in greenery of any kind will help to increase the probability of mystical thinking and enchanting experiences in our playscapes.

Things which are nonhuman or machine-made offer a level of meaning and support far beyond what is artificially available. Common sense and experience both tell us that we alter the natural environment at our peril. We read to our children of enchanted forests, wonderful briar patches, and mystical places "where the wild things are." Yet, look at the places that children actually have to play in! What can be done to close the gap, and how quickly can we begin? After all, weren't most of the places we remember as magical also predominantly natural?

Tradition has it that the world is made up of four main elements: earth, air, fire, and water. As children learn concrete operations and learn to interact with the physical world, it is important that they gain knowledge of its major components. Only when they are adept at the manipulation of these basic building blocks can abstract thinking freely take place.

Figure 12.2. Gardens, woods, jungles, groves, and orchards have always been potent sources of enchantment (*photo by James Talbot*).

Make sure that the playground offers ample opportunity to interact safely in many ways with earth, air, fire, and water. Gardening, for example, is an excellent way of learning how to balance the four elements to create life (Talbot, 1985). What could be more magical than the growth process? Observing raw materials blossom into a beautiful flower or an ear of corn is a spiritual experience indeed.

Make sure that playgrounds offer sand and water play. Can some kind of paddle pool be provided? How about a fireplace, or at least an occasional bonfire or cookout in which the kids can take part? Or a safe tower or treehouse with a spyglass for sky watching and a cockpit of some sort with a steering wheel for "flying." Have an ecology pond, digging place, giant boulders, or even some plain old mud puddles.

Line Quality and Shape

For a child, there is more intrigue in a circle than a square, in a curved line than a straight one, in a multi-faceted crystal than a tube. Why this is so doesn't matter so much as taking advantage of the fact and acting on it when we are creating places for children.

Why make a rectangular door when you can have an arched one? Why make a square-shaped platform when it could be cloud-shaped? Why have a cylindrically-shaped tunnel when with a little more effort you can have a biomorphically-shaped interior reminiscent of Jonah's whale? Why build a straight bridge when you can make it topsy-turvy, arched, or hanging? Why have a beeline walkway when it can meander? And what about portholes for windows, or a large old dead tree instead of a regimented jungle gym?

Children relate more easily to softened edges and curves, to anthropomorphic shapes, to eccentricity and whimsicality. What can we do to playgrounds to improve their line quality? Could we rout the sharp wood edges? Add an arched gateway? Install some rolling hills? Paint some friendly shapes? Add a winding trike track with tunnels and hills?

Sensuality

Places which engage the senses are more enchanting and remain more profoundly in our memories than those with little sensual stimulation. Rich color, fragrances, pleasant sounds, engaging textures, varied light qualities—all of these give heightened significance to any experience. Consider again your own memories; sycamores whispering in the breeze, the feel of lamb's ear against one's cheek, a tart pear from grandmother's yard, the dank feeling under the porch.

For infants and toddlers in your play yard, create a sensory walk, with textures, sounds, and fragrant blossoms, even impregnated smells, or simple vegetation and other natural elements. Fluid or viscous materials like sand, dirt, clay, and water also engage the senses while enhancing the construction and symbolic play schemes of children.

Layering

Another aspect of magical ambience is layering, a term we use loosely. One of its meanings involves looking through things at other things. Objects or views in the background are "framed" by layers of foreground objects or massing (such as walls, hills, or vegetation). The sense of depth is heightened and a feeling of richness is obtained. Discovery and mystery are also enhanced because things are often hidden by other things, and movement by the child is required to see all parts of the environment.

Thus a sequential revelation or a fragmented perception takes place, which intrigues the imagination and requires effort to fully

Figure 12.3. The exotic feeling of a jungle tree hut is suggested by the use of large tree trunks, split log steps, natural rope, stockade walls and a layer of hemp fringe "thatch" around the top edge (*photo by James Talbot*).

penetrate the environment and then find and fit all the pieces into a whole. The resulting totality is less preordained and more enriched with meaning supplied by the child than, say, a play yard that is taken in by a single look. This opens the door to mystical thinking, transforming the environment to fit the fancies of the child.

The concept of layering may also pertain to levels of meaning. An object may have several levels of interpretation, or degrees of complexity. These are discovered and perhaps enhanced by the child over time. For instance, imagine a large sculpture set in a playscape which is approached from the rear and appears to be, at first viewing, a large mammal of some kind with splayed legs. As it is approached, however, the front legs turn out to be wings. Upon further examination, the wings turn out to also be slides, and yet another set of legs comes into view, which turns out to double as low sitting benches. Furthermore, it is discovered that when the nose is pressed, water comes out of the mouth. A simpler example would be those large, open-mouthed lion or hippo sculptures that are also trash receptacles. A "not only/but also" rather than a merely "either/or" situation is thereby created.

Novelty

Rarity, unusualness, specialness, unpredictability, and incongruity—these are all things that intrigue youngsters. To come upon something that cannot be immediately categorized stretches the limits of a child, again opening the way for a multitude of interpretations. A playground having something not found anywhere else in town is unique. A sense of pride and specialness is endowed to those using it—an elevated state that a mere catalogue playscape will never provide.

What if your playground had a nicely made totem pole with neat, funny, and scary faces, one that a child could even climb? Or what about the famous giant Rukugo Tire Dinosaur in the Ota-ku, Tokyo playground? Or an extensive music center including Trinidadian steel drums, a real oriental brass gong, and a giant xylophone? Wouldn't the mere novelty alter and expand children's perceptions of their world? Shouldn't the playground super-structure integrate some novel elements—a pipe telephone system, or a unique enclosure for house play?

Mystery

What is it about fog or snow that can so transform any landscape into a wonderland? And what is it about twilight that can render the most mundane and known places into magical realms? Children love surprises and discovery. The game of hide-and-seek is as popular as ever, and we know how intrigued kids are by the unfamiliar, if only by the popularity of spook houses and scary stories. And we also know, from our own lives, how refusing to acknowledge and face those "things that go bump in the night" can ultimately confound our ability to function later as whole and centered adults.

Let's admit that the mysterious is an integral part of life. Allow a few areas in their world to remain a bit secret and obscure. Keep the playground such that it can't be comprehended at once at the child's eye-level. Leave a few nooks, crannies, and hidey-holes, or consider how the play yard might be softly lit and used in the evenings. Create an "enchanted forest" with vines, bushes, tall grass, hills, bridges, tunnels, and other features children love so much and add some appropriate music or sounds to complete the mood.

Brilliance

The mesmeric and transporting qualities of things that sparkle, glitter, and shine are as old as history. "Every paradise abounds in gems" (Huxley, 1954, p. 101). In earlier times there were ancient bonfires, the stained glass of Gothic churches, the fireworks of the Chinese, Christmas tree decorations, and the rich pageantry of the Olympic games. In recent times we've experienced the full, transporting power of modern stage lighting, outdoor floodlighting, neon, the colorful, stroboscopic light shows and fireworks spectaculars, the enveloping OMNIMAX-IMAX motion picture, and laser sculptures. Probably our all-time favorite light spectacle throughout the millennia has remained the glowing, colorful sunset. Children, who have not yet been exposed to these various entrancing art forms, are especially delighted by them. Infants and toddlers are enraptured during their early trips to the kitchen, with all its gleaming chrome, porcelain, and tile. To them, all that glitters really *is* gold. Crystals are especially intriguing to youngsters as are fire, glitter, the metallic colors in their crayon sets, and polished surfaces.

There are countless ways to make sure that play spaces offer these kinds of experiences. Surface mosaics of tile, polished stone, marbles, mirrors, and even shells are not only attractive to children, but are also something they can create themselves. What about the use of gold, silver, and copper enamel to paint a door? Or embedding quartz crystals into a wall or tunnel? Or perhaps one could impregnate clear polyurethane resin with color, glitter, and other shiny objects. Could prisms be hung to liven up a wall at a certain time of day? Could we fit a play yard with low-voltage colored night lights having dimmer switches simple enough for the children to safely use at night? Even a mural using rich saturated colors or a densely planted bed of brilliant flowers with a mirror ball could create an extra-special effect that would open up new vistas.

Juxtaposition of Opposites

A certain epic quality, a grand totality, becomes present when opposites are at play with each other. When high contrasts occur the effect is dramatic, sometimes exciting, and a largeness of purpose is suggested. The graphic technique of chiaroscuro is a bold example.

How opposites—male/female, sun/moon, day/night, hard/soft, pink/blue, light/shadow, void/solid, happy/sad, dead/alive, good/evil, positive/negative, hot/cold—are expressed in the playground will probably be up to the adults; how they are resolved will be up to each child over and over.

The world is made up of opposites, and major systems of thought revolve around how this is expressed, be it in terms of one struggling against the other, or one complementing and balancing the other. Children will not be dealing with these dichotomies in a rational sense, but they will be dealing with them all the same. Coming to terms with the polar nature of life is in essence a magical process, and the environment can either highlight and assist in the process, or ignore or deny it.

The playground will provide a richer, more enchanting atmosphere if we try such things as: sculpting a high-relief surface that creates dramatic contrasts with sunlight and shadow; painting with pairs of complementary colors so that they vibrate together; making a climbing structure as a series of solids and shadowy voids rather than just an open network; having contrasting materials close together; juxtaposing smooth, rounded shapes with straighter and more angular ones; having both an ornamental, possibly rounded entrance or gateway and some form of obelisk or tower-like sculpture near each other; or having soft as well as hard elements in the play yard. With encouragement and experience, children themselves will be able to come up with many other ways to express this facet of life.

Richness and Abundance

So many yards and play spaces remind us more of sensory-deprivation chambers or post-holocaust deserts than anything else.

There is no magic in them because very little can be created in a vacuum. We prefer an environment rich in possibilities, abounding with *stuff*, with no sense of scarcity.

Children feel freer, more powerful, and better about themselves, when they're not constantly scraping the bottom of the junk barrel, re-using the same old toys, or having to ration whatever is available. The environment must say, "As part of a rich and abundant universe, I support you fully." Whether it be in terms of details, things, building supplies and tools, vegetation, events, color and other sensual experiences, or merely time, the play environment should be a varied cornucopia of endless possibilities. Yet more is not always better when it comes to play environments for kids. More raw materials for creativity and more natural features does not mean showering children with an endless stream of store bought trinkets and toys.

Connection with Other Times, Other Places

Age and history bestow a mystical aura. A hoary old oak has more magic than a sapling. It may be because in previous times magical thinking was more prevalent and purely rational thinking did not dominate. Perhaps it is simply the richness of implied experience. Or could it be the unknown quality that leads to speculation as to what it may have been like back then, thus expanding the use of the imagination? It's as if an old place or object, having been through so much, is somehow alive and has more tales to tell.

It seems to be the nature of things past to develop a patina, an aura of the dream state. So important is this evocation that in the late 1800s there was a cult movement of Romantics who, longing for antiquity and all it suggested to them, would go so far as to build "ruins" from scratch! The underlying attraction to old things, often wrapped up in a fear of the de-humanizing tendencies of the Industrial Age, is still with us today. For instance, it is not often that modern fairy tales and modes of illustration affect us the way the older ones do. Ancient, ivy-covered walls are "hallowed"; new bare ones are not. And it wasn't until the Velveteen Rabbit was really used that he became real.

Creating "instant age" can be touchy business, but often choices will arise in creating an environment that will allow one to opt either for something brand new, mechanical, and hard or something soft enough to show the passage of time, or already having a sense of history. Many builders will scrape a site bare of all trees and stones, no matter what their age, before building. Right there is an opportu-

Figure 12.4. We prefer an environment rich in possibilities, abounding with *stuff* with no sense of scarcity (*photo by Joe Frost*).

nity to keep the older elements of the site intact. Whether to have child care in a new or older building is an opportunity to tap into the past. Choosing between new, fired brick and used, unfired brick for your patio or walkway is another. In general, when choosing materials for any building project, think of which material "feels" older, which ones will gracefully reflect the effects of time and use (Alexander, 1977). Isn't that a major reason we seem to prefer, for instance, tile to concrete, or additive building methods such as brick to poured or monolithic materials such as asphalt; or thicker and more solid walls and columns to thin modern ones?

Children's imaginations are also piqued by the exotic, that which is foreign, intriguingly not of their culture. Ali Baba's cave, Tarzan's jungle, King Arthur's court, the Taj Mahal, Oz, Morroco, China, even Hawaii—these are places that all conjure up potent images to the child in all of us. Many children's stories and movies get plenty of mileage from the fact that they take place in a "far-off land" where everything's strange and anything could happen. Since children don't know what it's actually like there, they are forced to fill the gaps, and that is where they gain their magical power over such worlds, very unlike their own everyday world where all the answers are accomplished facts.

What seems exotic to children? Spiral columns? Onion-shaped domes? Pointed arches? Filigree? "Jewels" and metallic colors? A yurt? Mosaics? Hieroglyphics? A sculpture of an elephant, or lion? Palm trees? A turret? Zebra skin patterns? Foo dog statues? Keep an eye out for what intrigues them and put it in their play space. Make it as detailed, multi-faceted, lavish, and lovingly as you can.

"Is-ness"

In driving through a neighborhood of hideous architecture Huxley (1954) discovered that "within sameness there is difference" (p. 61). A bank of geraniums was entirely different from a special stucco wall, but the "isness" or "eternal quality of their transience" was the same.

Objects, beings, and places that have no other purpose than just to *be* express a meaning beyond utility and apparent reasoning. Much vision-producing art and architecture, magical in intent and rich with potential, don't really *do* anything. They merely are. The cherubim and heroic figures of antiquity, the great mausoleums and monuments of old, fountains whose function is to elicit reflection and awareness of a larger order of things, Oldenberg's great floppy canvas fan, the Olympic flame, mandalas, natural cloudscapes, all of these have suggestive and transporting qualities far beyond their static natures. Their very uselessness allows them to do or mean whatever the beholder wishes and suggests transcendency and ritual in a larger sense.

Not everything in the play yard needs to be functional. Add something whose sole appeal is in its "thing-ness": a statue, large sphere or other geometric solid; a flower garden; a tree hanging; a freestanding arch or vault; some graphic design, symbol, or map of an imaginary country. Whatever it is, it can be heraldic, whimsical, archetypal, mysterious, anything, as long as it has a profound, attractive, and tangible energy, which speaks to that which is not yet expressed in the children, something you know they will feel and notice.

Loose Parts and Simple Tools

Places built by kids themselves, even children with special needs, using scrap or natural materials are often more magical to them than those designed and built by adults. A hammer is the child's magic wand, and we are constantly amazed at how, with a little support and

Figure 12.5. Risk is necessary in play, and children will instinctively seek it out in unsafe places if it is not offered in safe ones (*photo by Joe Frost*).

encouragement, children can bring about the transformation of mere junk into Rube Goldberg-ian wonderlands. The Japanese author Daisaku Ikeda (1979) understood this when he spoke of the overindulged as "glass children." Many children in industrialized countries have no toughness, so weak you expect them to break. Their fearful parents won't allow them to use tools for fear they might injure themselves so ready-made plastic kits have supplanted the need. Seemingly minor matters such as these, repeated over and over, tend to shape the direction of the child's life.

The Illusion of Risk

There's no magic in avoiding challenge. The peak experience that occurs during a moment of risk is a potent one; the mind is in a state of alertness, resourcefulness, and expectancy; the body is ready and open to change. The two are aligned in the face of perceived danger. It is a thrilling, exhilarating moment. Mastering the threat results in a concentrated, almost tangible growth spurt with transformational and empowering qualities. Each success has the potential to be a triumphant affirmation of life and personal power. The focus is on the timeless present, and this is a heady place to be. This is one face of rapture. This is a magical state of being.

On the other hand, not being allowed to take chances causes a debilitating timidity and fearfulness in later life. Risk is necessary in play, and children (not to mention adults deprived in childhood) will instinctively seek it out in unsafe and life-threatening places if it is not offered in safe ones. Growth simply demands the making and overcoming of mistakes. Play experiences can include heights without actual exposure to long falls, speed (such as zip lines, long slides, tall swings, bikes, sleds, skateboards), motion of all kinds (especially spinning), darkness, adventure hikes in a wilderness, diving, super-

Figure 12.6. Contemporary children live in a tightly structured world of lessons, practices, and schedules—a world that no longer values recess, leisure, or time for reflection. Those responsible for designing childrens' playscopes must help change this and restore the magical in childhood (*photo by Joe Frost*).

vised playing with fire, using scissors, saws, and hammers, and difficult balancing and climbing events (with resilient surfaces below). A common error of adults is assuming that "safe" on playgrounds means less challenging. With skillful planning we can have it both ways.

Doing Nothing

When Christopher Robin told Pooh, "What I like doing best is nothing" (Milne, 1928), he was living in a world that allowed daydreaming, reflecting, and playing or not playing. Few contemporary children enjoy such luxuries. Rather, theirs is a tightly structured world of lessons, practices, and schedules—a world that no longer values recess, free time, leisure, and fun for fun's sake. Adults unwittingly assume that television fills the need for privacy and reflection or reading but in reality television structures time, distorts reality, channels thought, and *robs children of their own reflection and dreams.*

The wise play leader understands that children must have *time* and *places* for truly free play; opportunities for selecting their own playthings and themes; freedom from adults and society's rules and restrictions; opportunities for messing around with valued friends in enchanting places; time to just be kids and have fun.

Conclusion

The power to visualize, create, and risk in a safe setting, these are the elements of childhood enchantment. They are important steps in the development cycle and a sound basis for developing children who are thinkers, wonderers, and builders and who at the same time are confident, resilient, and tough.

In sum, we propose design principles intended to transform traditional, mundane, over-slick, sterile, or high-tech places into magical, enchanting playscapes. They are not the only qualities to be considered in designing playscapes, but they do address our children's need for the mystical and magical and their sense of wonder. Such playscapes extend possibilities, expand awareness, transcend the common, and enhance opportunities for children to wonder, create, and experiment—and thus to grow.

References

Alexander, C. (1977). *A pattern language: Towns, buildings, construction.* New York: Oxford University Press.

Huxley, A. (1954). *The doors of perception: Heaven and hell.* New York: Harper and Row.

Ikeda, D. (1979). *Glass children and other essays.* Translated by Burton Watson. Tokyo: Kodanska International.

Milne, A. A. (1928). *House at Pooh Corner.* New York: E. P. Dutton.

Poltarnees, W. (1986). The fascination of the miniature. In J. McCahn (Ed.), *The teenie weenie's book.* La Jolla, CA.: The Green Tiger Press.

Talbot, J. (1985). Plants in children's outdoor environments. In J. L. Frost & S. Sunderlin (Eds.), *When children play.* Wheaton, MD: Association for Childhood Education International.

Bibliography

Bengtsson, A. (1974). *The child's right to play.* Sheffield, England: Tartan Press.

Frost, J. L., & Sunderlin, S. (1985). *When children play.* Wheaton, MD: Association for Childhood Education International.

Hurtwood, L. A. (1968). *Planning for play.* Cambridge, MA: MIT Press.

Moore, R. (1986). *Childhood's domain.* Dover, NH: Croom Helm.

Sutton-Smith, B. (1986). *Toys as culture.* New York: Gardner Press.

APPENDICES

Appendix A

Mission Statement for the Committee on Play

Appendix B

Trained Volunteer Survey Administrators

Appendix C

Playground Selection Process

Appendix D

Preschool Playground Survey Instrument

APPENDIX A
Mission Statement for the AALR-AAHPERD Committee on Play

The purposes of the AALR Committee on Play are:
- to understand the nature and function of play
- to support play
- to share information on play
- to educate for play with a focus on the individual, society, and setting.

APPENDIX B
Trained Volunteer Survey Administrators

National Preschool Center Playground Survey Trained Volunteers

Sincere appreciation is extended to the professionals named below who conducted the survey of preschool center playgrounds throughout the United States.

Kaye Adkins
Dawn Deena Allen
Viola Bahls
Denniese Barber
L. Bradford
Kayla Brazell
Phil Brown
Linda Brucato
Mary Buresh
Linda Caldwell
Claire Carpenter
Xiwei Chen
Mary Cline
Maddi Cox
Nancy Curtis
Karen Dietz
D'Layne Doherty
Nita Drescher
Janice Dulin
Harriet Field
Doris Fletcher

Donia Ford
Bettye Foster
Joe Frost
Patricia Harris
Monty Henderhan
M. Hernanden
Nancy Herrod
Olive Hipps
Mildred Holdnak
Kristen Holm
Patricia Hopp
Jay Jacox
Tom Jambor
Artie Johnson
Stephanie Keller
Jeen D. Koo
Don Krehbiel
Eileen Larkin
Janet Lipscomb
Dennis Majeskie
Martha Mendez

Sarah Moore
Shari Nelson
Judy Noteboom
Kari K. Patterson
Michael Peters
Kathy Picha
Christie Roe
Sherry Schmidt
B. Schwegmann
Nancy Scott
Marguerite Shannon
Ilisa Sinderbrand
Richard Stenner
M. Tattoon
Shellye Taylor
Gwen Terry
Donna Thompson
Joyce Wiley
Loyce Willet
Marshal Wortham
Sue Wortham

APPENDIX C
Playground Selection Process

AALR-AAHPERD-COP
(Committee On Play)

National Survey of Preschool Centers
Playground Equipment

1. Using your phone book yellow pages under Day Care or Early Childhood Center, compile a list of all potential administration sites for the geographic area you have chosen.
2. Number all of the centers starting with #1.
3. Select the centers you will survey, based on the 'Playground Selection Process' listed below.

Playground Selection Process
(Used to Pick the Centers to be Surveyed)

A. 0–10 centers in the area: assess 1 center
    #2B. 10–20 centers in the area: assess 2 centers
    #2, #18
C. 20–40 centers in the area: assess 4 centers
    #2, #18, #8, #17

D. 40–70 centers in the area: assess 7 centers
   #2, #18, #8, #17, #41, #13, #36
E. 70–100 centers in the area: assess 10 centers
   #2, #18, #8, #17, #41, #13, #36, #94, #26, #81
F. 100–150 centers in the area: assess 15 centers
   #2, #18, #8, #17, #41, #13, #36, #94, #26, #81, #97, #143, #111,
   #113, #124
G. 150–200 centers in the area: assess 20 centers
   #2, #18, #8, #17, #41, #13, #36, #94, #26, #81, #97, #143, #111,
   #113, #124, #125, #11, #152, #4, #112
H. 200–250 centers in the area: assess 25 centers
   #2, #18, #8, #17, #41, #13, #36, #94, #26, #81, #97, #143, #111,
   #113, #124, #125, #11, #152, #4, #112, #212, #131, #230, #25, #70
I. 250–300 centers in the area: assess 30 centers
   #2, #18, #8, #17, #41, #13, #36, #94, #26, #81, #97, #143, #111,
   #113, #124, #125, #11, #152, #4, #112, #212, #131, #230, #25, #70,
   #245, #220, #115, #107, #281
J. 300–350 centers in the area: assess 35 centers
   #2, #18, #8, #17, #41, #13, #36, #94, #26, #81, #97, #143, #111,
   #113, #124, #125, #11, #152, #4, #112, #212, #131, #230, #25, #70,
   #245, #220, #115, #107, #281, #309, #59, #176, #54, #160
K. 350–400 centers in the area: assess 40 centers
   #2, #18, #8, #17, #41, #13, #36, #94, #26, #81, #97, #143, #111,
   #113, #124, #125, #11, #152, #4, #112, #212, #131, #230, #25, #70,
   #245, #220, #115, #107, #281, #309, #59, #176, #54, #160, #351,
   #382, #282, #153, #114
L. 400–500 centers in the area: assess 50 centers
   #2, #18, #8, #17, #41, #13, #36, #94, #26, #81, #97, #143, #111,
   #113, #124, #125, #11, #152, #4, #112, #212, #131, #230, #25, #70,
   #245, #220, #115, #107, #281, #309, #59, #176, #54, #160, #351,
   #382, #282, #153, #114, #20, #257, #203, #423, #426, #396, #201,
   #354, #485, #172

*Note: For geographic areas with centers in excess of 500 call L. Bruya collect at 817/565-2651, leaving your name, phone, and the number of schools in the district. He will return your call with additional numbers of schools to survey.

Please survey each center listed on the list even if it has no play structure. If a center has no play structure, note it on the *National Survey of Playground Equipment* for Day Care/Early Childhood Centers and send it in.

Please list the # of the center selected on the survey instrument as well as the number of centers in the district.

Appendix D
Preschool Playground
Survey Instrument

AALR COMMITTEE ON
PLAY
PRESCHOOL
PLAYGROUND
EQUIPMENT SURVEY

_____

Name of Person Conducting Survey

_____

Date Survey Conducted

_____

Beginning Time Completion Time

_____

_____

Name and Address of Preschool
Playground

_____

Number of Children Enrolled in
Preschool

Section 1. Type and Numbers of Equipment. Record preschool playground numbers in left column; infant-toddler (age 0–36 months) playground (if separate) in right column.

1.1. List the numbers of each type of equipment located on school playground:

Permanent (fixed Equipment)		Portable Materials (movable parts)	
Record Number		Record number or circle yes or no	
Pre-school Infant-Toddler		Pre-school Infant-Toddler	
	slides		loose tires
	swing structures		barrels
	merry-go-rounds		loose boards or other
	seesaws	yes no yes no	building materials
	suspended bridges	yes no yes no	gardening tools
	balance beams	yes no yes no	carpentry tools
	rocking apparatus	yes no yes no	art materials
	geodesic domes		tricycles
	monkey bars (jungle gyms)		wagons
	trapeze bars (chinning bars)		wheelbarrows
	overhead (horizontal) ladders	other portable materials (List below)	
	fireman's poles		
	tire or net climbers		
	number of separate play structures		
	number of superstructures (interconnected structures)		

other permanent equipment
(List below)

	Other Provisions	
	Record number or circle yes or no	
Preschool	Infant- Toddler	
		separate sand play areas (not around or under equipment)
		water play areas
		hard surface area for games
		areas for digging soil
yes no	yes no	natural areas for plants
yes no	yes no	provisions for animal care
		accessible water supply-hose or faucets
		tables
		toilet facilities
		amphitheatre area
		storage for portable play materials
		storage for maintenance equipment
		grassy areas for organized
		play houses
		boats (for dramatic play)
		cars (for dramatic play)
		trucks (for dramatic play)
		shade structures (man-made)
other provisions (List below)		

For sections that follow, survey all equipment including infant/toddler and preschool.

Section 2: Location and Accessibility
_____ 2.1. Is the play equipment easily in view of nearby residents and/or passersby?

_____ 2.2 Is there a fence at least 4 feet high surrounding the playground?

_____ 2.3 Is access to the play equipment possible for children in wheelchairs, by means of a hard surface?

_____ 2.4 Can wheelchairs get *on* any of the play equipment?

Section 3: Size and Placement of Equipment
_____ 3.1. Is there at least 10 feet of space between each fixed piece of equipment?

_____ 3.2 How many concrete footings around support structures are exposed at or above ground level?

_____ 3.3 Is all equipment placed to avoid collision or interference with traffic patterns of children on wheel toys on hard surface pathways?

_____ 3.4 Is smaller sized play equipment, intended for infants and toddlers, present?

_____ 3.5 If so, is smaller equipment separated from larger equipment by a fence or other divider so as to avoid immediate crossover use?

Section 4: Swing Equipment (If no swings are present, go on to Section 5).
_____ 4.1 How many separate swing *structures* are present?

_____ 4.2 Number of swing *seats*?

_____ 4.3 How many of the swing seats are made of wood or metal or similar dense materials (e.g., animal swings)?

_____ 4.4 How many of the swing seats have a swivel type suspension?

_____ 4.5 How many swing *structures* are designed for infants and toddlers?

_____ 4.6 How many of the swing seats for infants and toddlers are on a separate structure from the other swings?

_____ 4.7 How many of the swing structures have barriers such as fences or hedges, which discourage children from running into swings while swings are in motion?

_____ 4.8 How many of the swing structures have support structures which are firmly anchored in the ground?

_____ 4.9 How many of the swing structures have sharp corners, edges, or projections on any part of the swing seat, chains, or swing structure?

_____ 4.10 How many of the swing structures have swings with moving parts in good working condition and not cracked or rusted so as to be in danger of breaking?

_____ 4.11 How many swings have chains covered with plastic or other material so that fingers cannot pass between chain links?

_____ 4.12 Which of the following surface material is found under and around the swings? ($\bar{x}$=average)

_____ concrete	_____ clay	_____ pea gravel
_____ asphalt	_____ sand	($\bar{x}$ depth)
_____ grass	($\bar{x}$ depth)	_____ commercial
	_____ mulch	matting
	($\bar{x}$ depth)	_____ other

Section 5: Slide Equipment (If no slides are present, go on to Section 6).

_____ 5.1 How many slides are present?

_____ 5.2 How many of the slides have missing or broken parts?

_____ 5.3 How many of the slides have sharp corners, edges or projections?

_____ 5.4 How many of the supporting structures are firmly fixed in the ground?

_____ 5.5 How many of the slides are wide enough to accommodate more than one child, sliding side by side at the same time?

_____ 5.6 How many of the sliding surfaces are stable, smooth, and even throughout their length?

_____ 5.7 How many of the exit regions of slides have angle and slope which decrease and cause deceleration before the child reaches the end of the slide?

_____ 5.8 How many inches high from ground level is the lower end of each slide?

_____ _____ _____ _____

_____ 5.9 How many feet from the ground is the highest vertical point for each of the slides?

_____ _____ _____ _____

_____ 5.10 Which of the following surface material is found under and around the slide?

_____ concrete	_____ clay	_____ pea gravel
_____ asphalt	_____ sand	($\bar{x}$ depth)
_____ grass	($\bar{x}$ depth)	_____ commercial
	_____ mulch	matting
	($\bar{x}$ depth)	_____ other

Section 6: Climbing Equipment (If no climbing equipment is present, go to Section 7).

_____ 6.1 How many separate climbing *structures* are present (count superstructures once)?

_____ 6.2 How many of the climbing structures have structural supports firmly fixed into the ground?

_____ 6.3 How many of the climbing structures have all parts securely fastened?

_____ 6.4 How many of the climbing structures have open holes at the end of the tubes or pipes in which fingers could fit?

_____ 6.5 How many of the climbing structures have small spaces where structures connect which could possibly trap hands or fingers?

_____ 6.6 How many of the climbing structures have sharp corners, edges, or projections?

_____ 6.7 How many of the climbing structures have distances between hand holds or foot supports (ladders, steps) which are between 7 and 11 inches?

_____ 6.8 What is the maximum height from the ground that a child can climb on each piece of equipment (include deck railings)?

_____ _____ _____ _____

_____ 6.9 How many of the climbing structures have a guard rail around the highest platform area?

_____ 6.10 How many of the climbing structures have openings which are between 4½ and 9 inches which could entrap a child's head?

_____ 6.11 Which of the following surface material is found under and around the climbing equipment?

_____ concrete	_____ clay	_____ pea gravel
_____ asphalt	_____ sand	($\bar{x}$ depth)
_____ grass	($\bar{x}$ depth)	_____ commercial
	_____ mulch	matting
	($\bar{x}$ depth)	_____ other

Section 7: Rotating Equipment (Merry-Go-Rounds, etc.) (If no rotating equipment is present, go on to Section 8).

_____ 7.1 How many rotating structures are present?

_____ 7.2 How many of the rotating structures have supports firmly fixed in ground?

_____ 7.3 How many of the rotating structures have all joints and fasteners holding the equipment firmly together?

_____ 7.4 How many of the rotating structures have sharp corners, edges, or projections?

_____ 7.5 How many of the rotating structures have an open space between the center post and the outer perimeter of the rotating structure?

_____ 7.6 How many of the rotating structures have shearing actions underneath the structure that could crush body parts?

_____ 7.7 How many of the rotating structures have exposed gear boxes that could shear or crush fingers?

_____ 7.8 How many of the rotating structures have a cleared area extending out 20 feet around the structure, so as to allow running space for children coming off the merry-go-round?

_____ 7.9 Which of the following surface material is found under and around the rotating equipment?

_____ concrete	_____ clay	_____ pea gravel
_____ asphalt	_____ sand	($\bar{x}$ depth)
_____ grass	($\bar{x}$ depth)	_____ commercial
	_____ mulch	matting
	($\bar{x}$ depth)	_____ other

Section 8: Spring Rocking Equipment, i.e., Rocket Ships, and Animals (If no spring rocking equipment is present, go on to Section 9).

_____ 8.1 How many spring rocking structures are present?

_____ 8.2 How many of the spring rocking structures have structural supports firmly fixed in the ground?

_____ 8.3 How many of the spring rocking structures have all parts of the equipment present?

_____ 8.4 How many of the spring rocking structures have sharp corners, edges or projections?

_____ 8.5 How many of the spring rocking structures have handholds at least 3 inches long?

_____ 8.6 How many of the spring rocking structures have footboards or footrests which extend at least 11 inches out from the base?

_____ 8.7 How many of the spring rocking structures have springs in which the fingers or toes can be pinched?

_____ 8.8 Which of the following surface material is found under and around the spring rocking equipment?

_____ concrete	_____ clay	_____ pea gravel
_____ asphalt	_____ sand	($\bar{x}$ depth)
_____ grass	($\bar{x}$ depth)	_____ commercial matting
	_____ mulch	_____ other
	($\bar{x}$ depth)	

Section 9: Seesaw Equipment (If seesaw equipment is not present, go to Section 10).

_____ 9.1 How many seesaw structures are present?

_____ 9.2 How many seesaws are present?

_____ 9.3 How high are the seats during their highest point of use?

_____ _____ _____ _____

_____ 9.4 How many of the seesaw structures are firmly fixed in the ground?

_____ 9.5 How many of the seesaw structures have internal moving parts or swivels accessible to fingers of children?

_____ 9.6 How many of the seesaw structures have all joints and fastenings secure?

_____ 9.7 How many of the seesaw structures have sharp corners, edges or projections?

_____ 9.8 How many of the seesaw structures have made provision for cushioning the impact of the seat striking the ground?

_____ 9.9 How many of the seesaw structures have handholds on each end which are at least 3 inches long?

_____ 9.10 Which of the following surface material is found under and around the seesaw structures?

_____ concrete	_____ clay	_____ pea gravel
_____ asphalt	_____ sand	($\bar{x}$ depth)
_____ grass	($\bar{x}$ depth)	_____ commercial matting
	_____ mulch	_____ other
	($\bar{x}$ depth)	

Section 10: Designated Sand Play Area—Sand Is Contained Within Area for Digging, etc. (If no sand play area is present, go to Section 11).

_____ 10.1 How many separated sand play areas are present?

_____ 10.2 How many of the sand play areas are clean and free of debris?

_____ 10.3 How many of the sand play areas drain of water?

_____ 10.4 How many of the sand play areas are elevated?

_____ 10.5 How many of the sand play areas are covered to exclude animals from gaining access?

_____ 10.6 How many benches for adult seating are provided adjacent to the sand play area?

Section 11: Designated Water Play Area—Water Is Contained Within Area (If no designated water play area is present, go to Section 12).

_____ 11.1 How many separate water play areas are present?

_____ 11.2 Which type are they? _____ pool _____ water fall _____ water cascade/sluice _____ spray _____ sprinkler/ sprayer _____ water canals _____ water wheel

_____ 11.3 How many of the pool areas are elevated and/or fenced and gated to exclude animals?

_____ 11.4 How many of the water play areas have water clear and free of debris?

_____ 11.5 How many inches deep is the water at the deepest part of each water play area?

	Stream or Canal	Pool	Other:	
Name	_____	_____	_____	_____
Depth	_____	_____	_____	_____

_____ 11.6 How many benches for adults are provided adjacent to the wading pool?

Section 12: Signs

_____ 12.1 Is there an overview map of the play area?

_____ 12.2 Are accessible facilities (e.g., restrooms, phones) designated?

_____ 12.3 Are there signs giving details of where to seek help in case of accidents?

_____ 12.4 Are there signs which direct wheel toy (trikes, bikes) traffic in the general vicinity of the play structure(s)?

_____ 12.5 Are there signs or arrow (→) indicators on the structure to direct traffic to options for play routes?

_____ 12.6 Are identification signs or the structures themselves color coded to indicate difficulty or challenge?

_____ 12.7 Are there signs prohibiting animals from the playground?

_____ 12.8 Are there signs which warn players of activities which they should not participate in?

_____ 12.9 Are there signs connected to the play structure which are designed to expand exploratory play by posing problems to solve?

_____ 12.10 Do signs which contain written words in English also contain instructions in other languages common to the area?

Section 13: Trees and Shade Structures

_____ 13.1 How many trees are located within 50 feet of each major playground equipment area?

_____ 13.2 Are any of the live trees planned as a part of a play structure?

_____ 13.3 Are there dead trees in the playground equipment area which are used as part of the play structure?

_____ 13.4 Are there tree houses built in any of the trees which are used for play?

_____ Built in tree, _____ Built around tree,
_____ Built under tree

_____ 13.5 Are trees planted on the perimeter of the structure to provide a break from prevailing wind?

_____ 13.6 Is a man-made shade structure available to shade adult seating?

Measurements:
_____ Width _____ Height _____ Length _____ Depth
Material Type:
_____ Wood   _____ Metal   _____ Plastic   _____ Concrete
_____ Cloth _____ Other

_____ 13.7 How many drinking fountains are located within the immediate playground equipment area?

Section 14: Pathways

_____ 14.1 Are there points on the playground where lines are likely to occur?

Number of occurrences:_____

_____ 14.2 Are hard surface pathways (sidewalks, trike paths, etc.) provided for use with wheeled toys (trikes, wagons, bikes . . .)?

_____ 14.3 Measure and list the width of the path at 1) one end, 2) middle, 3) other end, and record the overall length of the path.

Width: 1) _____, 2) _____, 3) _____

Length: _____

_____ 14.4 Record the material from which the hard surface path was made.

_____

_____ 14.5 Does the hard surface pathway contain at least one intersection?

Section 15: Wheel Toys—Riding

_____ 15.1 Are wheel toys available for use during play?

_____ 15.2 Are riding wheel toys available for play?

_____ 15.3 Are wheel toys to push available for play?

_____ 15.4 Are wheel toys to pull available for play?

Section 16: Manipulatives

_____ 16.1 Are wooden building blocks available for play?

_____ 16.2 Are tools and buckets available for play in the sand and/or water?

_____ 16.3 Are balls or other sporting equipment available for play?

_____ 16.4 Are trucks, cars, and other small toys available for play?

Section 17: Garden Area

_____ 17.1 Is there a garden area planted by children?

Return To: Dr. Louis Bowers, PED 206, Physical Education Department, University of South Florida, Tampa, Florida 33620-8600; (813) 974-3443.